MORE FIRST NIGHTS

MORE FIRST NIGHTS

by

JAMES AGATE

BENJAMIN BLOM  New York/London

To
A. W. DEVAS JONES
because
I am too busy
to write letters
to Kenya

First Published 1937
Reissued 1969 by
Benjamin Blom, Inc., Bronx, New York 10452
and 56 Doughty Street, London, W.C. 1

Library of Congress Catalog Card Number 74-86886

Printed in the United States of America

CONTENTS

SWEET KNELL OF OLD DRURY

THREE SISTERS. A musical play by Oscar Hammerstein. Music by Jerome Kern. Drury Lane Theatre, Monday, April 9, 1934.

COUNSELLOR-AT-LAW. A play by Elmer Rice. Piccadilly Theatre, Tuesday, April 10, 1934. [*April* 15, 1934]

> First—to each living thing, whate'er its kind,
> Some lot, some part, some station is assign'd.
> The feather'd race with pinions skim the air—
> Not so the mackerel, and still less the bear.
> —" The Progress of Man," by GEORGE CANNING.

WHAT LOT, part, or station is assigned to the providers of books for musical plays? Obviously, that of amusing the British public. Or shall we say persuading it to sit the piece through to the bitter end in the attitude of a public which is amused? I defy anybody to fault my argument so far as it has gone, unless he happens on the notion that it is wrong *in toto*. For it *is* wrong—lock, stock, and barrel, fore and aft, hip and thigh—and by this last token apt to be found fault with and even smitten. The British public does not go to a musical play to be amused in the sense that if it is not amused it stops away. If it goes to a musical comedy and is amused, all well and good: the amusement is gratuitous, thrown in, buckshee, money for jam. The plain truth is that the British public just goes to musical comedy:

> *While the moved* critics *sit in dumb despair,*
> *Like Hottentots, and at each other stare.*

The author of this good parody has appended the following footnote to this passage: " A beautiful figure of German literature. The Hottentots remarkable for staring at each other—God knows why." But the critics know why they stare. It is to ask each other how long Drury Lane is to be the asylum for American inanity. The answer is: For ever, dear heart !

A friend of mine was once tutor in the family of an English squire who looked like Mr. Rochester and had a mansion in the Peak district of Derbyshire. The squire insisted upon dressing for dinner, though the nearest house where anybody else did this was Chatsworth, forty miles away, and every night he would rise from a meal of utter solemnity saying: " Shall we go and see about that fire in the library ? " The formula never varied. But people cast in the mould of this fireside fetishist have to be entertained, and only inanity will entertain them. They are also the backbone of the nation, which backbone when it is in town flies instantly to Drury Lane ! This explains Mr. Oscar Hammerstein II, who has given the present production its words and stage shape.

Now the same questions are to be asked of a musical play as of the Cosmogony :

> *Whether some great, supreme o'er-ruling Power*
> *Stretch'd forth its arm at Nature's natal hour,*
> *Composed this mighty whole with plastic skill,*
> *Wielding the jarring elements at will ?*
> *Or whether sprung from Chaos' mingling storm,*
> *The mass of matter started into form ?*

There is, of course, the alternative view :

> *Whether material substance unrefined*
> *Owns the strong impulse of instinctive mind,*
> *Which to one centre points diverging lines,*
> *Confounds, refracts, invig'rates, and combines ?*

In the matter of the Cosmogony my views are tempered by what I remember of Sanconiathon, Manetho, Berosus, and Ocellus Lucanus. But in the matter of the musical play I must plump for the strong impulse and instinctive mind of Mr. Hammerstein. Nobody else has so firm and assured a drive in the matter of witlessness.

Mesdames Charlotte M. Yonge, Emma Jane Worboise, and the distinguished authors of *St. Elmo* and *Barriers Burned Away* could have put their heads together without equalling the lambent innocuousness of these three daughters of a travelling photographer at whom we belatedly arrive. The youngest (Miss Victoria Hopper) was deserted on her wedding night by her gipsy husband (Mr. Esmond Knight) because he preferred the company of a circus busker (Mr. Albert Burdon) and the joys of the road. In cold blood one thinks there must have been some other reason having to do with unfounded jealousy, though at the time one did not detect it, perhaps because the first act had been so full of lullabying, cradle-singing, and asking who wants to go to sleep, to which one playgoer at least affirmatively responded. The second daughter (Miss Adèle Dixon) married into the peerage (Mr. Richard Dolman), while the eldest (Miss Charlotte Greenwood) espoused a village policeman (Mr. Stanley Holloway). Presently the three husbands met in the War, and years after they and their wives and their families made whoopee at Boulter's Lock. " The way you describe me I don't seem very exciting to myself," says one of the characters. But what is a deficiency in a person may be, as has already been demonstrated, a virtue in a musical-comedy plot, and I see no reason why on this score this production should fail.

What, then, of the acting ? There isn't any, because nobody has a chance to act except Mr. Knight, who manages to give a thunder-and-lightning quality to the little gipsy.

That Mr. Burdon can be a brilliant comedian cannot even be guessed, and we have to hark back to the films to appreciate how much ecstasy and riot there can be in Miss Greenwood. Fortunately she is allowed one of those dances in which her high, effortless kicking resembles the raising of the Tower Bridge. There are some charming numbers by the chorus, and both Mr. Kern's music and Mrs. Calthrop's settings are exquisite. Probably there is no country in the world in which visual and aural embroidery of such delicacy is tacked on to calico so coarse. But the English like it like that, and are right to like it so.

> *Ah ! who has seen the mailed lobster rise,*
> *Clap her broad wings, and soaring claim the skies ?*
> *Or the young heifer plunge, with pliant limb,*
> *In the salt wave and, fish-like, strive to swim ?*

Answer and implication are obvious. Musical comedy must keep to its medium; and if it soars it must only be into the illimitable inane. The stuff of its plot must always be sackcloth, let the critics bestrew themselves with what ashes they may. Mr. Hammerstein is no Shakespeare, and that is why he reigns in our national theatre.

Counsellor-at-Law, if it were a symphonic-poem, would be hailed by the musical critics as piece of pogrom-music. Better perhaps anti-pogrom music, for fundamentally it is all about the American Jew and how much better he is than the American non-Jew. It is true that the hero's brother is a black sheep, but this again is instrumental in showing in still more shining light the bright virtues of the rest of the family. George Simon is a New York lawyer who has risen from small beginnings to a position in which, to satisfy his wife's caprice, he can turn down 100,000 dollar cases. His wife is of that icy, up-stage, aristocratic kind, as aristocracy goes in America, the kind which would be equally horrified at anybody who was deemed a Jew or dubbed a Christian. She is the stock stage-figure of birth, breeding, and selfish pre-occupation to which the proper answer would seem to be Groucho Marx.

Years ago Simon connived at perjury to save a young criminal from a life-sentence. It seems extraordinary that because it is his fourth offence a young man who has stolen twelve dollars can incur such a sentence. But Mr. Rice knows his job, and after all our own laws have their savageries, and there is the old behest about beams and motes. Anyhow, the point of this play is not that we should quarrel with American jurisprudence but note how excitingly Simon gets out of the pit which his own magnanimity has dug for him. The trouble arises when a rival and Christian lawyer, whom Simon has too often opposed and defeated, discovers his early lapse and intends to use his discovery as the lever to disbar Simon—the American equivalent of having him struck off the rolls. So Simon hunts about for evidence of Christian peccadillo, and discovers it in the shape of a little widow, whereby the enemies declare two blacks to make a white and are reconciled. But now Mrs. Simon goes off with her Christian lover to Europe, leaving our hero to be fussed by his admirably Jewish mother, though this does not keep him from thinking about jumping out of the window, from which he is saved by his adoring secretary, who ought to be a Jewess but by some oversight is not.

Such in bald outline is this exciting play, all of which happens in Simon's office. This gives Mr. Rice the opportunity to tell us a great deal about American types, a task of which your American playwright never tires. We have seen them all before—the amorous secretary, the telephone girl, with her confidante at the other end of the line, the office boys, the Semitic gumph who is also the *deus ex machina*—but have never seen them done with sharper effect. The

Birmingham players are very dexterous in giving each character his or her point, and, to the English playgoer, produce the American illusion. Miss Elspeth Duxbury is quite moving as the secretary, whose tongue is tied largely through the fast moving of her pencil. She is too busy to tell her love, and Simon would not have time to hear it. In any case, the end of the play shows him free of his wife, but with the advent of a new big case resuming marriage with his profession. Miss Edie Martin plays old Mrs. Simon with a drenched and faded sweetness that amounts to beauty, and Miss Netta Westcott presents Simon's wife as though she were descended from Tom Robertson's Marquissy. Mr. Charles Victor has five excellent minutes as a steely-purposed wander-wit. Last remains Mr. Hugh Miller, who is the play's life and soul and strength and passion. One says passion because of a first-class scene with a Communist, a small part finely rendered by an actor I cannot identify, in which the pair thrash out all that is most hotly to be said on the individualist issue. Mr. Miller's performance is all fire, and it is a treat to see full-blooded acting elsewhere than on the screen. If I have a fault to find, it is that he hardly suggests the Jew, and not at all the Jew who has risen in the world. My complaint is not that Simon has acquired culture, to which his kind takes as readily as a duck swims, but that he wears it with too austere a taste. The mark of your successful Simons is not only taste but an excess of it: a diamond scarf-pin, a glossier hair-oil, a starchier cuff, might have made all the difference. It is Mr. Miller's ascetic features which are the trouble. But then it must be very difficult for an actor who looks like Thomas à Becket when he was a minor canon to suggest that big shot—the Jew lawyer who is too much the gentleman.

THE CASE OF MR. LAUGHTON

[*May* 13, 1934]

So far as I know, it was George Henry Lewes who first differentiated between Shakespearean actors and actors of Shakespeare. In the first category he put Edmund Kean and Macready, in the second Charles Kean and G. V. Brooke. The point arises in an essay written eighty years ago, in which Lewes begins by saying: " If passion is the essence of tragedy, I ought to have gained experience enough from this week to last me a lifetime. In saying this I make one little supposition, viz. that tragic passion and a tragedian in a passion are one and the same thing. C'est une très forte supposition; mais enfin ! " Apart from the regrettable lapse into French, this strikes me as being first-rate ! But Lewes always is first-rate. In another essay he tells us that to impersonate a character three fundamental conditions are requisite. He calls these conditions respectively: (1) Conceptual Intelligence, (2) Representative Intelligence, (3) Physical Advantages. Under (1) he tells us that " high poetic culture, knowledge of human nature, sympathy with elemental states of passion, and all that we understand by a fine intellect, will assist the actor in his *study* of a character, but it will do no more. The finest intellect in the world would not enable a man to play Hamlet or Othello finely." Under (2) he talks of the command of gesture, look, and tone, the mimetic power of the actor. But it is (3) that we are going to be most concerned with in this article. Here Lewes says:

" The third requisite, which I have named physical advantages, includes person, deportment, voice, and physical power. Too little consideration is devoted to that, yet it is enough of itself to make or mar an actor. All the intellect in the world, all the representative intelligence in the world, could not enable a man with a weak voice, limited in its compass, to perform Othello, Macbeth, Shylock, etc., with success. Whereas a noble presence, a fine voice, and a moderate degree of representative intelligence, with no appreciable amount of conceptual intelligence, have sufficed to draw the town ere now, and make even critics believe a great actor has appeared."

I am sorry to bore readers, but if I am to make my point I must be allowed to continue a little with Lewes, because he was right in his day, and I do not believe that the canons of great acting and criticism have changed in eighty years. Of Macready this critic wrote:

" Certain peculiarities and defects prevent his representing the high, heroic, passionate characters; but nothing can surpass his representation of some others; and, connecting this representative intelligence with his physical advantages, we see how he can execute what he conceives, and thus become an actor. His voice—one primary requisite of an actor—is a fine one, powerful, extensive in compass, and containing tones that thrill, and tones that weep. His person is good, and his face very expressive. So that give him a character within his proper range and he will be great in it; and even the greatest actors can only perform certain characters for which their representative intelligence and physical organisation fit them."

Now have I hit the nail on the head often enough ? We have seen how in Lewes's opinion Macready could only become an actor through the coupling of representative intelligence with physical advantages, and how in his view the greatest actors must not venture beyond the range of their physical organisation. Let us apply all this to Mr. Laughton, and consider to what extent he would be wise in endeavouring to transform himself from a melodramatic and character actor of genius into an even passable tragedian.

Nobody is going to accuse me of lack of appreciation of Mr. Laughton, and if anybody does he will be confounded with chapter and verse. To the best of my recollection, and until this actor went to the Old Vic, I had seen him in seventeen parts, not counting his film performances. As I remember, they were these: One, Epikhodov, the frustrated young man in *The Cherry Orchard*. Two, the boor and lout of the Bohemian fair-ground in *Liliom*. Three, the sleepy-eyed, velvet-handed, senile Russian judge in *The Greater Love*. Four, the bumptious, oily Italian journalist in Pirandello's *Naked*. Five, the tyrant Creon in *Medea*. Six, the jealous American in *The Happy Husband*, who looked as if he came out of one of the glossier American magazines. Seven, Count Pahlen in *Paul I*, a performance of slow-moving, irresistible momentum. Eight, Mr. Prohack in Arnold Bennett's play of that name, a witty portrait drawn from contemporary life and manners. Nine, the Man with Red Hair, an excursion into the horrific indicating a good many unpleasant things which Mr. Hugh Walpole had glossed over. Ten, Ben Jonson in George Moore's *The Making of an Immortal*. Eleven, the French detective in *Alibi*. Twelve, Mr. Pickwick. Thirteen, the pathetically ugly fellow in *Beauty*. Fourteen, the footballer-hero of *The Silver Tassie*. Fifteen, the Brigadier in *French Leave*. Sixteen, Tony Perelli, the gangster, in *On the Spot*. Seventeen, Mr. Marble, the bank-clerk turned murderer, in *Payment Deferred*. I also bagged him, as the collectors say, in a little piece by Lady

Bell. Looking back over this catalogue I find that my best recollections are concerned with the Man with Red Hair, Tony Perelli, and Mr. Marble. I am persuaded that Mr. Laughton's essential genius—by which I mean the perfect alliance of conceptual intelligence, representative intelligence, and physical *disadvantages*—is concerned with the portrayal of the sinister, all the more horrific because of the fleshly suggestion. Your fat murderer must always be more horrible than your lean one, who has a predestinate look of the gallows about him. But Mr. Laughton is also a magnificent actor on the mimetic plane alone, and is a master of that kind of character-acting which is as much a matter of mind as of make-up.

Coming now to this actor's recent season at the Old Vic, we find exactly what, if the foregoing be correct, we should expect. His Lopakhin in *The Cherry Orchard* was a superb study of character in the best sense of that word, and that it was not hailed as the finest piece of acting in town, which it demonstrably was, can only be attributed to the fact that the part is not a spectacular one. Angelo in *Measure for Measure* was a subtle study in vice horribly self-aware, though you had to accept the theory that he who is driven by fleshly and sensual desires must himself look sensual and fleshly. Prospero was a failure because you wanted to pat the old gentleman and tell him to run away and play. Chasuble in *The Importance of Being Earnest* was easy, and Tattle in *Love for Love* a brilliant achievement in comedy, again an essay in the best kind of character-acting. Macbeth, finally, just wouldn't do at all ! From all this it is to be argued that Mr. Laughton is not a tragic actor and never will be, and I write this article because I have heard a whisper that he intends to devote the next twenty years to proving that he is a tragedian. That indeed will be a tragedy, because it will be a waste both of time and of genius. Mr. Laughton

needs no increase of intelligence, conceptual or representative, and his Macbeth will not be any better if he thinks
about it till he is ninety. It all comes back to the old question
of an actor's physical characteristics, which are beyond Mr.
Laughton's or any actor's power to control.

I shall conclude with words of the great critic already
quoted, and which, applied to Macready, will stand very
well for my views on Mr. Laughton:

> " We shall perhaps best understand the nature of his
> talent by thinking of the characters he most successfully
> personated. They were many and various, implying great
> flexibility in his powers; but they were not characters of
> grandeur, physical or moral. They were domestic rather
> than ideal, and made but slight appeal to the larger pas-
> sions which give strength to heroes. He was irritable where
> he should have been passionate, querulous where he should
> have been terrible. In Macbeth, for example, nothing
> could be finer than the indications he gave of a conscience
> wavering under the influence of ' fate and metaphysical
> aid,' superstitious, and weakly cherishing the suggestions
> of superstition; but nothing could have been less heroic
> than his presentation of the great criminal. He was fretful
> and impatient under the taunts and provocations of his
> wife; he was ignoble under the terrors of remorse; he stole
> into the sleeping-chamber of Duncan like a man going to
> purloin a purse, not like a warrior going to snatch a crown."

Yet Macready, on Lewes's own testimony, was a magnificent
actor. So, too, is Charles Laughton. But he is not and never
will be a tragedian.

A FRENCH CLASSIC

RUY-BLAS.   By Victor Hugo.   Cambridge Theatre, Wednesday, May 23, 1934.   [*May* 27, 1934]

No MAN can serve two masters, and the worst part of being a dramatic critic is that one is seldom called upon to do anything else. Is the play bad ? Yes, but there are the susceptibilities of the impresario to be considered. Is an actress indifferent ? Yes, but you played golf yesterday with her husband, a charming fellow. Did a production bore one to the verge of swooning ? Yes, but the audience lapped it up and wanted more. The critic is always torn between what he honestly holds and that which a sentimental public would prefer he should kid himself into thinking and therefore saying. This week your dramatic critic finds himself most precariously poised, for he must decide between giving his honest opinion of the drama of Victor Hugo as it affects a modern English audience, and the natural deference and courtesy he must offer to the distinguished artists of the most famous theatre in Europe paying an official visit. He must console himself with the thought that a French critic would be in exactly the same difficulty if the Old Vic, which is the nearest thing we possess to the Comédie Française, were to present, say, *The Lady of Lyons*, in Paris, with the *doyen* among English actors as the amorous gardener. But we should certainly not dream of ushering in *King Lear* with Lytton's balderdash, and may it not have been a mistake to spoil our palate for Sophocles and Molière by drenching it with Hugo's turgid insipidities? Readers need not remonstrate that Hugo was a greater writer than Bulwer; comparisons, besides being odious, are generally inaccurate.

Fortunately, we have at hand an ally in that blessed principle known as historical perspective. The point is not how effective in the theatre Hugo is to-day, but how much effect he achieved in 1838, the year of *Ruy-Blas*, which by a happy fluke is also the year of Bulwer's masterpiece. One word in Hugo's earlier *Hernani* had ushered in the new mode in playwriting. The King asked: " Quelle heure est-il ? " and received the simple reply, " Minuit." Whereas, says Mme. Hugo in her reminiscences, every previous dramatist must have put the answer in the form of:

> *Du haut de ma demeure,*
> *Seigneur, l'horloge enfin sonne la douzième heure.*

Eight years later Hugo was still storming the battlements of realism when he made Ruy-Blas launch himself into a tremendous recital beginning, " Un jour . . ." and then break off with the words: " Mais à quoi bon ceci ? " Once more the point is not what realism in poetic tragedy is to the English audiences of to-day, but what it was to the French audiences of one hundred years ago.

A much greater difficulty crops up when we begin to consider the quality of Hugo's dramatic poetry. To the English ear Racine's verse is still lovely; his drama may be bound in chains, but the chains are silver and gleaming. Whereas Hugo's dramatic verse, again to English ears, is as clumsy as the ropes and shackles in which one breaks a horse. How is it, asks the Queen of Ruy-Blas, that he speaks as kings should speak ? Ruy-Blas replies:

> *Parce que je vous aime ! . . .*
> *Parce que rien n'effraie une ardeur si profonde.*
> *Et que pour vous sauver je sauverais le monde !*

Je suis un malheureux qui vous aime d'amour.
Helas ! je pense à vous comme l'aveugle au jour.
Madame, écoutez-moi. J'ai des rêves sans nombre.
Je vous aime de loin, d'en bas, du fond de l'ombre;
Je n'oserais toucher le bout de votre doigt,
Et vous m'éblouissez comme un ange qu'on voit !

Leaving aside the question as to how one could be dazzled
by an angel one *didn't* see, is not this horribly flat ? Flat, not
judged by the standards of one who would build him a
willow-cabin at his mistress' gate and halloo her name to the
reverberate hills, but flat absolutely and without comparison.
Possibly an intentional flatness, since not even your French
dramatic poet can have his cake and eat it, and Hugo,
having turned his back on the bombastic school with the
simple word " Minuit," cannot return to it, even when he
pretends to be impassioned. Yet here, again, opinions have
differed. Swinburne tells us that *Ruy-Blas* is written in
such verse as none but Hugo could write, and Théophile
Gautier puts the play high up in his list of well-written
pieces.

It is to be remembered, too, that Hugo was out to do
something other than display heroic figures in action to the
accompaniment of noble verse. The hero of his play, he tells
us in his preface, is not Ruy-Blas, but the people : " It is the
people without a present, but looking to the future ; orphaned
poor, intelligent, and strong ; humble in station, yet aspiring
high, and with the premonition of genius ; wearing the badge
of servitude, yet worshipping in its wretchedness and dejec-
tion that one figure which in a crumbling society stands for
authority, loving-kindness, and prosperity." But the whole of
Hugo's preface is good stuff, and it is odd to note, on re-
reading, how much better than his fulfilment is Hugo's
promise of the nobleman to whom one fine morning arrives

the discovery that in his race to ruin he has outstripped the monarchy. We have to realise, however, that to the French audience of the period Don César was probably as good as Hugo's foreword about him.

Still continuing in our lucky vein of historical perspective, consider last what the acting of Hugo's day was like, at least in Hugo's opinion. " The acclamations of the house," he writes, " greeted Frédéric Lemaître at his first entrance and continued to the end. Darkly brooding in the first act, melancholy in the second, impassioned and sublime in the third, he attained in the fifth to one of those prodigious effects wherein the actor surpasses all who have gone before. For older playgoers Lemaître is a Lekain and a Garrick in one, for contemporary theatregoers he combines the technique of Kean with the sensibility of Talma." G. H. Lewes made short work of Hugo's ecstasy. He confessed to the smallest possible pleasure in any French actor who is being *rêveur et profond*, denied that there were any tears in Frédéric's Ruy-Blas, and said straight out that the actor's famous " explosions " left him wholly unmoved. But this again was an English point of view, and Lewes volunteered the statement that Hugo ought to be the better judge of a great French actor in his own play.

Then how about the galvanising effect of a great actress upon that limp rag, the Queen ? It was her success in this part, rehearsed under Hugo himself at the 1872 revival at the Odéon, which obtained for Sarah Bernhardt her engagement at the Français. Mr. Maurice Baring says that in this rôle Sarah " had poetry, passion, and grace and youth, and first love to express. She expressed it easily, with unerring poetical tact; there was no strain, not a harsh note, it was a symphony of golden flutes and muted strings; a summer dawn lit by lambent lightnings, soft stars, and a clear-cut crescent moon." Consider now the stuff upon which Sarah

had to work these wonders. Consider that apostrophe to
the young man who sheds his blood and risks his life:

> *Pour donner une fleur à la reine d'Espagne;*
> *Qui que tu sois, ami dont l'ombre m'accompagne,*
> *Puisque mon cœur subit une inflexible loi,*
> *Sois aimé par ta mère et sois béni par moi!*

Was there ever such an example of the *cheville*, that
padding forced by rhyme-necessity, as " ami dont l'ombre
m'accompagne " ? The truth, of course, is that with the
supreme alchemists it matters very little whether the stuff
is Shakespeare or Racine, Hugo or the multiplication-table.
Sarah knew this as well as anybody, and it was probably this
knowledge that lay behind her Monna Lisa-like but entirely
scrutable smile !

Summing up, one finds in the new approach to realism, the
cunning flattery of the people, the robust, well-intentioned
verse, and the magnificent chance it gave to the actors of the
period, sufficient reasons why in 1838 the piece should have
had an enormous success with French audiences. Sitting at
it a hundred years later we must agree with Mr. Shaw that
" Victor Hugo, on his spurious, violently romantic side, only
incommodes us."

There still remains the obligation to say something graceful about our visitors. Times have changed, and M. Albert-
Lambert gives me the impression of having changed to the
extent of knowing fustian when he reels it off. Hugo—how
persistently the old man recurs !—gave Horace's famous
reason for the effectiveness of Lemaître's tears in this part.
But the theory that an actor must be in tears before he can
provoke them amply explains our famous visitor's failure
to move us, since it is simply not thinkable that anybody living to-day can project himself into Ruy-Blas's factitious
emotions. Not even a great French actor can declaim much

of this verse without looking like a dying duck in a thunder-
storm, and though it is a noble fowl and a grandiose commo-
tion the simile holds. In this case what mastery of tradition
and a noble voice could do was done, and the tirade about
the condition of Spain in the seventeenth century was fine.
Mlle Vera Korène as the Queen spoke beautifully and
looked almost obstreperously handsome. The other rôles
were agreeably distributed.

MILTON IN REGENT'S PARK

Comus. Revival of Milton's Masque. The Comedy of
Errors. Revival of Shakespeare's Farce. Regent's
Park, Thursday afternoon, June 14, 1934.

Meeting at Night. A play by Margery Sharp. Globe
Theatre, Thursday, June 14, 1934.   [*June* 17, 1934]

"There is very little sense in a play without a curtain," said Jane Austen's Mrs. Norris. But this does not
apply to *Comus*, which Milton wrote to be performed in the
shade of the old apple-tree. Hazlitt went to see this masque
at Covent Garden, and declared that it had been "got up
with great splendour" and received "as much success as
was to be expected." I hope it will be not unamusing if I
devote a little space to recalling what Hazlitt thought and
said about Milton on the stage. The greatest of English
critics begins by insisting on the contrast between his subject
and Shakespeare, declaring that Milton saw all objects from
his own point of view, whereas Shakespeare "had no personal character and no moral principle except that of good
nature." Having paid Milton a perfunctory compliment for
the quality of his verse, Hazlitt goes on to say that the poetry,
when spoken, lost half of its effect, but that this was com-
pensated by every advantage of scenery and decoration, so
that in the end "this most delightful poem went off as well
as any pantomime."

There follows a long and involved passage, proving, or

attempting to prove, that fine writing which is not immediately reflected in action, of which the masque-form admits
little, " is at best but elegant impertinence." In support of
this two passages are quoted " to show how little the beauty
of the poetry adds to the interest on the stage." Venturing
to disagree entirely with Hazlitt here, I would cite some
instances where the enhancement is entirely pertinent. In
such a passage as that in which the Elder Brother bids:

> *some gentle taper,*
> *Though a rush-candle from the wicker hole*
> *Of some clay habitation, visit us*
> *With thy long levell'd rule of streaming light . . .*

the ear must hear before the mind can take in the full
beauty of that last line. The eye slips too quickly over such a
passage as:

> *Can any mortal mixture of earth's mould*
> *Breathe such divine enchanting ravishment ? . . .*
> *But such a sacred and home-felt delight,*
> *Such sober certainty of waking bliss*
> *I never heard till now. . . .*

which demands all that the actor can give it of quiet ecstasy.
It is very finely rendered by Mr. Clifford Evans. Modern
criticism is, I suggest, much nearer the mark in going all
out for essential loveliness, and seeing the truth about vice
and virtue quivering within the wave's intenser day, through
the pure gusto of Milton's verse. For even Hazlitt granted
that Milton had gusto. So much of it indeed that he was
" never satisfied till he had exhausted his subject," whereas
Shakespeare " never insists on anything as much as he might,
except a quibble." But why drag in Shakespeare ? Had not
each his own gusto ?

Another amusing thing might be to compare Milton's

laboured argument in favour of Enjoyment as against Niggard Abstinence with what other writers have had to say on the same subject. The case for enjoyment is the burden of the Pléïade, and better scholars than I will know where to look for it in antiquity. On the opposite side the Attendant Spirit is easily confuted. What if Circe's victims:

> *Not once perceive their foul disfigurement,*
> *But boast themselves more comely than before;*
> *And all their friends and native home forget,*
> *To roll with pleasure in a sensual sty . . . ?*

How came the Spirit not to know that where ignorance—of a changed state or of anything else—is bliss, 'tis folly to be wise? Samuel Butler nearly sums it up when he says: " The extremes of vice and virtue are alike detestable: absolute virtue is as sure to kill a man as absolute vice is, let alone the dullnesses of it and the pomposities of it." The absolute truth, of course, is that the man who has only tasted virtue will never know any state of happiness above the middling, whereas the man who has savoured vice will know ecstasy and lose his peace of mind for ever. This statement is what we look for in the Lady's counter-argument, but do not find. In compensation we get her view upon the great problem of the twentieth century, to wit, the sane and equable distribution of the world's wealth. The passage, which I recommend to the attention of politicians of every school, is as follows:

> *If every just man that now pines with want*
> *Had but a moderate and beseeming share*
> *Of that which lewdly-pamper'd Luxury*
> *Now heaps upon some few with vast excess,*
> *Nature's full blessings would be well dispens't*
> *In unsuperfluous even proportion,*
> *And she no whit encumber'd with her store.*

But I digress. It now becomes necessary to say how beautifully the little piece is put on in this enchanting setting, which has nothing to do with the gas-lit theatre but is an element of its own compounded of earth and air and sky. At night, I am told, and can well believe, that Beauty walks these gardens. The actors go perfectly about their job, and not only the spirit of poetry, but the air of intelligent enjoyment, has descended upon the least of them. On the afternoon I attended Miss Sybil Evers played the Lady, and did very nicely. But the brunt of the business, which consists in taking the spirit out of our bodies and giving it an airing in the realms of fancy, rests with the Attendant Spirit, who is rendered by Mr. Leslie French in terms of breathless rapture. This can, of course, only be done by having perfect command of one's breathing, which again denotes the highly skilled craftsman. To communicate the incommunicable requires a touch of genius, and we felt that this had been present when at the end this well graced actor came forward to bid farewell, and twitch'd his mantle blue.

Mr. Bernard Shaw once wrote a full-dress article on the Elizabethan Stage Society's performance of *The Comedy of Errors*. This article began with an account of the touring actor's expertness in the matter of travelling by rail and bullying theatrical landladies. It went on to discuss Mr. Pinero's views on the stock company, Barry Sullivan's temperament, Macready's ill-temper, Shakespearean forgery, the dramatic art—if any—of W. G. Wills and Tennyson, Ibsen's Bishop in *The Pretenders*, Mr. Bourchier's training as an amateur, and how much Mr. Penley had made out of *Charley's Aunt*. The article ended with a dozen lines in which Mr. Shaw dealt with the method of production, ignored the acting, and had not a word to say about the play. Who am I to improve upon this master ? I shall simply hold that Miss Margaretta Scott brought Adriana to charming life, that Mr. Dennis Hoey looked magnificent as Solinus, that the Antipholuses and Dromios of Messrs. Eddison, Carey, Leigh, and Tickle were as little boring as they have ever been, and that heartening quantities of nudery and drapeage flashed through the fernery and boskage.

Meeting at Night is a very nearly good play which suffers from what one might call divided direction. It appears to be steering one course, and it suddenly takes another. In the first act Delia Crowborough, expensive and minxish, is engaged to marry the dashing young airman Harold Parker, principally because it would look well in the shilling weeklies. She is really much more attracted by Nicky Bentall, ex-Army and an almost-howling cad. At the end of this act Parker is about to fly to Australia, and if Delia hopes he gets there safely it is only because she will have another triumph to talk about at parties.

The second act is after dinner, and a small but smart house-party is sitting over their coffee on the verandah waiting to hear, if not see, Harold's aeroplane pass over the house. And then Harold comes in; he has funked it and turned back. The play, which had threatened to be merely one of amorous entanglements, now turns into a psychological study of fear, almost as though Harold were another Lord Jim. This is excellent, but we feel that Miss Sharp wasted a good deal of time over her comic newspaper-reporters which she might have used to explain that Harold's first-act gloom is nerves and not the mindlessness one expects from people associated with the internal-combustion engine.

It now appears that the discovery that her lover's courage is a mask for cowardice awakens a better self in Delia, who falls in love with her hero as soon as he declares himself bogus. This is the untrue stuff out of which psychological novels are made, and at this point we remember that Miss

Sharp is a clever novelist. Anyhow, Harold and Delia spend the night together, and next morning Harold finds sufficient courage to start his flight in earnest, while Delia scampers all over the morning-room furniture like a chamois which has found its mate. She becomes all girlish and happy; the airman crashes, and Delia announces that henceforth her purpose in life will be serious. She will do such things, though she cannot particularise, which, as another of fate's victims said, will be the terrors of the earth. Will a baby be among them ? We rather hope so, since nothing less could sober down this distressingly effervescent young woman.

The piece is very well acted. Miss Leonora Corbett does full justice to Delia, though Miss Sharp in demanding that she should turn on a soul as easily as a bath-room tap has asked too much. Delia, being a minx, has no soul, and Miss Corbett's cleverly substituted soulfulness is not quite what is wanted. But this improving actress does the sauce and capers very well. As the aviator Mr. Roger Livesey works tremendously for an opening, and has the sympathy of the house quite tremulously with him. In the middle of the second act after his confession of cowardice he is like a footballer who, with the empty goal in front of him, is afraid to kick—or like a prize-fighter punch-bound. Mr. Whatmore, who produces, and Mr. Livesey should get together at once and see what can be done to wake up this scene. It wants more movement and at least one little bit of noise. At present it is the most moving near-success in town, and one feels that it can be made into the real thing. For the rest, Mr. George Curzon puts a pleasant veneer on the caddish Nicky, Miss Merle Tottenham scores a clever little success as a journalist, Dame May Whitty as Delia's fussy and dithering parent is admirable, and Miss Helen Haye as a tart impoverished sponger on country-house hospitality throws some admirable vinegar on these troubled waters.

RONALD MACKENZIE'S LAST PLAY

THE MAITLANDS. A play by Ronald Mackenzie. Wyndham's
Theatre, Wednesday, July 4, 1934. [*July* 8, 1934]

EVERYBODY knows families like the Maitlands. Families
which when they do not happen to live at the seaside are at
this time of the year busy visiting it. Families whose members
make no concealment of their positive or negative attitude
towards each other. Or to whelks, beach carnivals, film stars,
mother's rheumatism, road-houses, washing-up, cocktails,
child-bearing, and every other item in the gay round of love,
life, and laughter. But can you make a work of art out of such
a family, being every family that looks forward to its three
weeks in August or fortnight in September ? The answer is:
easily, if the form contemplated is the novel, for there you
have the advantage of the author's sentimental or witty
commentary. Whereas if the play-form is chosen the tub
has, so to speak, to stand on its own bottom with nobody to
appraise its workmanlike tautness or leaking seams.

The theme of *Little Eyolf* was once declared by Mr.
Shaw to be " as actual and near to us as the Brighton and
South Coast Railway." And again: " If you ask me where
you can find the Allmers household, the Helmer household,
the Solness household, the Rosmer household, and all the
other Ibsen households, I reply, ' Jump out of a train anywhere between Wimbledon and Haslemere; walk into the
first villa you come to; and there you are.' " But there, I

suggest—belatedly, since the quotation is nearly forty years old—there, I submit, you are not ! By some ghastly accident the Allmers couple, who spend the evening spiritually dis-embowelling each other, come together as the curtain falls. But consider the end of the other Ibsen plays. Nora walks out, Solness falls off a steeple, Rosmer and Rebecca jump into a mill-race, Borkman freezes to death. Hedda shoots herself, and if Mrs. Alving is left twining her hands in her hair it is because Ibsen didn't forgive her sufficiently to grant her the boon of dying. I am not saying that these things are not right and proper as endings to stage-plays; what I do say is that if such happenings were as universal as Mr. Shaw in his first fine careless rapture for Ibsen pretended, Wimble-don and Haslemere would be more deserted than any village Goldsmith ever heard of. In other words, a play, while having the air of being true to life, must have livelier incidents or end in direr catastrophe than that life affords, or it won't be good theatre. Two questions must be asked of any play. " Are the characters true to life ? "—in which case the answer must be Yes. And : " Do people do such things ? " —the answer to which can be either Yes or No. The play is still good if the dramatist, through theatrical necessity, pushes normal people to an end which, though abnormal, is logical.

This dull preambling will have served its turn if it provides an answer to the objection that the incidents in *The Maitlands* are laid on too thickly. I do not believe that a schoolboy who has just passed his examination is going to burst with the news into any seaside parlour between Brighton and Wey-mouth and find it littered with wounded bodies and maimed souls. Everybody in this play has got into a different jam at the same moment, and while this can happen in all seaside villas the odds are a million to one against it happening in any one of them. Or you might put it that if the author had

been a Russian it would have been a million to one on these
things happening to any family of holiday-makers, and that
a play showing how these things did not come to pass would
have been dubbed by Russian dramatic critics " a fantasia
in the English light-comedy manner." But perhaps this is too
abstruse !

The Maitlands is true to life in that it concerns one of those
muddled families in which step-sisters, daughters-in-law,
and second cousins abound; we all know the family which
alternately cherishes and bullies some distant relative because the poor girl has nowhere else to go. This being so,
you rightly guess that the widowed Mrs. Maitland (Dame
May Whitty) has been left some £200 or £300 a year, and
possibly the house. Or any sum at once large and small
enough to keep both starvation and contentment at arm's
length. Her son Roger (Mr. Gielgud) is an usher at some
local private school, to and from which we gather that he
cycles. He would be able to give his mother a good deal more
out of his £400 a year if it were not that he has an expensive
wife (Miss Joan Marion) who is holidaying abroad. There
is another son, Jack (Mr. Jack Hawkins), an actor upon
whom the London managers are beginning to look favourably. There is stray Cousin Phyllis (Miss Catherine Lacey),
who still keeps up with her school friend Joan (Miss Sophie
Stewart), a young woman unaccountably alleged to have
money. One says " unaccountably " because the straitened-
means atmosphere has reduced one to the condition in which
most people spend their lives—that of looking upon money as
something existing only in books. There is the imbecile Major
Luddington (Mr. Frederick Lloyd), who gives the impression
of continually popping in while never seeming to go. This is
not the normal impecunious major of farce, but the pecunious
widower of real life with a half-pay pension and a half-
witted son, Arnold (Mr. Stephen Haggard), whom Roger

Maitland is coaching for an examination which it is inconceivable that he should pass. Normally nothing would
happen to these people except that the actor-son might
perhaps marry the rich girl-friend and the Major pair off
with the cousin, while in the course of time Mrs. Maitland
would probably die and the expensive wife decide to have
a costly baby. All this happening over years, while excellent
material for a novel, would be useless for a play. Therefore
Roger must know that his wife has left him, which permits
him to pay court to Joan. Phyllis refuses the Major because
of a moonlit, passionate stroll with Jack, who has no intention of marrying her, but will consider, when he goes on
tour, including her in his personal luggage. So far so good ;
whatever goes on in the Maitland household Mrs. Maitland
will know nothing about it !

The morning of the last act dawns bringing an American
offer for Jack, who rushes off, completely forgetting that the
night before he has seduced Phyllis. She, poor girl, would
now willingly fall back on the Major if she had not five
minutes earlier crushingly turned him down. Then, of course,
Mrs. Roger must come back to the fold, her foreign admirer
having turned out to be pure bad egg, and it goes without
saying that she enters unannounced to find the rich little girl
hanging round her husband's neck. Seizing a convenient
pistol she rushes off stage, and Roger, hearing the bang,
knows that if the wound is not fatal he must return to his
bondage. This is bad news for the poor little rich girl, who
gazes out to sea and the Isle of Wight, presumably hating
both. It is on this multi-melancholy scene that young Arnold
now enters, waving his telegram. Previously, when everybody
else was laughing, he was always crying, and now he is a dry
blanket among wet ones. It is a fine stroke of theatre which
makes his face and the curtain fall simultaneously, and
Mackenzie showed himself to be a first-class dramatist when

of all the characters in this play he solicited our affection for this gaby alone.

It is the barest truth that Mr. Haggard's acting as Arnold overshadows everything else. In *The Laughing Woman* he had to display a mind too big for his body; now his head, like the cretin's, must be too large. A young actor who can brilliantly achieve two such feats and refrain from swelled head —of which malady in Mr. Haggard's case I hasten to say there is no indication—such an actor may go far. In this play his rueful comedy and the suggestion that beneath his oafishness the boy is being hurt bring a lump to everybody's throat. In my time I have never seen such promise. I shall severely refrain from criticising Mr. Gielgud, who is much too fine and romantic an actor to be happy away from rhetoric and robes. It was in *Musical Chairs* that Mr. Gielgud first worked the vein of elegant umbrage at this crude world, and now he repeats the performance. It is a way out, but no more; if this romantic must be modern, it should only be in a Russian blouse. All that goes with the bowler hat defeats him.

Some grand acting comes from the rest of the cast, with the exception of one little lady who is tried too high. Mr. Komisarjevsky's production is first-class, and one thinks that he must have lain awake chuckling over his masterful jugglery with seaside architecture. Nothing but an anchovy in its curled state could cope with that jumble of lobby, stairs, and kitchen-door, or negotiate that first-floor landing without falling into the sea. But seaside houses are like that, and perhaps the happiest moment of the evening is when Miss Isobel Ohmead, distressed by some basement calamity, noiselessly puts her cap round the door and as silently withdraws it.

IDLE THOUGHTS OF AN IDLE CRITIC

[*September* 2, 1934]

A THREE AT THE LAST HOLE at Littlehampton and the best that Worthing can do in the way of dinner prompted me to present myself at the Connaught Theatre to see what was the worst that local repertory could wreak upon one. " Ahse full ! " said Gold Braid. I still murmured that I would like to see the show. " Ahse full, I told yer ! " Gold Braid repeated. With a shade of annoyance, I said that Mr. Agate of the *Sunday Times* would like to go in. There was a look on Gold Braid's face which could only be translated into : " Git aht of it ! " But at that moment the More Than Courteous Management came skimming up and enquired as to the length of my stay at Worthing. Three evenings thence a seat could be provided, and on the following day two. Business, I gathered, was topping. I enquired the name of the play, which, since this was a repertory theatre, could, I thought, only be called *Dole Day in Dukinfield*. But it wasn't. The piece was *Ten Minute Alibi*, that genuine London success.

This might be the place for an essay on what constitutes a success, and everybody knows that the art of essay-writing is to enlarge and expatiate upon what everybody knows already ! A theatrical success is a piece which people want to see as distinct from one which they ought to want to see and don't. That was the thing to say and it is said now, as Mr.

Humbert Wolfe's parodist put it. That to which I more particularly want to draw the reader's attention is the picture of a dramatic critic, whose whole soul less than a month ago vomited at the bare mention of a first night, being turned languishing away. That it should come to this, as Hamlet said. But two months holiday'd, nay, not so much, not two ! Heaven and earth, let me not think on't ! O most wicked speed, to post with such dexterity to a mere repertory theatre and then be unable to gain admission ! There is, of course, another way of looking at it. This is that the Everlasting had taken the best means of securing his canon 'gainst self-slaughter. Anyhow I did not get in. That is the point I intended to make, and it is made now.

In a reasonable world your dramatic critic, returning to London with Ate by his side, whoever she or he may be, and ready to cry Havoc ! and let slip the dogs of war, would find something to cry havoc about and to let slip the dogs at. But this world is not reasonably constituted, and the past week has seen one all dressed up with nowhere to go. Mr. Cochran magnoperated last night at the Palace, Manchester, and yesterday afternoon the dramatic critic of this paper minoperated at a horse-show in a field adjacent to Manchester. But Browning was right: never the play and the place and the beloved critic all together. Though I was in Manchester I was not at Mr. Cochran's revue. I heard beforehand, however, that it was going to be a great success, and what more can anybody ask ? In theatrical matters the fault, dear Brutus, is not in ourselves but in our stars, and Mr. Cochran's bunch is beyond reproach. However, I seem to be straying off into the Tom Tiddler's Ground of Mr. Bishop's column, and had better be getting back to my own.

This is no place for a review of the season that is past; things without remedy should be without regard. Nor is this the place for an assessment of the season to come. The future, said Paula Tanqueray, is only the past entered again through another gate. " That's an awful belief ! " retorted Aubrey, and obviously every dramatic critic would give up the ghost if he believed that the season in front of him was going to bear any likeness to the one he has left behind. Hope, however, springs eternal in the human breast, and at this point it occurs to me that one of the best ways of making bricks without straw is to borrow the quotational bricks that somebody else has made. The instructed reader will have remarked this already.

I shall, therefore, cast no longing, lingering look behind, being fully determined to forget those last six months during which palsy shook a few sad, last grey hairs, and dramatic critics sat and heard each other groan. Away ! Away ! Though the dull brain perplexes and retards, tender is the night, and haply the Queen-Moon is on her throne clustered around by all her starry Fays. From which I gather that Miss Cooper is going to appear in a play with Miss Compton. But I gather wrong : both ladies are to appear this week, but at different theatres !

Mr. Maugham told us at the end of *Our Betters* that the most beautiful sight in the world was two ladies of title kissing one another. I conjure up a view even more luscious —that of two star-actresses handing the play's success to one another at curtain-fall with every appearance of cordial sincerity. But that is a dream never to be realised on this more than terrestrial planet. Nor would it be in accordance with cosmic law. The only reason the stars don't bump into each other is that they keep strictly to their own orbits, and the same holds good of theatrical stars. Yet somehow I wish it were different. I should like to have seen Kean and Irving in the same play, and why not Laughton matched against Jannings ?

In such an ideal exhibition there would be little cautious

sparring—no half-hits—no tapping and trifling, none of the *petit-maîtreship* of the art—they would be almost all knock-down blows; the fight would be a good stand-up fight. To see two rival players rise up with new strength and courage, stand ready to inflict or receive mortal offence, and rush upon each other " like two clouds over the Caspian "—this is the most astonishing thing of all : this is the high and heroic state of man ! So say all of us. Or at least those of us who have the wit to take their good where others, notably Hazlitt in his account of the fight between Bill Neate and the Gasman, found it.

That is why I want to see Miss Bergner matched against an actress of equal talent. But our younger writers on the stage tell us that Miss Bergner's talent is matchless, and therefore the wish is vain. The only possibility, then, is to match Miss Bergner against a part, and I suggest it should be a part in which other great actresses have found fame. There were great men before Alexander, and presumably there were great actresses before Miss Bergner. Now what part would one like to see her essay ? Lady Macbeth ? Hecuba ? Adrienne Lecouvreur ? I would suggest *A Doll's House* except for the fact that the British public has unmistakably let it be known that it does not intend to flock to any revivals of Ibsen in any considerable numbers. If the various banking-houses refuse to avail themselves of ¡Mr. Micawber's abilities, or receive the offer of them with contumely, what is the use of dwelling upon *that* idea ? If the various types of men and women who make up the playgoing community refuse to avail themselves of Mr. Ibsen's abilities and refuse the offer of them with contumely, what is the use of dwelling upon *that* notion ?

Therefore I am going to suggest that Mr. Cochran should get Mr. Romney Brent to re-translate *Frou-Frou*, an admirable play, and one of the best parts for an actress ever written. This piece was good enough for Aimée Desclée and

Bernhardt and Modjeska, and should suit Miss Bergner. A good Frou-Frou, said W. T. Arnold, " must be and do two things. She must be personally likeable by her audience, and she must be able to play the first two acts with the almost fatuous light-heartedness they require. In other words, an actress must have charm, and the power of appearing extremely young." What's the matter with that ? And again, of Modjeska's performance: " The opening of the fourth act was touchingly played with a kind of sad dignity which suited the part. The scene with Sartorys was moving and powerful, and the death scene in the fifth act touching. Its great merit was the continued thought for the child at the dying woman's feet. Sarah Bernhardt forgot him too soon. It was the one fault of her exquisite performance in this act. The scene is, however, but a purple patch upon the play in any case, and the English version is here necessarily inadequate. ' Pauvre Frou-Frou ! ' is untranslatable."

If Miss Bergner is the actress we all take her to be, I feel sure that she would find the right translation for " Pauvre Frou-Frou ! " However, if there is one thing of which I am certain, it is that we shall *not* see Miss Bergner in this part. Which is a pity, since comparisons, though odious, are the only method of ascertaining how far any player is entitled to be considered great. That is why I would rather see Miss Bergner in a revival, say, of *Mary Rose* than in a new play, even by such a master as Sir James. Fair as a star, wrote the poet, when only one is shining in the sky. I suppose that it never occurred to the old codger, ambling at Ambleside and mobled in sublimity, that this was as about as left-handed a compliment as any poet could pay.

Where, the reader may ask at this point, are we in the argument ? To which I triumphantly retort: Who said anything about an argument ? *Voilà l'article qu'il fallait faire, et maintenant ça y est !*

MISS COOPER ON ILKLA MOOR

THE SHINING HOUR. A play by Keith Winter. St. James's
Theatre, Tuesday, September 4, 1934.

MURDER IN MAYFAIR. A play by Ivor Novello. Globe
Theatre, Wednesday, September 5, 1934.

ROSE AND GLOVE. A play by Hugh Ross Williamson.
Westminster Theatre, Saturday, September 8, 1934.

[*September* 9, 1934]

" Rural audiences have not that analytical spirit which leads
the mind to fasten itself upon trivial details, and thereby to lose
the true perspective."   —Letter to the Press.

WOE IS ME, first that I am not a rural audience, and
second that a month's rustication has renewed the analytical
spirit ! Mr. Winter's play has four major characters—David
Linden and his wife Judy, David's brother Henry and his
wife Mariella. The house is David's, and Henry has brought
Mariella on a visit. The play is about two things, Yorkshire
farmhouses and the lengths of self-sacrifice to which a
farmer's wife will go that her husband may be happy with
another woman. Not being a married woman, I know
nothing about such lengths. But I have horse-dealt in Yorkshire, and I have never met a farmer who had an equally
good seat (*a*) on a horse, enabling him to win cups at shows,
and (*b*) on a piano-stool, enabling him to play a Rachmaninoff Concerto and for an encore the César Franck Violin

Sonata. Now I do not deny the existence of Yorkshire gentle-
man-farmers whose final meal is high tea. The point is that
if they and theirs speak with the accent of the St. James's
Theatre, then I know that they live in a largeish house
adjoining the farm, and employ a bailiff. Whereas if they live
within ten yards of the stables—which judged by a stop-
watch is the case in this play—and do their own calving and
foaling, why then I expect them to speak with a Yorkshire
accent and their womenfolk to look as though they had never
heard of bath salts. It must be one or the other.

The impression this piece makes is that it was conceived
in London and then forcibly transplanted to Yorkshire, on
the theory that an elaborate sweet made by a fashionable
chef becomes a Yorkshire pudding if it is set down on a
Yorkshire table. Mariella, the exotic visitant, with her simple
little gowns by Molyneux and her nose-in-the-air manner, is
perfectly true to life. I remember as a boy sitting opposite
some such creature at lunch in a country inn at Dovedale,
and hearing her ask of her flashing escort about a dish of
obvious custard: " Is that mayonnaise, do you suppose ? "
Mariella, not recognising a high tea when she sees one,
points to the cold ham and boiled eggs and asks whether
people are expected to eat all that amount before dinner.
She has your travelled insolence, because when somebody
asks her if she has ever seen such a sunset, she replies, " Yes,
lots ! " and goes on with her book. The daffodils must have
peered very hard indeed when so sophisticated a doxy came
over so simple a dale. But we have agreed that the lady is all
right; it is the dale which is so odd. What dale and in what
Riding ? Bloomsburyites will " get " me when I say that I
suspect it to be the Laura Riding, and that the only market
David could ever drive his pigs to must be Shepherd Market.
If the setting of the play were London I should not at all
object to its pattern, which is neat. Mariella never really

loved Henry and married him for reasons which really do not concern the playgoer. They happen to be that she found her own country, Holland, too flat, was bored with the windmills, and wanted to marry somebody. Henry, needless to say, is very much in love with her. In the case of the other couple the pattern is reversed. David never really loved Judy, though Judy passionately worships him. These premises being set forth, the play can only be about what is to happen when David and Mariella discover a mutual passion. Here I must take that carping view from which your rural audience is so fortunately free. In dramas of West End entanglement blameworthy husbands are doubtless discovered pressing to their lips in abstraction gloves discarded by their mistresses. Doubtless they are surprised gazing spaniel-like at doors through which their fair ladies have withdrawn.

By the way, what a quaint trick stage-heroines have of thinking they will go to their rooms and going there! Mariella does this about twenty times. It occurs to me that an admirable play might be written entirely in that room to which a distraught lady retires after this scene and that, and I suggest it to Mr. Priestley who is interested in technique. But to return to that farm-kitchen. Frankly I do not believe that David, being a Yorkshire farmer, would allow himself to be discovered fondling the jacket he has lent Mariella during a ride.

But there is a more important matter in which this play bears the London hall-mark. Whether the reader will agree with me depends upon whether he also believes that a complex in town takes on a different complexion in the country. Judy, having read *The Fountain* and been a member of the Gate Theatre, both from the beginning, would conceivably hand her husband over to Mariella on a sublimated plate. Whereas everything I know about the wives of

Yorkshire farmers tells me that Judy, accustomed to separators
and dividing sheep from goats, would take a totally different
view of the town-bred intruder. We are asked to believe that
Judy climbs a hill to put a sacrificial two and two together.
My view is that she would stand her ground in her own
living-room, fight for its sanctity with tooth, nail, and
tongue, and tell Mariella how many beans make five, where
she gets off, and that if she insists upon getting off it will have
to be with somebody else's husband. And how long does
Judy suppose the pair will remain happy ? She knows David
well enough to realise that he will get sick to death of dragging Mariella round the watering-places on the Yorkshire
coast and playing that Rachmaninoff Concerto on indifferent
hotel pianos and the viler ones of boarding-houses. In a word
this play, which is thoughtful and not vulgar, has nothing
wrong with it except the characters it is tacked on to. That is
to say, I do not believe in a Yorkshire Judy rushing to the
barn which has conveniently caught fire and flinging herself
under a crashing roof-tree. Whereas I should be perfectly
prepared to believe in Judy as a Mayfair *exaltée* descending
to the garage in the mews below and doing whatever it is
people do who asphyxiate themselves in garages.

Regarded as Yorkshire farm-people, the company come in
for the same criticism as the play; in so far as they were distinguished artists comporting themselves at the St. James's it
is inconceivable that they could have been better. Mr. Raymond Massey as David gave the impression that he knew a
great deal about the piano and nothing at all about top-
dressings; however, he rode the third-act storm very well.
Miss Adrianne Allen, deserting the pert for the wistful,
achieved it both wisely and winningly; this was a complete
success in the theatre, and it was the author's and not the
actress's fault if we felt that with such a farmer's wife mice
could trail their tails with impunity. Miss Gladys Cooper as

Mariella did not break her rule of always doing well; the part gives few opportunities, but the competence is so great that it takes on the air of something more. As Henry, the featureless husband, Mr. Cyril Raymond filled in perfectly. The piece has two other characters. One is the youngest male Linden, nicely presented by Mr. Derek Williams; the other, a female, dragonsome Linden, is the best part in the piece. Perhaps for that reason, and perhaps because the actress is unfamiliar as well as clever, Miss Marjorie Fielding ran off with what was left of the play after Miss Allen had done with it, bag and baggage, scrip and scrippage.

An alternative and better title for *Murder in Mayfair* would be *When Policemen Sleep*. There was an awful shindy in a mews, as a result of which a slut, brilliantly acted by Miss Edna Best, was shot. Three characters were in the running for the crime. There was Miss Fay Compton's peeress, who on an excessively hot night when nobody else was wearing any kind of wrap went to a mews party in a cumbersome fur coat. Perhaps it was the sort of a fur-coat peeresses in the Agony Column are prepared to sacrifice. Somehow or other we didn't think this peeress did it. Nor could we assign the crime to the French pianist, impersonated by Mr. Novello and the victim of all that contumely and misunderstanding which go so well with the rising inflection in this actor's voice. " You do not want to hear me play Bach's Chromatic Fantasia ? You must talk while I play ? You believe a great pianist has nothing in his private life except dope and drink and women ? Of course you believe these things ! " Then with a descending inflection : " Well, for once in a way, my dear friends, you are right ! I have not played one bar of the Fantaisie Chromatique since that woman told me she loved me. She told me she was going to have a baby. You think that baby was mine, *hein* ? Well, my friends, for once you are wrong ! " No, although Mr. Novello brought his usual skill, charm, and gusto to the rôle of saint slightly the worse for wear, we did not think he shot the slut.

This left only Mr. Robert Andrews, the slut's boy-lover, pure of heart. Now, Mr. Andrews is always a much better actor than anybody ever supposes, and his performance in this piece is the best but one. But the leopard cannot change his spots, and vice versa ! What I mean is that this actor has bounced up and down with a tennis-racket on too many of Miss Marie Tempest's sofas to steep his hand in murder. And perhaps, after all, it didn't matter who killed the slut. The police took not the slightest interest in the question, and it seemed almost gratuitous of Mr. Novello to assemble the trio for a conference on the material as well as the sentimental aspects of the crime. " It's all right, old boy," said the French pianist to the betrayed lover. " You just toddle along to Paris. I've no doubt that the jury will put it down to some Person Unknown. Let me see, this is the —— division, isn't it ? The —— police are pretty decent about this sort of thing."

Why was it necessary for the slut to become shot ? Well, that's a long story, and I am afraid not interesting enough to tell in detail. Miss Best, who gave by far the finest performance of the evening, completely negatived the play by the inability to suggest foulness of mind. Having explained what she understood by love—" Something that always was and will be, before I was born and after I shall have died " —in the clear tones of the Constant Nymph, Miss Best could do no more than suggest the foul temper of a pure mind, and this has nothing to do with sluttishness. Within this interpretation her performance was subtle and full of interest, arousing expectation by some little bit of significance, satisfying it, and using the satisfaction to provide fresh expectation—whereas everybody else in the play plastered one with Mr. Novello's clichés and exhibitions of acting that had served a hundred times before.

I don't quite know what to say about Miss Compton; she really must contrive distortion or some way of bringing expression to lovely features which too many years of light and sunny comedies have rendered as placid as Bassenthwaite, that lakeland jewel which persists in shining whether the sun is out or not. The play has a long part which might have been written for Miss Braithwaite or Miss Collier in grotesque mood. Actually it is played by Miss Zena Dare, about whose performance I do know what to say—though I hardly like to say it. May I just hint to this well-meaning actress that throughout the evening she continually breaks the first rule of acting, which is that a player shall not be obviously conscious of his or her audience ? The performance would be effective enough if Miss Dare would only consent to keep it within the framework of the play. As, however, the entire audience disagreed with me and applauded Miss Dare to the echo, I should not, if I were she, take my advice.

The blurb to the printed version of *Rose and Glove* contains the sentence: " The play takes certain liberties with the facts of history, though none with its truth." As I do not know what this means, I will go on with the next: " Inevitably it will recall Marlowe's *Edward II*, but the relationship between the King and Gaveston is shown here in an entirely different light, since Marlowe's thesis is both psychologically improbable and historically unproved." Mr. Williamson is entirely at liberty to think this way. Hitherto Piers Gaveston has been regarded as Edward II's favourite in a pejorative sense, and again Mr. Williamson is entitled to the view that they were the best of pals only in the sense that the Chairman and the Vice-Chairman of an Urban District Council are hand-in-glove. But the friendship theme recurs throughout this play like the fences in a point-to-point race, with the horse consistently refusing. Then why give the piece this particular historical label ? Why not postulate any idealistic king and any flatulent adviser who, having inherited a war, seek to get out of it ? The best criticism of this play I can think of is contained in Mr. Evelyn Waugh's description of Hetton Abbey: " Between the villages of Hetton and Compton Last lies the extensive park of Hetton Abbey. This, formerly one of the notable houses of the county, was entirely rebuilt in 1864 in the Gothic style and is now devoid of interest. It contains some good portraits and furniture." It seems to me that Mr. Williamson's play is without interest, that the portraits are poor likenesses, and that I do not know any old song which I would exchange for the furniture.

The acting of a distinguished cast is undistinguished, though the cast may reasonably plead the absence of any spur to distinction.

MR. PRIESTLEY'S TRIUMPH

EDEN END. A play by J. B. Priestley. Duchess Theatre,
Thursday, September 13, 1934.   [*September* 16, 1934]

A HALF-WIT SAID to me the other-day: " Did you enjoy
Treacle Tart? " I said: " No ! " The half-wit went on: " But
you gave it a good notice." I said: " I thought it an excellent
musical comedy ! " and left him. After the first night of
Mr. Priestley's play another conversation of like refreshing
clarity took place, this time between a distinguished intellectual and a dramatic critic:

D.I.—I read your notice of *The Busy Bee*. I must say that
play entertained me immensely, though you say there
wasn't a word of truth in it. Now, to-night's play may be
true. But I just didn't want to see it.

D.C.—Oh !

D.I.—You see, I go to the theatre purely to be entertained.

D.C.—Ah !

D.I.—And therefore I don't care whether a play is true
or not. The kind of falsehood which you say upsets you in
a theatre upsets me if I find it in a book. But then I take my
reading seriously.

D.C.—Yes ?

D.I.—You see, I don't think the theatre's the place for
serious plays !

D.C.—No ?

D.I.—Of course there's Tchehov. But that's different.

D.C.—Oh ?

D.I.—What I mean is . . . Sorry, here's my car. Good-night ! Intellectual disappears, and Critic turns into the Strand wondering how an art can survive when the half-wits only like it when it is bad and the intellectuals won't have it when it is good.

I have decided that what follows shall be addressed neither to the one class nor the other, but to that utterly reasonable person, the middle-brow, who will not scoff if I mention the name of William Archer. Archer laid it down that there were three things to be asked of any play. (1) Is it true to the visible and audible surfaces of life ? (2) Does it use the mechanism of the theatre in such a way as to beget " interest, suspense, anticipation, sudden and vivid realisa-tion " ? (3) Does the end of the play find the audience morally the better and intellectually the richer for it, and does the play say and mean something ? I shall return to these three questions presently. The point is now to report Mr. Priestley's play as accurately as memory and the neces-sary condensation permit.

It is October, 1912, when the curtain rises on the sitting-room of Dr. Kirby's house at Eden End in the North of England. Sarah (Miss Nellie Bowman), the old Yorkshire nurse in the Doctor's family, is alternately petting and scolding Wilfred Kirby (Mr. John Teed), a callow youth on leave from Africa where he has a job with a trading-com-pany. He is at the stage when barmaids attract, and we feel that she will be a lucky Hebe who does not get him for a husband. Wilfred has a sister called Lilian (Miss Alison Leggatt), a hard, unlovable creature who if she ever gets a husband will make him feel meaner than he really is. She hankers after Geoffrey Farrant (Mr. Franklyn Bellamy), a neighbouring gentleman-farmer, whose poetic needs are satisfied by Kipling and who could not spell " Rach-maninoff," let alone play his concertos ! We feel that

DN

Geoffrey will be a lucky fellow if he does not fall a victim to Lilian's spidery lure. Then there is old Kirby himself (Mr. Edward Irwin), a country doctor who, after taking his degree, deemed provincial discretion a safer card to play than London valour. Life's more glittering prizes have passed him by, and it is his half-regrets which hold the play together.

They would be whole regrets if it were not for his elder daughter Stella (Miss Beatrix Lehmann), who eight years before the play opens ran away to become a great actress, and has achieved her object. Or so her fond parent believes. This affectionate gullibility is the play's single weakness; the old man is too shrewd in other matters not to know the truth in this one, and, in any case, the jealous Lilian's viperish tongue must have undeceived him. The difference between this anomaly and concerto-playing farmers is the difference between a good suit of armour with a flaw in it, and one which isn't sword-proof anywhere. It is a structural weakness rather than an imperfect realisation of character.

Now Stella enters, and we realise from the actress's mien and aura that Stella is not really a famous player even in the repertory sense. Ostensibly home for a holiday, she is obviously tired out and sick to death of playing second leads in Number Three towns and on colonial tours. You might put it that she is anxious to shake the yoke of being an inauspicious star from her world-wearied flesh. By the end of the first act Lilian has wormed out of her sister that she is married, though separated from her husband; she will leave it to Stella to tell her father in her own time and way. In the interval Lilian has been busy, for when the curtain rises three days later, we find that she has telegraphed for Charles Appleby (Mr. Ralph Richardson), Stella's husband and a fifth-rate actor and "good sort" whose spiritual home is the saloon bar. Why has Lilian telegraphed? Because Stella has been setting her cap at Geoffrey, that innocent fly half caught, or so Lilian thinks, in Lilian's web. Here we come upon the play's strength, which is its steady truth to life as it is really lived, and not as it is imagined by greensickly playwrights with Oxford insufficiently out of their systems. Does Lilian, improving the shining hour, swallow half the contents of her father's medicine-shelves so that the way is clear for Stella to marry Geoffrey after divorcing Charles? No. Instead she has a heart-to-heart talk with Stella, and Mr. Priestley is a sufficiently good dramatist to arrange that you cannot easily tell it from a slanging match. Lilian points out to her sister that she has made a mess of everything she has attempted. She ran away to become a famous actress and failed. She has tried marriage with Charles and failed. Now she comes quoting Wordsworth and a lot of guff about starry skies and lonely hills to poor Geoffrey who is perfectly happy with a gun and a few rabbits. In a few months' time she will drop him like a hot potato, and where will they all be then? Lilian is just not going to stand for it, and Stella has the sense to see that right is entirely on her sister's side. There is nothing left to do except pack up, which she literally does. Pretending to her father that she and Charles have two important offers, Stella makes it up with that bemused numskull, who asks for nothing better than to take the road again in double harness. The end of the play finds the Doctor with his dream of vicarious content unbroken, and the curtain descends on a delightful touch. This is that Geoffrey, who cannot have Stella and will not have Lilian, also packs a bag and goes off to a cousin in New Zealand.

Now, is this a good play, or isn't it? Let us go back to Archer's criteria. (1) I suggest that, apart from the unique discrepancy to which allusion has been made, the play is entirely true to the visible and audible surfaces of the life it sets out to present. Wilfred, Lilian and Stella are brother and two sisters, the daughters of this father and not four gowned-and-tailored, unrelated mannequins only to be brought to life when fashionable players consent to put on their clothes. Mr. Priestley's characters move by their own volition before he has started to do and after he has done with them. Charles is the kind of man Stella would marry, and Geoffrey is the kind of gentleman-farmer who would be potting rabbits in that vicinity. In other words, the characters exist and cohere. (2) Is the play all that is conveniently summed up in the word " interesting " ? That depends upon the playgoer. If the playgoer must have Lido-haunting duchesses upbraided by their dukes for choosing their gondolas according to their gondoliers, and cannot bemean himself to a milieu where nobody has more than a few paltry hundreds a year, why then this play is not for him. I am afraid my word will have to be taken for Mr. Priestley's craftsmanship and manipulation of incident, which are admirable. This is not one of those plays written round a dozen heads stuck out of a dozen railway-carriage windows to see why a train has stopped and pressing their owners into some fortuitous imbroglio.

(3) Permit me to leave moral improvement out of the question. Archer had to put that in because he was a Scot. Is the playgoer intellectually the richer for this play ? That again depends upon the playgoer. If he be a low-brow he has no intellect to be enriched; if he is a distinguished intellectual like my friend of the other evening he wants his theatre to make him not richer but poorer. I am convinced that this play will give the middle-brow something to think about and talk over. What does it say, and what does it mean ? I doubt whether Archer himself could have given a satisfactory answer to this question about any play. In connection with the first production of *Little Eyolf* we find him writing: " I should be puzzled to say off-hand what is ' the good of ' the *Œdipus* or of *Othello*." And again: " I

must premise with emphasis that it is no set ' doctrine,' or
' moral,' or ' message,' that I profess to expound. I do not
even assert that Ibsen deliberately put in the play all that
I make out of it. He simply took a cutting from the tree of
life, and, planting it in the rich soil of his imagination, let it
ramify and burgeon as it would."

Similarly I shall be content to say that Mr. Priestley has
taken a cutting from the tree of Yorkshire life and that its
ramifications and burgeonings, with their gentle melancholy
and rich humour, moved and amused me as I like to be
moved and amused in a theatre. Why 1912 ? Not for the
easy irony of the " good time coming," but because of the
greater poignancy of that passing moment which has all the
illusion of urgent life and that we know to be in yesterday's
grave. If *Eden End* is not a good play, then all that I know
and have learned about plays is wrong, and I must go to
school again. My half-wit who enjoyed *Treacle Tart* will
probably say to me, provided he retains even that half of
wit which he hath: " I thought *Eden End* was an excellent
play. I did not enjoy it."

On the first night I thought that Miss Lehmann was a
little shy of the immensely difficult part of Stella. It is a comparatively easy thing for a great actress to come flaunting
on to the stage as a genuine world-famous actress like
Sudermann's Magda; all that is necessary is for the player
to abound in her own glamour. Miss Lehmann had to tackle
the far more difficult job of suggesting an actress trailing
clouds of failure. But even unsuccessful actresses visiting the
home that lay about them in their infancy bring with them
the smell of grease-paint, and the fact that they have not
made good only increases their pretentiousness. In other
words, Miss Lehmann was not quite actressy enough for
Stella. This lovely player is first and foremost an intellectual
actress, and I half-suspected her underplaying to be due

to the old intellectual snare of team-work. Away with all such repertory nonsense ! Stella is a leading part, and whoever plays it must lead. May I then suggest to an actress of extraordinary perception and quality that she should first of all speak up a little more, and then consult some Mrs. Vincent Crummles or other old trouper as to how she may make her gestures and the outline of her acting a little less woolly ? If Miss Lehmann can be persuaded to throw her weight about a little more, this beautiful play will draw the town; her colleagues, one and all, are sheer perfection. The production of Miss Irene Hentschel is exceedingly sensitive and skilful, though as a sop to those who go to the theatre "for entertainment" she would do well to speed it up here and there.

OLD VIC AND OLD NILE

ANTONY AND CLEOPATRA. Revival of Shakespeare's Tragedy. Old Vic Theatre, Monday, September 17, 1934.

MOONLIGHT IS SILVER. A play by Clemence Dane. Queen's Theatre, Wednesday, September 19, 1934.

No MORE LADIES. A comedy by A. E. Thomas. Wyndham's Theatre, Tuesday, September 18. [*September 23, 1934*]

To STRIKE TWELVE at once is no mean feat for an actor; it is a still greater feat for a whole company. This is what any company must do which tackles *Antony and Cleopatra*, and the question is how near the new players at the Old Vic have come to doing it. Two things are essential for this kind of success. The first is that the actor shall at once throw the spectator back into the time of which Shakespeare was writing; this is largely a matter of appearance. The second is that he shall act Shakespeare like a Shakespearean actor, which is largely a matter of voice. In my view all but three of the company fail, for reasons to be particularised presently. The three successes are Mr. Abraham Sofaer's Messenger, who looks exactly right and with each and every one of his small scraps of verse fills the theatre with Shakespearean music. The second success is Mr. Maurice Evans's Octavius, though I think a chillier note should be struck by this master of chicane. The third is Mr. David Horne's Enobarbus, though he imperils the time-factor by looking a little too like the late Lord Salisbury. When these three actors are about we have the fleeting sensation that this is Shakespeare's tragedy of *Antony and Cleopatra.*

No other play by this or any other dramatist plunges so directly into the middle of things. The opening sentence: " Nay, but this dotage of our general's O'erflows the measure " shows the piece well on its way. The next eight lines promise everything that we are to see. Incidentally, I wish some better instructed Shakespearean commentator would tell me whether the coincidences in which this play is peculiarly rich really are coincidences or intentional echoes and recapitulations. In the first speech Philo talks of his captain's heart having in the scuffles of great fights burst the buckles on his breast, and in his last scuffle with fortune Antony bids his heart be stronger than its continent and crack its frail case. Was it conscious art or something in Shakespeare's physiology which made him subconsciously repeat the pattern? Perhaps we may say of the poet what Antony himself says of the Soothsayer: " Be it art or hap, he has spoken true." However this may be, Philo's first speech presents us with the whole of this tragedy of looking backward.

" Money lost, little lost; honour lost, much lost; pluck lost, all lost." Mr. Granville-Barker says in his admirable Preface to this play: " Losers ought not to whine. Antony stays a soldier and a sportsman—and a gentleman, by his lights—to the end." But a gentleman in ruins, and with a partiality for harping on earlier pomp and circumstance. Over and over again Antony insists upon what a lad he has been, and there is such magic in the poetry of his regret that it is as though Autumn should call attention to the glory of its former Summer. Cleopatra makes tremendous catalogue of all that Antony has been; and the freed slave's " noble countenance Wherein the worship of the whole world lies " is neither compliment nor lip-service. These things are the mind's-eye portrait of all those vestiges and remnants which the actor must present to the spectator's physical eye and ear. Here, the spectator must say to himself, of his own accord and without prompting, are the ruins of the world's arch-romantic, master of largesse and unparalleled spendthrift. Though when the play opens Antony may be at the end of his tether, the actor's concern is not with this, but with the royally ranging fellow Antony has been before his tether runs out. Now I have great respect, and have often expressed that respect, for Mr. Wilfrid Lawson as a character actor. But this must not debar me from saying that Antony is a rôle which, though Mr. Lawson may conceive it perfectly, he can neither look nor voice. His first appearance with a shock of hair kept tidy by a gold band suggests a leading member of Peter Quince's troupe, and his voice is quite staggeringly unfitted for heroic verse. " Grates me : the sum ! " says Antony to the messenger from Rome. Alas, it is not the news that grates Antony so much as Antony's voice which grates on us ! In addition, the articulation is so indistinct that in many places the meaning is quite incomprehensible. Thus Antony nowhere justifies all that the other characters say about him, or our own preconceived view.

Miss Mary Newcombe's Cleopatra is a very good performance—of some other character. Of, say, a brilliantly clever, highly complex, neurotic lady of our own times. Perhaps not quite our own times, for Miss Newcombe has thought back, though not far enough back ; not further than Portia or Beatrice. Her dresses, of which the principal feature is a fringed tippet, could be worn at any of to-day's dinner-parties without exciting comment. On the other hand, her verse-speaking is so far on the right lines that it has obviously to do with verse, though I think she should mouth it more, and in the line : " rather make My country's

high pyramides my gibbet," give the word " pyramides "
its four syllables. Let me say that within the actress's conception her playing is always subtle and at the end moving.
Mr. Shaw said, apropos of the Manchester production of
1897, that if managers will only take care of the minor
actors the leading ones will take care of themselves. Either
insufficient care or something else has gone wrong with the
casting of Charmian and Iras. Charmian is acted as though
she were a replica of the parts played by Miss Helen Spencer
in modern comedy, and Iras is just a round-faced little
Miss from Kensington Gore. Now, if the atmosphere of the
East is to be brought into this play, these are the two
characters to do it, since it then gives Cleopatra time to
get on with the business of inveigling and betraying Antony.
Iras is mute almost throughout, but when she speaks it is
immensely to the point, and she has two extraordinarily
lovely lines:

> *Finish, good lady; the bright day is done,*
> *And we are for the dark.*

In Manchester they made Iras into a low-browed, walnut-
stained Egyptian, who throughout lay on her stomach and
gazed at Cleopatra in a mood half-way between breathless
adoration and sphinx-like criticism. She knew all that was
going on, and told Cleopatra when it was time to throw in
her hand. Whereas the present Iras is dumbly inefficient,
and Charmian gabbles to no purpose.

Despite the foregoing, the fact remains that Shakespeare's
play has come between me and every other I have seen this
week. The production by Mr. Henry Cass is for the most
part excellent, though I dislike the Chorus recruited from
the canvases of Marcus Stone. Mr. Menges' music is colourful
and happily remote from that facile Egyptologist, Luigini,
though near the end there is a horrid concession to what is

left of Victorian taste in the form of a voluntary which might
have been ladled out by the lamented Liddle. If there is
need for a concession to the senses, why not incense?

Moonlight is Silver is about a bundle of charm. Josephine,
while married to a stupidly jealous husband, and knowing
him to be both jealous and stupid, does openly all those
things which a minx does surreptitiously, and is annoyed
when the green light comes into her husband's eye. She
will go out of her way to spend every afternoon for three
months furnishing a country-house under the ægis and
personal supervision of her husband's friend, Charles.
The reason Josephine does not tell Stephen about these
confabbings and closetings is that the country-house is to
be a wifely surprise. So far, so good. It is Charles's wife who
becomes alarmed, or pretends to, and starts yammering
about a divorce. You would think, wouldn't you, that
Josephine, having done enough in the way of arousing suspicion, would lay off a little. But nothing of the sort. She
must always let Stephen surprise her talking to Charles over
the phone or holding his hand in sisterly farewell. In fact,
she is more irritating than Desdemona, because that young
woman was gormless by nature, whereas Josephine is supposed to be electric with gumption. In fact, the difficulty
one has with Miss Dane's play is, that if Josephine would for
one moment consent to demobilise her charm and behave
like an ordinary woman there would be no play. But perhaps
there isn't one anyhow!

Against this must be set the view that, up to a point, the
piece is very amusing. At the end of the second act Josephine,
to avoid further tormenting by her jealous tyrant, confesses
to the misconduct which she has not in fact committed.
This means a third act to prove to Stephen that Josephine
has been lying. Now the long speech which is alleged to
convince Stephen is all tosh. It is based upon the true love

in Josephine's regard and mien, just as though this were not the first thing any competent gadabout learns to achieve ! I permit myself to hold that this would be a much better play if the third act were abolished and the play made to end with the second-act curtain, which should run: " Very well, then. Since you *will* have it, I have been unfaithful ! " The whole point is Stephen's realisation in a flash that he *never can know* the truth, and it is the first law of tedium to inflict a third act upon an audience which has also realised in a flash that the play is over. Let me invite Miss Dane to read again Maupassant's story entitled *L'Inutile Beauté*, which is the last word anybody ought to write on this subject. Again, the characters in this play are obviously extremely well-off, and I estimate that Josephine's pocket-money runs into thousands. One feels that in real life she would simply say to her husband: " My dear Stephen, as you have obviously gone out of your mind, I am off to Sardinia, or Salzburg, or Southend ! " And go. One feels that tears are wasted on so arrogant a muff as this husband, and that this wife would simply not spend them. (There is some psychological business about Stephen's inferiority complex which is both pretentious and meaningless.)

Miss Lawrence's second-act frock of black velvet has a *chevaux de frise* of black tulle round the shoulders, so exorbitant and breath-taking that, looking at it, play and player vanish. Also one knows perfectly well that any woman wearing such a frock for the first time would not notice if her husband throttled her; her self-approbation would be proof against Othello himself. Miss Lawrence's fireworks explode to the normal pattern, though with a higher degree of incandescence than ever; Mr. Douglas Fairbanks, jun., sets the match to them likeably, with a good deal of power and discretion; and nice things should be said about Mr. Cecil Parker and Mesdames Martita Hunt,

Helen Haye, and Alexis France. But the treat of the evening, to my mind, is provided by Mr. Barry Jones, as Charles. Why Mr. Jones should throw over his definite matinée charm and take to inventing an odd, woolly, and entirely credible human being is one of those things no box-office can understand. But then part of the credit for this should be given to Miss Dane, whose play, until it begins to bore us by pretending to be serious, is very entertaining. The leg of mutton may be indifferent, but the trimmings are riotous and unusual.

Edward Warren and Diana Townsend in *No More Ladies* are the Antony and Cleopatra *de nos jours*. Edward runs after women, and Diana picks out luxurious hours with pugilists and other ornaments of the not too *beau monde*. She makes her first entry with a bandaged hand and, asked why, explains that it is through barking her knuckles on the front teeth of a young gentleman who has been seeing her home from a night-club. This is more or less the first act. In the second act Edward and Diana are married, and while he continues the noisy tenor of his way she has gone all soulful. Diana, you see, is that most tedious of all the theatre's puppets, the minx with a heart of gold. She has thought marriage with Edward was going to be a perdurable hypostasis, and Edward's attitude to this may be summed up in the phrase, " nothing doing." Diana invites to a bridge party all the riff-raff of Edward's acquaintance, so that in the third act the pair may compose their differences. Why this means should have that effect I have no notion. This play's assumption that there are no more ladies is backed by the author's inability to discover any more gentlemen. This may be true; indeed, modern society works day and night, especially night, to give such a theory plausibility. But from the point of view of the drama, I suggest that if it be true that ladies and gentlemen have ceased to exist, it will be necessary to re-invent them, for the reason that the preposterousness which has become normal loses all its tang. If conduct is not three parts of life, there can be nothing left remarkable, as Cleopatra would say, on the other fourth. Insult to the intelligence is added to the injury of the mind by the fact that the dialogue is entirely composed of laboriously unsuccessful epigrams.

Mr. Arthur Margetson acts cheerily, and Miss Ann Todd discovers a wholly unjustifiable spirituality. Miss Ellis Jeffreys, in a large part which has nothing to do with the play, is like a famous prize-fighter compelled to enthral an Albert Hall audience without any opponent. Her over-emphasis is therefore to be excused on the ground that shadow-boxing must be over-emphatic or it is nothing. I have little else to remark about this play, except that it contains two butlers, and that its presentation has required the connivance of four impresarios.

CAN LEAR BE ACTED?

KING LEAR. Revival of Shakespeare's Tragedy. Westminster Theatre, Monday, October 8, 1934.

[*October* 14, 1934]

Two of the prime cuts in the body of cant are the statements that Shakespeare did not mean his play of *King Lear* to be acted, and that it is in fact unactable. Both statements are nonsense, and Lamb when he inaugurated the second of them was for once in a way out of joint. That Shakespeare had the stage very much in mind is proved by the dramatic business of the trumpets sounding on behalf of Edmund, which is nothing to read, and again when the doctor says at Lear's waking: " Louder the music there ! " If ever there was a stage-direction in Shakespeare's spoken word, this is it. I have a fancy, too, that there is a pointer inserted in this play not for the benefit of any possible reader but for the slower-witted playgoer. I am aware that Shakespeare did not contemplate the printing of the plays, and that when we talk of *King Lear* not being meant for the stage we are really thinking of the poet giving rein to his full mind without caring whether the result could be fastened down to a stage performance. The passage I have in mind occurs when Kent is warned by " a Gentleman " that Lear:

> *Strives in his little world of man to outscorn*
> *The to-and-fro conflicting wind and rain.*

May we not take it that this is as much a pointer to the immediately ensuing: " Blow, wind, and crack your cheeks " scene as the steeple of St. Martin Ludgate is to St. Paul's ? In the theatre a bolt from the blue may be too sudden, and Lear's next appearance is so terrific and so *outsize* that I can imagine Burbage saying to the author: " You must give 'em a lead here or they'll laugh ! " We know that Shakespeare prepared us for Lear's entrance " fantastically dressed with wild flowers " in Cordelia's speech beginning: " Alack, 'tis he ! " This speech is generally cut, perhaps because the talk of rank fumiter, burdocks, hemlock, nettles, cuckoo-flowers, and darnel reads too much like a brochure with the title, *Garden Weeds and How to Get Rid of Them.*

It is even more demonstrable that Lear can be acted, as anybody can be convinced who takes the trouble to see how the great players of the past have come off in the alleged unequal and unfair contest. According to Forster, Betterton's performances of Lear between the years 1663 and 1671 " are recorded to have been the greatest efforts of his genius." But Forster does not mention who were the recorders, perhaps for the reason that Steele, the first accredited dramatic critic, was not born until the year after Betterton relinquished Lear. A hundred years later Spranger Barry and Garrick divided the town in this part. Of Barry it was said that he was " every inch a king " ; of Garrick that he was " every inch King Lear." According to Hazlitt, the impression made by the latter on Dr. Johnson was so terrific that he could never again see him in the part. Johnson, however, in his preface to the play does not allude to this, saying merely: " If my sensations could add anything to the general suffrage, I might relate that I was many years ago shocked by Cordelia's death, that I know not whether I ever endured to read again the last scenes of the play till I undertook to revise them as an editor."

I had hoped to prove that all the greatest actors have been greatest in Lear, and that the mark of second-raters like

Edwin Forrest, Vandenhoff and Charles Kean was to fail in
the part. But facts are stubborn things, particularly theatrical
facts. According to Hazlitt, Kean, whom I have always
regarded as the greatest of all English actors, merely
" chipped off a bit of the character here and there." My
father, who ran away from school to see Macready, implied
in after life that if he had not played truant he should not
have thought so much of him. I can never get it into my
head that Macready was really first-class. Yet here is Lewes
saying that Lear was his finest Shakespearean character, and
Forster opining that Macready's was the only perfect picture
of Lear since the age of Betterton. Then, of course, there was
Irving's mishap. Of this Mr. Graham Robertson has written :
" I saw the play again on the fifth night, and Irving's rendering was magnificent, its pathos terrible. I can still see him,
weary and half dazed, sitting up on his couch and staring at
the daughter he had banished, as she bent tenderly over
him. ' You are a spirit, I know. When did you die ? ' he
whispered ; and I can almost weep now when I recall his
voice." The trouble on the first night was Irving's nervousness, and I shall always believe that his Lear was a sublime
failure in the sense that it was a failure on the first night and
sublime for the rest of the run. In any case, I personally had
always more pleasure in seeing Irving fail than any other six
actors succeed. To sum up, the part of Lear can be played
by a great actor—if he is the kind of great actor who can
play Lear.

There is a sense in which a very young player Shakespeareanly bent is not ill-advised to tackle Lear ; nobody is
to be blamed for not climbing Everest, whereas he is a fool
who falls off Skiddaw. About Mr. William Devlin, who is
twenty-two, I shall say straight away that his acting in
the part is good enough for me to disregard his age. As the
performance of a youngster and a beginner it is incomparably

finer than anything I have ever seen; in fact, I have never seen anything at all like it. Setting this against the performances of mature actors in the part, I find that, with the exception of Benson's Lear, it is again incomparably the best I have known. Whatever one may have politely said about individual performances, I know none in my time that began to be Shakespeare's character, whereas Mr. Devlin's starts by being Lear. This is a snuffy, rather dirty old king, made out of the earth of Britain, and not your intellectual actor's octogenarian, *soigné*, redolent of the pouncet box, and breathing Oxford's youngest accent.

With that logic which so pains readers of this column, I shall now explain why the rest of it will probably be devoted to dispraise of Mr. Devlin, the point being that, whereas I have given marks to other actors for their little victories over nothing, I may have to take marks off Mr. Devlin for occasionally falling short of perfection. For example, he is not tall enough, and when this Lear talks about being every inch a king he has not enough full height to draw himself up to ! Over and over again throughout the play one feels that Lear must look as though he had stepped out of a canvas of Michael Angelo or a drawing by Blake—that is to say, just a shade bigger than life-size. But things without remedy, of which height is one, should be without regard, and Mr. Devlin has that with which Garrick and Kean made up for their lack of inches, a magnificent voice full of oak-cleaving thunderbolts and all the rest of it. He would do well, by the way, to devote attention to the middle register, which is a trifle weak. He has abundance of gesture, skilfully contrived in the grand manner, and is obviously an actor who has no difficulty in acting. Mr. Devlin presents Lear along the traditional lines without any annoying intellectuality and with due attention to each point as it comes along. I think that presently—in the course of the next forty years—he will

be able to elaborate the physical characteristics a little more
and show how as mind and body crumble the spirit becomes
more and more towering. Lear, who at the beginning has
still some vigour, comes at the end to physical babyhood;
contrariwise, the childish mentality with which he sets out
becomes the greatest mind, though disordered, that Shakespeare ever drew. It was wise of Mr. Devlin not to insist too
much upon the presentation of senility, which is the mark of
your second-rate actor; there will be time to make more of
this when he is confident of taking it in his stride. His understanding of the text and his sense of beauty are everywhere
apparent, and the whole of his conception hangs well
together. His most moving passage is perhaps the " Come,
let's away to prison " speech, and his pathos is as good as
any young man can be expected to achieve, though here one
thinks the actor must have years. " Nature's above art in
that respect," as Lear remarks. But the sovereign merit of
the performance—aided by the superb Goneril of Miss
Dorothy Green, the unusually effective Oswald of Mr.
Julian Somers, and the goodish Kent and Edmund of Mr.
Neil Porter and Mr. Francis James—is that it enables the
play to be seen as a whole. Here Mr. Hugh Hunt helps
through having the extraordinary notion of presenting the
play as a whole, or very nearly. This is attained through the
use of curtains and a simple, stylised setting having nothing
to do with those geometrical arrangements whereby Goneril
and Regan must stand on the apices of triangles while Lear
sinks back into a parallelepiped. The result is that the
philosophy of the play comes through as well as its poetry,
and to a greater degree than I have ever known before.

The reader will note that I make no claim for Mr. Devlin
as a great actor. I merely say that, apart from Sir Frank
Benson, his is the best Lear I have ever seen. On the other
hand, Mr. Devlin may be the worst possible Hamlet and an

incomparably fatuous Macbeth. Or he may not; it is impossible to tell. One cannot estimate an actor's facial expression or mobility of features when they are obliterated by the papier-mâché and horsehair of the make-up for Lear. Mr. Devlin creates for himself in this part a magnificent head, which, however, remains the same throughout, except that he holds it at different angles like a figure in a carnival. The simile is apt because the head is too big for the body, a fault which would be less noticeable in parts not of the Father Christmas order.

RICHARD NOT HIMSELF AGAIN

RICHARD II. Revival of Shakespeare's Tragedy. Old Vic
Theatre, Monday, October 15, 1934.

IMMORTAL GARDEN. A play by H. C. G. Stevens. Whitehall
Theatre, Thursday, October 18, 1934.

[*October* 21, 1934]

EITHER ONE is becoming a more attentive playgoer or the
method of Shakespearean production is getting more lucid.
Or was it that in the old days the star-actor appeared, did
his bit, and went off to have a breather but allowing no
more of the business of the play than was necessary for him
to recover breath ? There was a time when Shakespearean
playgoers who gathered their Shakespeare entirely from the
stage could hardly know what any play was about. The production of *Richard II* at the Old Vic is admirable in this
respect. So much of the play is left that one can even gather
whose son Richard is. The staging is excellent, the return
from Ireland being indicated by a single mast and sail quite
breath-taking in assurance, and very nearly as good as the
cromlech in the Westminster production of *King Lear*. The
mind once being satisfied, everything that the characters say
will be granted them. " Barkloughly Castle call they this at
hand ? " says Richard looking up at the upper box on the
O.P. side, and Barkloughly Castle that upper box promptly
becomes. " My lords of England," says York, and now that
we are in the mood the very supers become noblemen and
the ground they stand on is England. Talking of the ground,

one remembers that it was of this same cube erected in the middle of the stage like a monster packing-case that one recently said: " This is Egypt ! " Let me drop the shadow of a hint to Mr. Henry Cass, the producer, that if all the Kings of England are going to get themselves crowned and un-crowned on the top of Cleopatra's Monument, there is a faint danger of his mounting becoming stereotyped.

One of the best jokes of this production is the miscasting of Miss Mary Newcombe for the Duchess of York. Or perhaps I should say Miss Newcombe's refusal to cast herself properly. The Duchess is wife to the Duke—so much even the can-tankerous will not gainsay. York is brother to John of Gaunt, notoriously in his dotage, and it is sufficiently plain that York himself is a doddering old fool. Whence it follows that the Duchess is no chicken. " Have we more sons ? " she says. " Or are we like to have ? Is not my teeming date drunk up with time ? " There is no doubt that the Duke and Duchess are this play's two comics, for, if they were not, Shakespeare would have found some other two. Whence it follows that if York is, as the text dictates, a garrulous time-server and cackling old idiot, his Duchess must be at the beldam stage with her knees creaking with rheumatism. In the face of all this Miss Newcombe, coming to plead for her son Aumerle's pardon, makes skimming entry like a swallow down wind or a seagull lighting on a pier—virtuosity in motion of which any dancer in the Russian Ballet would be proud. Whereat Bolingbroke, who is thirty-three, the gentleman of the period, and solicitous for the old lady, has to say: " Good aunt, stand up ! " In addition Miss Newcombe gives herself such big round eyes and is so beautifully becoiffed that she could go on at a moment's notice for the Nun in *The Miracle*. Mr. Abraham Sofaer's Bolingbroke is a rich, resonant, and finely controlled performance; here is the man who is master not only of England but of himself. Mr. David Horne gives weight and authority to Northumberland, and I dissociate myself from those who appear to think that Mr. Horne is not a good Shakespearean actor. He lends weight to a company which is inclined to be on the young side. After all, even in the jimp and modish dawn of the Renaissance some of the men must have been full grown.

Mr. Maurice Evans is faced with one of the most difficult of all Shakespearean rôles. It was Sir Frank Benson who first discovered Shakespeare's Richard. Or perhaps it would be better to say that it was Montague who discovered what Sir Frank had discovered in the part, since when we have all gone on re-discovering Montague. The whole of this great piece of criticism hangs upon Richard's repetition of his last two words—" to die." " Mr. Benson half rises from the ground with a brightened face and repeats the two last words with a sudden return of animation and interest, the eager spirit leaping up, with a last flicker before it goes quite out, to seize on this new ' idea of ' the death of the body." Anti-Bensonians—for there have been some of this school—have said that on this occasion Richard, engrossed in the simulation of death, forgot whether he had said this line or not and so repeated it to make sure ! Mr. Evans restores the balance by leaving the last two words out and just looking them, which is very clever of him. There have been other great exponents. There was Beerbohm Tree, who made the play look and sound like the sweet knell of Old Jewry. And of course nobody has forgotten Mr. Gielgud's poetic study, which must always satisfy those who never saw Benson. Mr. Evans must be said to do remarkably well in view of the fact that he is the last person one would cast for Richard. The first and last pitfall of the acting profession is for the actor to think that by imagination, cerebration, or sheer acting he can play any part. This is just not true. Henry Irving could no more pretend to be a bluff, gormandising hearty than

Ellen Terry could " get away with " malevolence. Mr. Evans is of the Hotspur type. His body and mind are wiry, quick to active decision, and hence the very opposite of Richard's luxury and indolence. Whether Richard is conceived as conscious artist or minor poet uttering a good deal of major verse makes no difference to our acceptance of this Richard, which is just not forthcoming. The whole performance, then, is, as it were, surrounded by a thin circumference of disbelief. Yet Mr. Evans is so good an actor that, given the rim of non-acceptance, we unhesitatingly believe everything within the circle. That which should be petulance becomes genuine passion, and as passion is very fine indeed; this Richard would not say these things, but we realise that Mr. Evans is saying them very well. His speech beginning: " We are amazed " is a magnificent piece of declamation, and he renders the metaphysics of the last soliloquy with greater cogency than anybody else I have seen. Where this clever young actor is most at home is in the early scenes, in which he achieves a glittering impertinence. And the serious half of the play, though not lying within the actor's physical scope, is at least as well done as the handicap permits.

One of the commonplaces about spiritualism is that, though it may not be true, its use in moderation does no harm. The same may be said about Mr. Stevens's agreeable fantasy, *Immortal Garden*, which takes a wholly benevolent view of the hereafter. The next world is pictured as a garden which, we feel, would meet with the entire approval of Mr. Beverley Nichols. People about whom on the earthly plane bulletins are being issued foregather in this cheerful pleasaunce; those who are going to recover are made free of a tiny bit of the garden, while those who are about to pass over are seen wandering about it at will. There is a path up which these are ultimately led, and down which they never return. 'Tis a discriminating garden

where falls nor hail, nor rain, nor any snow, nor ever wind
blows loudly. Or if it does it is discreetly tempered to the
gentlemen in evening-dress and the young lady with the
permanent wave and the frock cut low. This suggests the
twofold reflection, that Infinity is the only dimension in
which a wave can be permanent, and that if you are a spirit
you cannot catch cold. However, it is a reassuring garden
which has nothing whatever to do with imprisonment in the
" viewless winds " blowing one " with restless violence
round about the pendent world."

It is apparently always late evening in summer, just before
dinner, the time being what the French call *l'heure bleue*. It
is a funerary garden in which one suspects nothing grows
except tuberoses and arum-lilies. It is an uncrowded garden
in which only one person dies at a time; *tot homines, quot
horti*. One person, one garden; this is a metaphysical grot
which can be multiplied in proportion to the population.
Music, by Mr. Leslie Bridgewater, attends the passing of
each individual, and I see no difficulty in the score being of
the kind which Norman O'Neill used to compose. This is
Limbo, and presumably if the characters were Elizabethans
we should hear lutes and recorders, while if they were
Ptolemaic our metaphysical sense would translate it in terms
of shawms and sackbuts. Probably one is putting this play
to the wrong kind of test. Like the Queen in *Hamlet*, we may
say to its author: " Come, come, you answer with an idle
tongue ! " It is certainly feasible for Mr. Stevens to retort:
" Go, go, you question with a wicked tongue ! " The point
is—does the spectator enter into, or does his mind reject,
these lush friskings in the unknowable ? Does he like the
manner in which Mr. Stevens gyres and his characters
gimble. The author will not deny that his next world is a
wabe. Is it, then, as good a wabe as Sir James Barrie found
for *Mary Rose* and Mr. Sutton Vane for *Outward Bound* ? And

if it is only a competent wabe, is competence enough ? My difficulty in plays of this order is to find something else to think about what time cerebration is prorogued. I found resource the other evening in wondering why the county cricketer who passed over did not wear skeleton pads. *Ex nihilo nihil fit* may be applied to the actors in this unfortunate experiment. Perhaps a word may be allowed about little Miss Mary Casson, impersonating the only character in the piece who was not half or quite dead. This pleasant little actress was clever enough to play for sanity, in which she was assisted by two smart frocks and a satin night-gown.

A TEMPESTUOUS EVENING

THEATRE ROYAL. A play by Edna Ferber and George
Kaufman. Lyric Theatre, Tuesday, October 23, 1934.

LOVERS' LEAP. A comedy by Philip Johnson. Vaudeville
Theatre, Thursday, October 25, 1934.

LINE ENGAGED. A play by Jack de Leon and Jack Celestin.
Duke of York's Theatre, Wednesday, October 24, 1934.

[*October* 28, 1934]

THE CAVENDISHES, though English-born, are the leading
theatrical family of America. The head of it used to be
Aubrey, a Macreadyish exponent of the classics, who took his
celestial call immediately on top of a dozen mundane ones.
In plain English, he dropped down dead on a Saturday night
after a week of playing to full houses. To him succeeded his
wife Fanny, now well on in years spent in Ill., Mass., and
Pa., and never missing a performance except to give birth
to Julie and Anthony. At the moment she is pulling up after
an illness, and the children are looking after the family fame.
Perhaps " notoriety " would be better, for though Julie
functions as a splurgy actress of good repute, Anthony is a
zany who treats the drama's principalities and powers very
much in the way that Petruchio treated Kate. Does a play
or film producer not see eye to eye with him ? Anthony will
spit him with quattrocento rapier or modern toasting-fork.
Does some New York reporter pester too much ? Anthony
throws him overboard from the liner's top deck. These

things are permitted to Anthony because of a nostril quivering with passion like a Derby winner's. Of the nose itself, Hyperbole is incompetent to speak; her finest flight—that from a feminine point of view it is America's Bridge of Sighs —is a lame and impotent conclusion since it has contained no hint of the quality of this world-wonder. Continually the possessor of this miraculous organ irrupts into the Cavendish apartment like some antique general about to sack a city; his costume bespeaks a mind as original as it is various— trunks and codpiece from some Florentine tragedy, silk and claret-coloured Russian blouse, the gold and quilted dressing-gown of Talma.

The fact that this piece has no plot does not prevent it thickening. There is a moment at which (a) Fanny Cavendish in collapse has been carried upstairs; (b) Anthony is yelling the house down for an immediate passport to Europe; (c) Julie is clamantly deciding to give up the stage that she may marry a South American millionaire; (d) Julie's daughter Gwen is vociferously breaking off her engagement with a boy in the insurance business who will not let her be an actress; (e) Fanny's brother Bertie is trying to borrow money and get his appalling wife into Julie's next play; (f) the house is besieged by florists, duns, reporters, callers on the telephone; and (g) everybody is taking a different kind of meal on a separate tray. " Is it always like this ? " asks the millionaire inopportunely calling. And Julie answers: " No ! As a matter of fact, you've arrived during the rest hour ! " This play is not a picture of normal theatrical life but a skit upon one family's way of living it. It is not pretended that much progress can be made with the study of, say Hecuba or Hamlet at a moment when one artist is being carried upstairs in a coma and another is sliding down the banisters in a frenzy. What is pretended is that Dryden was right when he said:

Great wits are sure to madness near allied,
And thin partitions do their bounds divide.

Only in the case of two of the Cavendish family the partitions
are down. Nothing can have been farther from the mind of
the authors than the indictment of a hard-working class.
Normality is represented at either end of the scale by the
oldest Cavendish, who intends to die in harness, and by
the youngest, who is beginning to realise that husband and
child must be minor personages in the life of one who would
be a stage-player.

The acting is a joy. The brilliantly written parts of Bertie,
the ham actor, and his wife, are most amusingly filled by
Mr. George Zucco and Miss Mary Merrall; indeed, one
could write a whole essay round Miss Merrall's hard-bitten
etching of the tenth-rate actress who contrives to be humble
and pretentious, haggard and jaunty, all at the same time.
Mr. Laurence Olivier gives a Cain-and-hair-raising performance of the Theatre Royal's imp of fame; the portrait is
lifesize and lifelike, which is not necessarily the same thing.
Miss Madge Titheradge endows Julie with her personal
sense of exquisite fun. This is not so much an impersonation
as an insinuation of one who, abroad a lioness, is at home
an ever so slightly malicious mouse. Miss Margaret Vines,
playing the granddaughter, has enormously improved.

Miss Tempest has obviously had no illusions as to who is
the head not only of the Cavendish family but of this cast
also. In the bright lexicon of Mr. Coward's youth there has
never been any such word as " fail." But I surmise that at
last there would have been if, as producer, he had attempted
to tell Miss Tempest that gowns of such bedazzlement were
surely never worn by snuffy old ladies lagging superfluous
on the stages of Ill., Mass., and Pa. Fanny's dresses are lovely.
The first, in cardinal, is pure Sargent, the black one in the

middle act is sheer Renoir, while the white radiance of the last is Sir John Lavery at his most expensive.

About this study of old age there is nothing of what Rupert Brooke called the " unhoped serene." On the contrary, it is fractious and imperious, full of gaiety and courage —no regretful withdrawal from life but a tingling coda. Indeed, the one mistake in a production lively to the point of breakneck is the close. Bravado at the expense of dying, and not death itself, is the matter for this play, and Fanny Cavendish should be alive at its finish. To stage a solemn death-scene with a slow curtain is an artistic error. Worse still, it will militate against the run of this glorious farce. Or will it ?

That noble army of martyrs, the panners or runners-down of new ventures, were at full strength at the first night of *Lovers' Leap*. They presented their case against this play on the well-known model of the defendant who says that his dog didn't bite the old lady, and, alternatively, if it did it wasn't his dog ! They stoutly denied that Mr. Johnson's play was witty, and, being asked to account for the machine-gun crackle of its reception, asseverated that the wit was borrowed from Mr. Coward. This is the kind of lying stuff which is so mischievous because it is based on a modicum of truth. It is true that Cedric, making conversation about Scotland and Ireland, and " not forgetting little Wales," repeats Richard and Jackie's tabloid tour in *Hay Fever*. But then, Mr. Coward himself repeats this trick when, in the first act of *Private Lives*, Amanda and Elyot throw off monosyllables about India, China, and Japan. In condonation of Mr. Johnson I shall suggest that experienced playwrights who repeat themselves must expect to be repeated by the inexperienced. Further, I suggest that this thing may very well be common form. Cedric is making his first appearance in the London drawing-room of Helen, whose sister Sarah he hopes to marry. Obviously, he desires to stand well with Helen, and his allusion to his actual castle in Scotland is a delicate hint that it is not a castle in Spain. I take it that Cedric is not cribbing from Mr. Coward's Jackie or Elyot, but volunteering answers to Lady Bracknell's—in this case Helen's—legitimate inquiries as to his eligibility. But grant—though I do not admit—echoes conscious or sub-conscious here and in half a dozen other places, and I still think a substantial residuum of originality must be ceded. Let anybody shut himself up with sufficient paper and Mr. Coward's recently published *Play Parade*, and see what sort of artificial comedy he can produce which shall get past an audience knowing most of these plays by heart. The thing just can't be done.

Now look at it another way. The piece, as is the manner of all these quadrilaterals, has no plot, or a very tenuous one. Helen and Roger have made a mess of their marriage, and it is because of this mess that Cedric and Sarah are shy of the marriage vow. The young people are going to take the less risky course of living together, and to prevent this and win them over to respectability Roger and Helen simulate reconciliation. The play then resolves itself into two questions. Will the young couple see through the show of reconciliation? And will that show bring about the reality? In the end the play shelves these dusty answers, Cedric deciding to join Roger as an Egyptologist raking in the dust of centuries. A weightier complaint would be that the author has bagged Mr. Maugham's ending to *Home and Beauty*. But here again the thing must be common form, at least for any dramatist determined to avoid the sticky, sentimental ending.

Returning to the argument, how does anybody expect such plotlessness to last out two and a half hours in the absence of wit? Shall I put it that a ship may not be seaworthy, but that if it keeps on crossing the Atlantic without foundering it must have some quality deputising for sea-worthiness ? If Mr. Johnson's play is without wit it must have some other quality which does as well. Though it is a futile thing to put the spoken word to the test of black-and-white. I will risk a sample, because a sample seems called for. Roger, provoking Helen's jealousy, alleges attachment to a lady Egyptologist, and this follows:

ROGER: Here's her photograph on a camel.
HELEN: Do all camels look like this ?
ROGER: Look like what ?
HELEN: Sneery. . . .

So far as I remember, none of Mr. Coward's plays contains any allusion to camels. Need I add that " sneery " is the camel's criticism on the other woman ? And, of course, the reader has sensed the overtone here. If this were a French play the wife would in her own mind be calling the other woman " ce chameau," the inevitable word for ladies dis-approved of. But I will not insist further, or ask the panners straining at their own gnat to swallow too much of my camel. The piece has four delicious studies. Of Helen's termagancy by Miss Nora Swinburne, of Sarah's virginal idiocy by Miss Ursula Jeans, of Cedric's nervous embarrassment by Mr. Walter Hudd, and of Roger's obtuse virility by Mr. Owen Nares. Taking my courage in both hands, I advise readers to spare an evening for the wittiest little comedy in town.

As a piece of dramatic carpentry *Line Engaged* will neither wash nor hold water. One just refused to believe that the hero would go out and murder a man hoping that his father, who was detective-inspector for the district, would come to his help and do some monkeying with pistols while the police-surgeon was examining the body. Also, there were so many bullets in the play that one lost count of the billets. Ethically the thing may be all right. The villain beat his wife, though it may be argued that this is what wives are for. What was really heinous was that he also blackmailed his mother-in-law, the helpmeet of a canon. This graver offence strikes at the whole foundation of Society.

I solved the play's problem by the simple method of looking round the cast and seeing which of the highly paid artists had least to say in the first two acts. In fact, I won a shilling, and left the theatre hoping it would be better than the play. Mr. Sam Livesey stood out of the ocean of melodramatic nonsense like a Needle off the Isle of Wight. The rest of the cast seemed to be suffering from coast erosion; they acted very well, but the play kept giving way under them.

EVEREST HALF SCALED

HAMLET. Revival of Shakespeare's Tragedy. New Theatre, Wednesday, November 14, 1934. [*November* 18, 1934]

WHEN a piece of acting is as good as Mr. Gielgud's Hamlet is known to be, it becomes the critic's duty to say not how far it exceeds the lowest standard but by how much it falls short of the highest. He must, when the highest honours are at stake, " find quarrel in a straw." Roundly, then, this Hamlet, beginning where most leave off, is fine; yet by a curious perversity it is only half as fine as this perfectly graced actor could make it. Now gather, and surmise.

The soldiers have stopped marvelling, and the curtain has risen on the first Court scene. Their Majesties are already seated, in a setting of such rich, if sombre, magnificence that the house breaks into applause. The King has made his opening speech and is asking Laertes what he wants, and we have still not made up our minds which among the courtiers is Hamlet ! Or would not be able to do so if we were strangers to the London theatre and did not know Mr. Gielgud. Can it be that they are going to play Hamlet without the Prince ? No; for at last we spot him, as much withdrawn as the width of the stage permits. Is he a trifle too spectacularly in the shade, a thought too determined to be the unobserved of all observers ? Is there too petulant a charm in the sweep of chin and throat, like Byron sitting for his portrait ? There may be, but these things are imme-diately forgotten in the exquisite and touching delivery of the " Seems, madam " speech and the " Too, too solid flesh " soliloquy. When Mr. Gielgud played the part four years ago I suggested that while knowing when he ought to be pathetic he had not, in fact, much pathos. This has been remedied to a very remarkable degree, and the spectator must have a heart of stone not to be moved by Hamlet's obvious affection for his dead father, made manifest in the little " Take him for all in all " colloquy with Horatio. Mr. Jack Hawkins plays very well here, being staggered at Hamlet's " Methinks I see my father," a little disappointed to find that his news is no news, and not sorry to hear that Hamlet is talking only of his mind's eye.

The scene on the platform is well done, though Hamlet omits the longish and rather dull speech about the " mole of nature." Something, of course, has to be cut, and this is a good bit to be rid of, except that its retention underlines a point which cannot be made too often in connection with this play. This is that Shakespeare is a writer, not of acute psychological treatises to be pored over by obtuse Germans, but of stage plays of which one part can be inconsistent with another, provided each passes muster at the moment of per-formance. Nobody can be more natural than Shakespeare when being natural is his cue; and nobody can do more violence to nature if unnaturalness is the more paying pro-position. For example, every reader of Shakespeare must have asked why Horatio does not tell Hamlet about Ophelia's death when he meets him at the railway-station, and every Shakespearean playgoer knows that the answer is to permit of the tragi-comic colloquy with the Grave-diggers and the revelation to Hamlet *in view of the audience*. It is not conceiv-able that any human being, expecting at any moment to meet his father's ghost, could or would embark upon that long and involved tirade about the power of a single flaw to undermine a character. That Shakespeare violates nature here is due to one of two causes—either the itch for spilling moral beans, or the mere dramatic necessity for prolonging the suspense. Owlish professors blinking at the passage will see in it elucidation of Hamlet's character, whereas Shakespeare probably puts it in to keep Hamlet, Horatio, and Marcellus a little longer in the dark. But that is by the way.

In all that immediately follows the Ghost's speech Mr. Gielgud a little disappoints, as here almost all exponents have a little disappointed. Oddly enough, of all the Hamlets I have seen, Tree fell least short here because, being an actor-manager æsthetically unencumbered, he had a spotlight by which to see him working hysterically up to that astonishing, romantic cry: " Hillo, ho, ho, boy ! come, bird, come." Mr. Gielgud has to do this in the dark on a staircase, so that the working-up can only be vocal, and the actor's voice despite its range and melodic outline is not quite up to this feat. A spectator who did not know the words: " Come, bird, come," would not hear them. Nor do I think that this Hamlet makes quite enough—if indeed he says it—of the little speech ending " for mine own poor part Look you, I'll go pray." It was here that Forbes-Robertson made Hamlet suddenly perceive that he is a doomed man; in saying: " For every man hath business and desire, such as it is," his Hamlet realised that whereas business and desire may be sorry things, it is his unhappiness that he must abstain from both. Mr. Gielgud's rendering of the " fellow in the cellar-age " is ineffective, and singularly little is made of the promise to put on an antic disposition. This is perhaps intentional because, except for one subsequent hurried disarrangement of hair and garments, there is never any question, so far as I can detect, of the Dane being either mad or pretending to be. He is not even mad north-north-west; whatever winds blow he remains a model of lucidity.

It is at this point that the spectator becomes aware of

a fixed determination on the actor's part to make as little as possible of anything that can be called the orthodox " acting " of the part, to throw away—in the actor's sense—everything except the highest of its poetry and the most sensitive of its philosophy. The result, strange to say, is not an enhancement but a diminishment of the character. Hamlet, interrupted in his reading by Polonius, should put on a mock solemnity whereby the old man does not know that he is being made fun of. Mr. Gielgud is cheeky here, so that we wonder that the old fellow does not resent the boyish impertinence. But then, in my view, all the play's urbanity is given insufficient value.

Mr. Gielgud pulls himself together for the " Rogue and peasant slave " soliloquy, which he delivers grandly, rendering it like the first movement of some tremendous concerto and so that the " To be or not to be " speech, which follows almost immediately, has the tenderness of a Mozartian slow movement. The scene with Ophelia must always beat any actor who is not content to take it as music, unless, of course, he is prepared to accept Sir Arthur Quiller-Couch's contention that this is a jumble of Shakespeare's play and that earlier story in which the bait used by the King and Polonius to discover Hamlet's secret was not Ophelia but a courtesan. Nothing else that I know of, except the madness motive, explains Hamlet's : " I never gave you aught," which occurs at the beginning of the scene before he realises he is being watched. The confusion of the two texts justifies Hamlet's planting upon Ophelia the vices of the courtesan, always on the supposition that Shakespeare jumped at this chance of invective and wasn't going to discard it because of its inconsistency with Hamlet's knowledge of Ophelia's character. Anyhow, the madness and Sir Arthur's contention between them accomplish the trick making the scene feasible. But the most fascinating speculations must not lure us out of playhouse logic. Since Mr. Gielgud jettisons all suggestion of madness and since not one playgoer in a thousand has read Sir Arthur's lectures, we come back willy-nilly to the scene played as sheer music. Our present Hamlet, realising that this is one of the great things in the play, tackles it for all his vocal grace and physical and mental elegance are worth, and his pathos here is again extraordinary. This in the present version brings the first part of the play to an end. After " throwing away " the Advice to the Players, perhaps on the score that it is hackneyed, Mr. Gielgud again commands the most of our admiration for the rapt beauty of his speech to Horatio: " Nay, do not think I flatter." Then follows some more deliberate underplaying, and so rapid and casual is the dialogue here that I cannot remember having heard about either " hobby-horse " or " miching mallecho." And surely Hamlet's lightning " The Mouse-trap " should be a dagger driven up to the hilt into the King's conscience? Whereas when Claudius asks: " What do you call the play? " Hamlet makes so little of the reply that the King could conceivably not hear him.

The end of the Play Scene is given effectively and prestis-simo, after which there is another lapse, the scene with the recorders being given too slowly and as a dialectical exercise instead of being the ground-swell of a storm which has still to subside. And frankly it is permissible to hold that the scene with the Queen could do with a little less intellectual passion and a little more of the other sort. Here Mr. Gielgud receives insufficient help from Miss Laura Cowie's Gertrude, and what should be an emotional duet becomes a cold lecture on moderation in second marriages. But perhaps the cooling off is again deliberate since Mr. Gielgud has no intention of giving the magnificent postscript about the " convocation of politic worms." How any actor can omit this beats me utterly, since half of Hamlet is portrayed here.

The player returns to his best self in the almost mathematical exposition of the " How all occasions " soliloquy, though the omission of the scene with the King and the resulting joining up of two lots of moralising make this over-nice debater a colder-blooded fellow than the real Hamlet of the full text. If the concluding scenes do not wholly satisfy it is because we feel the want of something, though it is difficult to say what. The impression we have by this time gathered is of a Hamlet who can fly into the most shattering of pets. He has accesses of grief, but they do not leave him moody, there is no melancholy in him, his mind has not the richness of its words, he is not fey or marked for death, and his talk of ripeness is academic and not the ultimate philosophy of a man who feels that his course is run. To sum up, this Hamlet's specific gravity is akin to Romeo's, and when he dies we are conscious of losing no more than a gay, gallant, romantic companion; we do not feel that part of ourselves has died with him.

I hope that the foregoing is not an ungenerous estimate. If it is, it is because the actor so wantonly sacrifices the acting strength of the play to no discoverable purpose. If he would reconsider this and give to the prose passages that loving attention he has given to the poetry, one would modify one's attitude almost without knowing it. One would then say wholeheartedly that this is Mr. Gielgud's intensest fulfilment of himself, and not inquire too closely whether an Irving or a Forbes-Robertson had richer stores of magic upon which to draw. This Hamlet abounds in loveliness, but one feels that the actor's treasury could yield more. It would be wrong not to insist upon the wealth of beauty and accomplishment contained in that half of the character which is fully explored. Elsewhere it is as though Hamlet had taken his own advice to the players too much to heart. And didn't the first dramatic critic say something about considering " some necessary question of the play " ? If Mr. Gielgud will reconsider the many necessary questions of this play he will make his performance the whole which at present it is not. The poetic half, having attained perfection, should be left severely alone.

The ladies who call themselves Motley have provided some enchanting scenery and dresses. Mr. Vosper's King is satisfying, and would be even better if Nature had not made the player's cheeks creaseless; this being so Mr. Vosper has to rely on his voice, which he uses excellently. Mr. George Howe makes Polonius a most engaging old fool; Mr. William Devlin's Ghost is insufficiently ghostly though beautifully spoken; and Mr. Glen Byam Shaw's Laertes looks like one of the naughty children whom Struwwelpeter's tall Agrippa dipped into the inkpot. Laertes and Ophelia are of the company of Shakespeare's golden lads and lasses and should be played as such. The rest is silence, including Ophelia, for whom in my opinion that charming little actress, Miss Jessica Tandy, is quite pathetically miscast.

WEBSTER AND THE MODERN MIND

THE DUCHESS OF MALFI. Revival of John Webster's Tragedy.
Embassy Theatre, Monday, January 14, 1935.

[*January* 20, 1935]

THERE ARE SO MANY THINGS to be said about Webster,
so many reasons for liking or disliking him, that one hardly
knows where to begin. Let me kick off by saying that *The
Duchess of Malfi* is done at the Embassy in a number of
simple settings ranging from the pleasing to the ominous
and not overdoing either extremity. Now what of the play
itself? Are we to rank Webster, as Mr. Shaw did exactly
forty years ago, as among " the whole crew of insufferable
bunglers and dullards whose work stands out as vile even
at the beginning of the seventeenth century, when every
art was corrupted to the marrow by the orgy called the
Renaissance " ? Is he just one of the Elizabethan literary
rabble who, formulating in rhetorical blank-verse cheap
ideas about murder, lust, and obscenity, " made the stage
pestiferous with plays that have no ray of noble feeling, no
touch of faith, beauty, or even common kindness in them
from beginning to end " ? Or is Webster a great dramatist
whom the froth of criticism can no more destroy than the
fleck and foam of two seas can wear away Gibraltar ? How
seriously are we to take Mr. Shaw, and how far was his
attack the lusty crowing, kicking, and laying about him of a
full-grown dramatic critic who was also an infant playwright
getting himself born into a world at the opposite pole from

Webster's ? Sitting at this play the other evening, I could not help wondering what sort of man Webster must have been that, at one time the friend of Shakespeare—so it is surmised —and presumably having witnessed the great Shakespearean tragedies with their deepening message of moral responsibility, he could still stick to his Punch and Judy themes.

Those rascals, Ferdinand and his brother the Cardinal, between them do not possess an ounce of what Hamlet would call " the motive and the cue " for the passion they work themselves into about their sister. Why should they be in such a frenzy to keep the Duchess from marrying again? Late in the play Ferdinand says something about inheriting vast sums if his sister dies husbandless. This passage was omitted at Swiss Cottage, and I think rightly, since it is a belated explanation stuck in doubtless to meet the objection of some snarling *Sunday Times* critic of the period ! Besides it isn't valid, since the Duchess has a perfectly good infant son by her first husband. Nor can snobbishness on the brothers' part be alleged, since not knowing upon whom their sister looks favourably, they cannot complain that he is only her steward.

The play starts, as it were, *in vacuo*. Webster asks us to suppose that if the Duchess marries again, her two brothers will for no reason tear her limb from limb. All right, let us suppose it ! He next asks us to suppose that one Bosola, whom the brothers have " forced " upon the Duchess, cannot discover who her new husband is, though she keeps having children all over the place ; and that for two years the villainous pair are perfectly content to do nothing, which is out of all keeping with their filthy temper at the beginning. Well, we'll agree to this complicated nonsense also. Two questions at once emerge : What is there about this play which made it acceptable to the playgoer of 1614 ? Is there that about it which makes it acceptable to the playgoer of 1935 ?

To answer the first question one must go to the scholars; for an answer to the second one need only consult oneself. But even the scholars have perhaps not insisted strongly enough upon the consciousness of the first audience that it was watching carryings-on not in England but in " furrin parts," and would therefore not be more flabbergasted into disbelief in these knaveries than we are by our modern plays of the underworld in Chicago. Mr. F. L. Lucas, in his admirable edition of Webster, recently reminded us that things were different in an age and land in which, for instance, the six sons of Lelio Massimo, on their father's second marriage, entered the bridal-chamber next morning and shot the bride in bed, because she was a cast-off mistress of Marcantonio Colonna. There is also the story of the professional cut-throat who, being offered a higher price by the victim to murder his employer instead, accepted but insisted on first fulfilling his original contract ! In the light of such happenings there is nothing essentially improbable about the action of *The Duchess of Malfi*; the point is that to the Elizabethan mind such action was acceptable whether it exceeded probability or not. Here again, what Webster's audience wanted was something full-blooded; so long as it got that, it cared very little for the logic which set the full-blooded thing going. Further, the play is full of examples tending to show that the habit of the centuries is much nearer to kissing and commingling than to drawing apart. The incident of the dead hand and the wax figure is pure Grand Guignol. There is some confusion about the Masque of Madmen. A colleague has made the point that, as done at the Embassy, this is not terrifying: Mr. Lucas gives cogent reasons for thinking that Webster did not intend it to be. Masques of lunatics were a popular " turn " at that time, and it is arguable that this particular masque, while intended to mortify the Duchess, was meant to amuse the spectator. Compare the knocking in Shakespeare's play, which has the double effect of striking terror into the heart of Macbeth and at the same time of bringing about the one comic scene in the play. Incidentally, and begging everybody's pardon, I think one should not ask a dozen of Hampstead's walking ladies and gentlemen to horrify an audience accustomed to the extravagances of modern Russian Ballet. And now, perhaps, that is enough about the playgoer of 1614.

Victor Hugo's " Insensé, qui crois que tu n'es pas moi ! " —any School of Languages will translate this for a shilling— must be my excuse for saying how this play affected me. I found that the tragedy's improbabilities did not worry me in the least, and that I had no need to justify them on the score that Webster was merely hashing up an old joint that half a dozen earlier story-tellers had cut and carved each after his own fashion. Never once did I have to murmur the word " Renaissance," that magic cloth from behind which your sixteenth-century story-teller produces cardinals and noblemen splashing about in Machiavellian wickedness like goldfish in a conjurer's bowl. At Swiss Cottage Webster's gloomy gentry seemed good enough without any suggestion of magic, given that the black dog of sixteenth-century melancholy was gnawing at their vitals.

The same dog bites the heels of that very Shakespearean character, Bosola, who is Don John plus Iago, but also with a touch of Thersites plus Jacques. Bosola would be honest if he thought that there were any such thing as honesty; he is a hard-up Hamlet whose poverty and not his will consents to villainy. His acts, though they are those of a hypocrite, do not make him one; he is in the wretched case of a Hyde who cannot help every now and then turning into a Jekyll. Indeed, it occurred to me that an age which can accept Stevenson's balderdash, supposing you call it so, ought not to boggle at Webster's bunkum. Nor did I find the end too

long drawn-out, though perhaps this is due to the prevailing
taste for the modern crime-novel which tends to expatiate
on why a murder is committed rather than how. After all,
the three villains must have something to say for themselves,
and one wanted to hear it. About Bosola we know; his
melancholy has been fashionable in Denmark. The Cardinal
is a more difficult problem, though I think straightforward
guilt answers for him.

> *How tedious is a guilty conscience !*
> *When I look into the fish-ponds in my garden,*
> *Methinks I see a thing arm'd with a rake,*
> *That seems to strike at me.*

Surely this is only the visual form of Macbeth's " How is't
with me, when every noise appals me ? "

Obviously a great deal depends upon how these two parts
are played, and I thought they were done admirably on this
occasion. Mr. Roy Graham made Bosola a fair-haired
rogue, a slippery thing of naught with diamonds in its ears.
Almost a waterfly, whose presence at Court might well seem
to the Duchess to be innocuous. Yet, by an ingenious disposition of the ruff, the head seemed to the spectator to
be sunk so so low into the shoulders as to connote dishonesty;
here, you said to yourself, was a moral hunchback. Mr. Neil
Porter's Cardinal was also in excellent key; his Eminence
walked about like a poker, and was much too straight in the
back to have anything but a tortuous mind. This brings me
to Ferdinand, who has to be taken as a figure of pure evil,
the case for any other motive being too thin. Or you can
think of this character as possessed; that he ends as a lycan-
thropist is not an accidental horror, since his remark about
the strangled children :

> *The death*
> *Of young wolves is never to be pitied—*

shows him to have wolfishness on the brain. Webster doesn't make it too easy for the actor, because he cannot resist the line which has since become so famous:

Cover her face: mine eyes dazzle: she died young.

I do not believe that anybody in the theatre believed that Ferdinand would have said this, which is the kind of thing Stephen Phillips, if he had been enough of a poet, would have given to Giovanni to say over the dead body of Francesca. Indeed, I have always thought that—

I did not know the dead could have such hair.
Hide them. They look like children fast asleep !

was a barefaced plagiarism. Having got on to this sentimental tack, Webster followed it up with Ferdinand's remark about being his sister's twin, which is unlikely but effective. It is the old argument of whether Hamlet had a real existence apart from his fashioner, or whether Shakespeare exercised the right to do what he liked with his puppet even at the cost of consistency. Here Webster certainly exercised this right. As Ferdinand Mr. John Laurie did not fall into the trap of playing for sentiment; he just did what any clever actor would do and skated swiftly and imposingly over both passages so that they meant nothing at all. My difficulty with this Ferdinand was that Mr. Laurie, despite his rantings, writhings, reelings, never came near frightening me; one brushed him off the mind like a fly. This actor's voice is too light, and what he falls into is a pet rather than a rage; the harder he acts, the more peevish that pet becomes. But one felt that Mr. Laurie knew what the part was about, which is always something, whereas another actor, say Mr. Ernest Milton, would have shown us, which is something else.

Miss Joyce Bland's Duchess? The difficulty is that the part starts off by being a good one, and then somehow isn't. She begins by being like Shakespeare's Beatrice, then courts Antonio with Portia-like largesse, fills in a Lady Macduff-like picture of domestic felicity, and is then struck more or less dumb while the mortification takes place, though in the course of this she must give out two terrific sentences: " Am not I thy Duchess?" and " I am Duchess of Malfi still." These must boom like Big Ben or they are nothing, and the play here calls for a Rachel or a Siddons. Miss Bland does not pretend to be an actress of this force, and, while she did everything that charm and intelligence and a conscientious reading of her part could do, her performance remained too bland. Last, Mr. Torin Thatcher gave all possible graciousness of presence, voice, and manner to that poor fish Antonio. But the truth is that this is the very whale of a play. Burbage acted in it, and if I were to cast it within living memory I should choose Irving for the Cardinal, his son Laurence for Ferdinand, Ernest Milton for Bosola, Henry Ainley for Antonio, and Ellen Terry for the Duchess. I should rehearse these for three months to shake their schools together, engage Gielgud to produce, with music by Delius, and then see whether an instructed audience would endorse Mr. Shaw's " Tussaud laureate " and Archer's " ramshackle looseness of structure and barbarous violence of effect . . . hideous cacophonies, neither verse nor prose . . . Bedlam-broke-loose . . . poor Webster." I have had no room to say anything about the play's poetry, or its even more magnificent prose, but I must not omit to declare that all honour is due to the Embassy Theatre for its gallant and, on the whole, successful enterprise. Honour to the good folk of Hampstead also, for crowding the theatre ! This, of course, is a play the Old Vic ought to do. As I came away I found myself humming: " Lilian, where art thou ? "

OLD LIGHT ON IAGO

OTHELLO. Revival of Shakespeare's Tragedy. Old Vic Theatre, Monday, January 21, 1935.

PAGANINI. A play by David Wells. Whitehall Theatre, Friday afternoon, January 25, 1935. *[January 27, 1935]*

EVER SINCE there has been dramatic criticism, dramatic critics have puzzled their heads about Iago's insufficient motive. Nobody has ever been gammoned by the excuse which he himself puts forward:

> *I hate the Moor;*
> *And it is thought abroad that 'twixt my sheets*
> *He has done my office: I know not if't be true;*
> *But I for mere suspicion in that kind*
> *Will do as if for surety.*

"I know not if't be true" is altogether too weak. Most critics have taken refuge in the fellow's inherent diabolism, to which colour is lent by the fact that, apart from Hamlet, Iago has more brains than anybody else in the plays. The great wonder to me is that the more recondite critics do not seem to have taken the trouble to look up Shakespeare's sources, and a minor wonder is that it did not occur to me to do this until yesterday, when I had the inspiration to cock an eye at the tale as told by Gian Battista Giraldi-Cinthio, whose dates are 1504–1573.

Now I have no more Italian than enables me to order a dish of macaroni; I am blessed, however, in a secretary who

mastered that language in Glasgow ! Further the War years
gave me some knowledge of the Provençal and the works of
Mistral, familiarity with whose golden couplets I have not
yet disclosed, though threatening to at any moment ! Now I
assert that whoever has no difficulty with the cicala's motto,
" Lou soulèu me fai canta," ought to be able to get the better
of a simple Italian *novella*. Let me, then, put in my own words
what I find in the original :

" There was in the Moor's company a standard-bearer
of very handsome appearance, but in his secret nature
one of the most depraved of men. The Moor had for him
much affection and regard, being unaware of his many
vices. For though he was of a most vile character, he hid
this behind proud and high-flown language and fair
seeming, so that despite his black heart he looked more like
to a Hector or an Achilles. This villain had brought his
wife to Cyprus, a fair and honest young woman who,
being Italian, was much loved of the Moor's wife, and
spent the greater part of the day with her.

" In the same company was also a certain captain
much beloved of the Moor. This captain was a frequent
visitor at the Moor's house and dined with him and his
wife. Thus the wife, who knew the captain to be well
liked of her husband, showed herself well disposed towards
him, whereby the Moor was greatly pleased. The wicked
standard-bearer, regardless of his wife's trust in him, of
friendship and faith and his duty to the Moor, was
violently enamoured of Disdemona, and his sole thought
was how he might possess her. This he dared not to show,
fearing that if the Moor discovered his passion he would
straightway slay him. By various means he tried, with all
secrecy, to make the lady aware of his love, but she,
thoughtful of none but the Moor, had no regard for the

standard-bearer, nor for any man else. So his love for the lady changed to deadly hatred. He determined that if he might not possess the lady, the Moor should not possess her either."

But this is admirable ! Iago in love with Desdemona has reason for more bitterness than the average rejected suitor, since there is offence to vanity in that she preferred not one of his colour, but a blackamoor. Now comes the vital question. What made Shakespeare decide not to use this motive, of which he must have known ? What made him think that a motiveless Iago would be more dramatic ? And is it ? Shakespeare's *flair* in this matter is unerring, and he probably saw that to make Iago in love with Desdemona would weaken the play's main interest instead of strengthening it. In any case it would have turned out a totally different play, which it is impossible for us to judge, for the simple reason that Shakespeare preferred not to write it ! Almost the most dramatic thing in the play we have is Desdemona's : " Hark ! who is't that knocks ? " and Emilia's reply : " It's the wind." This knock occurs in Cinthio, who now continues as follows :

" In the morning the rumour of the captain's death spread over the town, and at length reached Disdemona's ears. She, a tender woman, little suspectful that any harm might come of it, showed herself much distressed. This much displeased the Moor, who, going to the standard-bearer, said to him : ' You know well that this wretch, my wife, is grieved by the news of the captain, and even like to lose her wits in sorrow. Is he, then, all she has to live for ? ' And so they fell to discussing whether the lady should die by poison or by dagger. At length, and after failing to agree, the standard-bearer said : ' I have thought of a way which no one will suspect. Your house is old and the floor of your chamber is cracked. Let me strike Disdemona with a stocking filled with sand, so that she may die without any sign of wounding. We may then pretend that a beam has fallen and has killed her, and all will be allowed to accident.'

The Moor was much pleased with this wicked counsel. Having awaited a convenient time, being in bed with his lady one night and having concealed the standard-bearer in an ante-chamber, the latter did by arrangement make a noise in his closet whereby the Moor said suddenly to his wife: ' Didst hear a noise ? ' whereat the lady arose to see what this might be. As soon as the unfortunate Disdemona came to the door of the closet the standard-bearer lustily did strike her so that she fell, and, with what little breath was left to her, called the Moor to her aid. To her the Moor: ' Strumpet, this is thy reward, and let such be the reward of all who make their spouses cuckolds ! ' The poor lady saw her death before her, the murderer striking her yet again, and called on divine justice as witness of her fidelity, since worldly justice had availed her nought. Calling on her God, she was stricken again and killed by the impious standard-bearer. Having placed her upon the bed, he and the Moor caused the floor of the room to fall, whereafter the Moor summoned help because the house was falling down. At this the neighbours came running and found the lady dead beneath the fallen beams."

The conclusion of the *novella* is long and improbable. Both the Moor and the standard-bearer get into all sorts of troubles alien to Shakespeare's play, the upshot being that both are tortured and put to death.

It is perhaps lawful to say that " Othello " will always

be a pretty good play so long as the Moor is played by a pretty good actor. Watching Mr. Abraham Sofaer the other night I could not get out of my mind a picture in words of an earlier player who produced upon a critic of his day the exact effect that Mr. Sofaer produced on me. When I got home I rummaged about, and in Leigh Hunt found this:

" It is in the acknowledgment of gesture and attitude, but more particularly in the variation of countenance, in the adaptation of look to feeling, that the actor is best known. Mr. Pope, in his general style, has but two gestures, which follow each other in monotonous alternation, like the jerks of a toyshop harlequin: one is a mere extension of the arms, and is used on all occasions of candour, of acknowledgment, of remonstrance, and of explanation; the other, for occasions of vehemence or of grandeur, is an elevation of the arms, like the gesture of Raphael's St. Paul preaching at Athens, an action which becomes the more absurd on common occasions, from its real sublimity. If Mr. Pope, however, is confined to two expressions in his gesture, he has but two expressions in his look: a flat indifference, which is used on all sober occasions, and an angry frown, which is used on all impassioned ones. With these two looks he undertakes to represent all the passions, gentle as well as violent; he is like a quack who, with a phial in each hand, undertakes to perform every possible wonder, while the only thing to be wondered at is his cheating the mob. The best character he performs is Othello, because he performs it in a mask: for when an actor's face is not exactly seen, an audience is content to supply by its own imagination the want of expression, just as in reading a book we figure to ourselves the countenance of the persons interested. But when we are presented with the real countenance, we are disappointed if our imagination is not assisted in its turn; the picture presented to our eyes should animate the picture presented to our mind; if either of them differ, or if the former is less lively than the latter, a sensation of discord is produced, and destroys the effect of nature, which is always harmonious."

Almost every word of this describes my view of Mr. Sofaer's performance. This Othello may be said to be acted in a mask because it is played with one set of features which never alters. Except for the movement of the lips in speaking, not a muscle in the actor's face is moved to differentiate between joy, tenderness, perplexity, and rage; the player has, as we say, no facial expression. The voice, though noble, is monotony itself, being, except for the differences of loud and soft, the same throughout; the spectator who had no English would have difficulty in knowing what kind of passion the actor was in.

In the following passage:

> *I know, Iago,*
> *Thy honesty and love doth mince this matter,*
> *Making it light to Cassio. Cassio, I love thee;*
> *But never more be officer of mine.*
> *Look, if my gentle love be not raised up!*
> *I'll make thee an example*

there are four changes of voice. The sentence addressed to Iago is normal and civil. That addressed to Cassio shows deep emotion struggling with duty. That to Desdemona should be marked by great annoyance, and it is this vexation which causes Othello to turn and rend Cassio. Mr. Sofaer made hardly any difference between the tone of these four sentences. It is obvious that this part, more than any other in Shakespeare, requires physical attractiveness in the

actor, who must not add other handicap to Othello beyond
his colour. Mr. Sofaer has stature and presence, but, alas:
" Le voilà donc ce nez qui des traits de son maître a détruit
l'harmonie ! " This matters nothing at all in the case of
your Bolingbrokes and Mortimers, but as Cyrano well knew,
it bars the way to romantic passion. In the matter of gesture
Mr. Sofaer is as limited as was Pope. He, also, has two
gestures. The first is when in unimpassioned moments the
arms are raised either full or half-cock like railway signals;
the second is when in impassioned moments the fist is shaken
on a level with the forehead.

All this is not to say that Mr. Sofaer's performance is not
an understanding one; it is understanding in the sense that
we are persuaded that Mr. Sofaer understands it. But the
business of the player is summed up in the Witches': " Show
his eyes, and grieve his heart." The player must wring our
hearts by exhibiting something shocking to our eyes; this,
and not interior thinking, is the whole business of acting.
In the actor's sense Mr. Sofaer does nothing with the part
except exhibit its dignity, which may or may not be the same
thing as suggesting, as one of my colleagues does, that it
is a performance " masterly in the flowing urgency of its
thought." In my view a little less urgent thinking and a
little more practical doing is what is wanted in the theatre,
and I shall stand by my guns and say that the first demand to
make of any player is that he shall show us not what he has
thought in the study but what he can do on the stage. In
other words he must be *theatrical* in the first sense of that
word, and Mr. Sofaer's Othello is the last word in untheatricality. I conceive this actor as extremely valuable in performances where a cold northern dominance and austerity are
the note; when the wind is southerly he has little to give us.
In other words, he lacks that on which the whole nature
of Othello is built—to wit, temperament. May I put it

that Mr. Sofaer is a fine actor in a school of acting whose validity I deny, though conceding that it is all a matter of opinion ? As Johnson remarked in *The Rambler*: " In things which are not immediately subject to religious or moral consideration, it is dangerous to be too rigidly in the right."

As Iago Mr. Maurice Evans acted from the moment he came on to the stage. And went on acting, in the sense that you may take pleasure in a pianist's finger-work apart from his intellectual conception of the composer's idea. This was a boyish, eager Iago, perhaps a little too light in colour, but vivid and full of variety, making you feel that his words were the coinage of an ecstasy now first minted, and not the measured delivery of something conned and pondered. The Desdemona of Miss Vivienne Bennett was exceedingly moving, despite a dimpling, dumpling countenance which suggests that domestic pathos and not high tragedy will be her better medium. Can this, by the way, be the actress we saw as the telephone operator in *Counsellor-at-Law*? If so, she is an actress indeed. Miss Mary Newcombe as Emilia was temperamentally much more Moorish than the Moor, though I thought her a trifle too ladylike; Emilia should be more tart, with the tartness of peasant stock which has been taken into a great lady's household. However, Miss Newcombe went after the part like a shark after a nigger's leg, and took huge and successful bites out of it to everybody's delectation. A brilliant performance of a part which every actress with brains knows to be a grand one.

I think everybody in the theatre on Friday afternoon at *Paganini* must have recalled the story of how Oscar Browning, introducing himself to Tennyson, said: " I'm Browning." Tennyson replied: " No, by God, you're not !" Somebody at Paganini's threadbare At Home kept saying: " This is Chopin ! " " This is Liszt ! " " This is Berlioz ! " And one couldn't help murmuring: "No, by gad, it isn't!" The fault was not with the actors who, not being low comedians, could not utter more words than were set down for them. How can anybody, be he steeped in histrionics to the very lips, convince us that he is Chopin or Berlioz merely by looking like or even unlike him and mooning wordlessly in a group as static as one of Madame Tussaud's? George Sand was a bit more like it, because she was given a spate of words in which to abound Dudevantishly, and trail the dust of Nohant behind her elegant heels. Incidentally the part was very cleverly played by Miss Chris Castor, a most accomplished actress, the infrequency of whose appearances can only be due to the fact that whatever modern English plays call for, it can't be actresses!

Now how about Paganini? Here I have a confession to make, which is that I have never been able to leave a plaguey sense of humour in the cloak-room with hat and coat. But the mishap was also largely the fault of your theatrical archæologist, always misled by his passion for accuracy. I have no doubt that every inch of Paganini's tall hat was historically justifiable. But to my eye its tapering was of the witch-and-broomstick order, suggesting a magician at a children's party, and once that line of thought is started I just have to follow it. In this case it led straight to Bunthorne and, moreover, to Sir Henry Lytton's impersonation of Bunthorne. Especially when a young woman who had been to his concert said in the very accents of Angela or Saphir: "Maestro, you were transcendental!" Did this Paganini know what it was to be heart-hungry? Was his cynic smile but a wile of guile? And so on. I am not going to suggest that Mr. Ernest Milton did not act very well. He did. He seemed to feel Paganini's position acutely, but alas, appearances were against him!

The play? Well, mostly a thing of unhallowed shreds and

metaphysical patches. Was Paganini in league with the Devil ? Aren't we all ? The whole trouble was that Marlowe and Marie Corelli between them couldn't have made a play out of Paganini, that Sphinx without an actable secret. If this piece survives the experimental stage, I earnestly beseech Mr. Milton to do three things. The first is to lop off that ending in which the corpse of the maestro plays a ghostly fiddle to a posse of pussies. This, which was respectfully received by a sycophantic audience of intellectuals, can only wake normal playgoers to hilarity. The second is to find Paganini's dæmonism not in a make-up box but in his own great talent as an actor, which I assure him will amply suffice. The third is to change the play's title, for which, since it is all about dissolution I suggest *Death Returns to Business*.

A LANCASHIRE PROBLEM

LOVE ON THE DOLE. A play by Ronald Gow and Walter
Greenwood. Garrick Theatre. Wednesday, January 30,
1935.   [*February* 3, 1935]

ON THE PRINCIPLE of horses for courses I amused
myself after the first act of this play—which is all about
unemployment in that part of Salford where I happen to
have been born—in wondering which among the great
dramatic critics of my time would best have dealt with it.
A. B. Walkley? But then I remembered a sentence of his
which ran something like this: " M. Morand has wandered
over London from Ebury Street to the confines of Epping
Forest, from Upper Tooting to the route of Motor-bus No.
19, which (he asserts) takes you to Islington." No, it would
not, I think, have been safe to trust this play about short time
and short commons to one so delicately nescient. Mr. Max
Beerbohm? I have a feeling that our ever regretted dilettante,
instinctively shrinking from this tragedy of unfilled working-
class bellies, might have given his essay the form of a parody
of contemporary Mr. Kipling:

> *And the Devil whispered behind the leaves,*
> " *It's squalid, but is it art?* "

Mr. Shaw? I recalled an article on Shakespeare's *Henry IV*,
in which our All Wisest treated himself and us, but more
particularly himself, to a dissertation on quite a number of
things. On the incompetence of shoemakers. On the new

medical practice of painting the tonsils with caustic to cure kidney disease. On the technique of Paderewski. On the reason why the bass part in Mendelssohn's " Son and Stranger" consists of only one note. On Christy Minstrelsy.

No ! Despite the fact that this article contained a sentence beginning: " When the operative at his mule in the cotton mill pieces the broken yarn . . ." I did not feel that our Puckish Solon was the man for Mr. Greenwood's play; I felt that we should have got not so much a criticism of a particular set of hard cases as an indictment of that short-sighted, somnolent, supine, spineless, shirking, shameful, sottish stupidity on the part of our economic rulers which has led to China's dwindling consumption of shirtings and India's decreasing demand for dhootis. Montague ? Here there was the risk that the clothes-pegs on Mrs. Hardcastle's clothes-line would have become jewels on the thread of that exquisite prose. Archer ? But surely the very name of Hard-castle must have lured that learned Scot into long-winded comparison between the state of the drama to-day and its condition in 1773, the year of *She Stoops to Conquer* ? One giant remains—Clement Scott. That over-despised critic may not have been overburdened with taste, discrimination, style, though I suspect that these charges are generally preferred by those who have never read a word of him. But he had three essential qualities—a great heart, enthusiasm for a play as something to be acted before a full and excited house, and a capacity for seeing what the point was and making that point in straightforward, understandable English. Clement Scott was the Dickens of dramatic criti-cism, and he would have been the play's ideal critic just as Dickens would have been the ideal spectator of this tragi-comedy. But, you say quickly, *Love on the Dole* is not a tragi-comedy, since in it the comic quality does not enter into and transfuse the tragic as it does in, say, *Juno and the Paycock*.

You say that Mr. Greenwood's play is the sum of alternating chunks of both commodities. I agree, and that is the reason why Dickens would have been our ideal spectator, because that is the way in which he wrote his novels.

Following in Scott's footsteps I must perceive what is *not* the point about this piece acted in a London theatre before a London audience. I am to realise that the house cared no jot about the author's narrative skill, type of humour (whether Hogarthian or Dickensian), characterisation, and other matters normally the province of the literary critic. No jot about the degree of faithfulness with which these things have been transplanted to the stage, the first business on these occasions of the dramatic critic. No jot about the ironic, even Greek quality of the happy ending which, if the thing is a work of art, must be established beyond question. I am to see that what moved the house was not the art with which the father's, mother's, daughter's, son's predicament was presented—though the attained effect obviously connotes recognition, even if subconscious, of the skill used to produce it—but the predicament itself. Since Scott would not have been ashamed of adjectives like " naked," " raw," and " bleeding " to describe such a situation as that with which this play ends, I must not be ashamed either. The play moved me terribly, and must move anybody who still has about him that old-fashioned thing—a heart.

In case there are readers who do not know what Mr. Greenwood's situation is, I shall briefly recapitulate it. Sally Hardcastle, a mill hand, has lost her lover, killed in a skirmish with the police during an unemployment demonstration. He was consumptive and would have died anyhow. All the family except Sally is out of work, so that she has to keep father, mother, herself, her brother, and the girl whom her brother has got into trouble. There is the dole, but that does not last for ever. And now a wealthy bookmaker makes Sally a proposition. He is married, but if the girl will consent to be his nominal housekeeper he will provide not only for her but for her family also. It was at this point that I feared Walkley's filigree-work on the theme of: " They drink the champagne wot she sends them, but they never can forgive ! "

It occurs to me here that some of our moralists might give us the benefit of their cogitations on this theme and tell us what Sally should do. I would ask some bishop, except that bishops do not provide solutions: they deplore. The way for Sally's ultimate decision has been paved in an earlier conversation between her mother and a neighbour who has her head screwed on—in the wrong or right way, but any-how on ! Mrs. Bull's argument is as follows:

> Y'want to forget y'self for a bit an' try to understand how t'young 'uns must feel about all these here goings-on in t'world to-day. Every cent they earn being tuk in keeping their owld folks an' any o't'family what comes out o'work. If your Sal had gone on brooding as she was, she'd ha' done what poor sowl did in t'next street yesterday. Guardians towld him he'd t'give five bob to his people what had come under t'Means Test, an' him married wi' a wife and family o' his own. An' what did *he* do ? Cut his froat an' jumped through bedroom winder, poor sowl.

There are some terrible passages before Sally finally decides. Her father calls her unspeakable names. But Sally goes on making her point. She faces up to her father: " Y'kicked our Harry out because he got married, an' y're kicking me out 'cause Ah ain't." He knocks her down. Sally goes on: " Ay, an' Ah'll tell y'summat else. It's sick Ah am o' codging owd clothes t'mek 'em luk summat like. An' sick Ah am o' working week after week an' seeing nowt for it. Ah'm sick o' never havin' nowt but what's bin in

pawnshops an' crawling wi' vermin." In the end Sally
goes off with her bookmaker, and we know that some force
in her other than her own luxury and riot is driving her to a
career which may not wholly displease her though the man
does. As she goes she pours money into her mother's lap
and leaves on the table those letters from her protector which
are to obtain jobs for her father and brother. In a scene for
which the only parallel is César Birotteau's fall to his knees
on the news of his bankruptcy, we have already heard Sally's
father pray for work and take the name of God not in vain.
The end of the play finds him an angry, beaten man, and
his last words are: " Oh, God, Ah've done me best ! Ah've
done me best, haven't Ah ? " Well, hasn't he ?—I imagine
Scott would have asked. And I ask readers of the *Sunday Times*
the same question. In the days before booms and slumps,
when virtue was as stabilised as the currency, such a father
would have plunged the bread-knife into his daughter's
bosom, saying with Macaulay's Virginius:

> *And now, mine own dear little girl,*
> *There is no way but this.*

Are we to-day to condemn Sally ? Or her father ? How
far is a man justified in using his daughter's immoral
earnings to keep a roof over her mother's head ? It may be
that in the light of later reason such earnings may not be
immoral. Are they, then, moral ? Since we have mentioned
old Hardcastle, perhaps we might echo Lady Teazle and
agree to leave honour, which to-day we should call morality,
out of the argument. Out of the argument, that is, when
there is question of empty bellies and babies coming into a
starving world.

Whether the play is or is not a work of art in the sense that
it will endure when the Lancashire looms are going full time
again, and Chinese and Indians have unlearned the trick

we taught them of weaving their own calicoes and preferring them to the imported ones—is a matter of purely academic interest. The matter of this play is here and now. Here is something which brings home to us the fact that whereas London is one luxurious traffic jam, many a street in Lancashire has no traffic, and in many a Lancashire home is neither jam nor the bread to put it on. But it is still my business to declare that Mr. Gow has made a shapely play out of Mr. Greenwood's novel, though what one might call the idealistic parts of the book are beyond any manipulation. Nobody is going to believe the scene on the moors, which is only another little bit of *Autumn Pocus*. I personally don't believe in the young workman who, looking at the smoke-cloud hanging like a pall over the distant city, says: " It's a queer thing that all that foul smoke should make beauty for us." This agitator is played by Mr. Ballard Berkeley. Now Mr. Berkeley, if I mistake not, is a London actor, and when it comes to playing Lancashire plays London players, however good they are, just won't do. They won't do because they bring with them overtones and echoes from scores of familiar performances. That Miss Marie Ault was born in Wigan is no matter; however skilfully she acts, at some time or other we are going to be reminded that the Amah in *East of Suez* spoke with that voice. Miss Drusilla Wills is a lovely person, but here *Yellow Sands* crops up. The same thing applies to Miss Cathleen Nesbitt and Mr. Arthur Chesney, who give brilliant performances whose brilliance sticks out a mile. This is their undoing, since all this gloss and polish and careful obliteration of gentility in favour of Lancashire roughcast is shown up for the artistic, and therefore make-believe, thing it is the moment it is seen in juxtaposition with the absolute authenticity of Mr. Alex Grandison's Harry Hardcastle, Mr. Julien Mitchell's Mr. Hardcastle, Miss Beatrice Varley's Mrs. Bull.

Cézanne's drawing of a brick may be more real than any brick that was ever made, *but not when somebody hits you with it.* Mr. Grandison's loutish hobbledehoy, growing out of his clothes and into man's estate, and his two equal and urgent demands for the right to wear long trousers and the right to look after his girl—these are tremendous things to watch; they hit you in the face, and perhaps the play would have been still nearer to life if this character had been unbearably killed, instead of the agitator, which was bearable. Is Mr. Grandison an actor ? I don't know and shall not ask until he is seen in something else. Is Mr. Mitchell an actor, and could he play any other part except Hardcastle ? Here again this is not the time to enquire. If Mr. Mitchell should be a London player his virtue is in being a London player unknown to me. And Miss Varley ? Again the same thing. There is more truth and reality and vigour in one corner of Mrs. Bull's shawl than in the entire casts of the six most popular drawing-room plays now drawing the West End. Miss Wendy Hiller impresses me as having a foot in each camp. As Sally she is very, very good indeed, though there are moments when she is inclined to become actressy; in these she is indistinguishable from a London actress trying to be non-actressy. I wish to state that I am not under the impression that the actors I like in this play are actually out-of-work cotton-operatives. They may be, or they may not, and anyhow it is difficult to believe that they are superlative artists concealing their artistry, because that doctrine is all moonshine. I would prefer to say that they are Lancashire players who know everything about Lancashire life and not enough about London acting to spoil that knowledge. Now let Miss Hiller beware ! I can see that six months ago she was a magnificent Sally. On Wednesday night I had the glimmer of a ghost of a notion that here was a very promising young actress giving a magnificent *performance of* Sally.

SHAKESPEARE AND MR. ROBEY

King Henry IV. Part I. Revival of Shakespeare's Play.
His Majesty's Theatre, Thursday, February 28, 1935.

For The Defence. A play, by John Hastings Turner. Duke
of York's Theatre, Tuesday, February 26, 1935.

[*March* 3, 1935]

So much preluding and fanfaring, so much use of
tucket answered by sennet prompted my neighbour to ask
me whether I thought Mr. Sydney Carroll intended to turn
the play into an opera. I said it was quite possible, my revered
colleague being, like Habbakuk, *capable de tout*. Presently,
however, the cheerful din, elegantly assembled for the
occasion by Mr. Ernest Irving, subsided and the curtain
went up to reveal a highly Plantagenet London exceedingly
unlike Regent's Park. It was an interesting experience to
hear the King's opening speech unpunctuated by the sough
of cedars, the twitter of robins, and the cry of " love-fifteen "
from the neighbouring lawn tennis courts. That this was
very much an indoor performance was proved by the vagaries
of the limelight man, who, less sure of himself than Nature's
luminary, kept trying to marry his colleague's amber with
various shades of blue. Perhaps this was intended to be
deepening twilight or the drawing-on of early afternoon?
Apart from this Mr. Carroll has done grandly, in equal
measure of valour and discretion.

The difficulty about Shakespeare criticism is that one must

HN

speak by the book, or the P's and Q's are going to give a lot of trouble. It would be easy to fault Mr. John Drinkwater for lack of exhilaration in the title rôle if one did not remember that whoever plays the part must take his cue from the opening line: " So shaken as we are, so wan with care." One did, however, think that the actor overdid the part's sobriety; after all, this was once Henry Bolingbroke and the fire should still be there though it has burned low, whereas Mr. Drinkwater gave one the impression of being a personage who had become extinct without ever having been a volcano. In any case he had a deal of history to get off the royal chest, and the extent to which any given spectator found His Majesty long-winded must have been governed by that spectator's degree of liking for Shakespearean history. For myself, Shakespearean history is like beer and like chamber-music; some is better than other some, but none is bad. I could sit for hours and listen entranced to such cataloguing as:

> *The Earl of Douglas is discomfited:*
> *Ten thousand bold Scots, two and twenty knights,*
> *Balk'd in their own blood did Sir Walter see*
> *On Holmedon's plains. Of prisoners, Hotspur took*
> *Mordake the Earl of Fife, and eldest son*
> *To beaten Douglas; and the Earl of Athol,*
> *Of Murray, Angus and Menteith. . . .*

Even so, it was a bit dull until Hotspur came along to stir the royal stumps.

Hotspur was very valiantly played by Mr. Edmund Willard, always given that while the part is one for a silver trumpet the note of Mr. Willard is Coleridge's loud bassoon. And surely the text calls for the impetuosity of youth and not the morose pugnacity of middle-age ? I very much liked Mr. Lewis Casson's Owen Glendower, who, having conjured up musicians to accompany his daughter, listened to her singing with his arms held in the air and the ferocious, rapt expression of a Chief Bard at an Eisteddfod. He only wanted a wreath of mistletoe to be the spit and image of the Celtic, intarissable bore. Mr. Patrick Waddington was inclined to over-accentuate the priggish aspect of the Prince. If there is a more revolting passage in Shakespeare than that which begins: " Yet herein will I imitate the sun," I have still to read it. The gorge of Pecksniff himself must have risen at the hypocrisy of:

> *And like bright metal on a sullen ground,*
> *My reformation, glittering o'er my fault,*
> *Shall show more goodly and attract more eyes*
> *Than that which hath no foil to set it off.*
> *I'll so offend, to make offence a skill;*
> *Redeeming time when men think least I will.*

Sir Arthur Quiller-Couch says that this speech, if we accept it, poisons all of Harry that follows: " Most of us can forgive youth, hot blood, riot: but a prig of a rake, rioting on a calculated scale, confessing that he does it coldly, intellectually, and that he proposes to desert his comrades at the right moment to better his own repute—*that* kind of rake surely all honest men abhor." The lines are obviously Shakespeare's. " Who doth permit the base contagious clouds To smother up his beauty from the world " must be by the same hand that wrote the sonnet lines: " Anon permit the basest clouds to ride With ugly rack on his celestial face." Sir Arthur tries to avoid holding that the priggishness is not Harry's but Shakespeare's—which, of course, it must be, *vide* Walkley's denial of the precedent *état d'âme* theory which I have quoted too often to need more than reference here— by suggesting that Burbage or somebody came to the poet and said at a later date: " Look here, they [meaning the

audience] are not going to stand for a rapscallion turned
Sunday-school teacher. You've got to get them right about
him in the beginning ! " Whereupon, according to Sir
Arthur, Shakespeare went back and obediently inserted the
miserable stuff. I am afraid that this argument won't wash,
and that Shakespeare himself had the priggish strain. Are
there not other lines of the immortal bard which, according
to Mr. Shaw, in their " canting, snivelling, hypocritical
unctuousness " perfectly catch the atmosphere of the rented
pew ? And then Burbage's case was no case at all, since at the
end of Part I Harry has already become reasonably noble;
indeed his parleyings with and about Hotspur are in the
very best temper of the king he afterwards became. The high-
placed ragtag and bobtail, who in the histories lay plots,
get executed for them, and spend their entire time splitting
on one another, were very well acted by Messrs. Leslie
Frith, Henry Oscar, Cecil Ramage, George Skillan, W. E.
Holloway, and John Laurie.

This brings me to the comedians, and probably not too
soon, since I believe the whole of the foregoing has been so
much wasted effort. Just as nobody would have dreamed of
going to see this play at His Majesty's without Mr. Robey—
which was Mr. Carroll's legitimate reason for this extraordinary casting—so I do not believe that any reader wants
to bother with anything about the present production, or the
play, or the poet, or anything at all except how Mr. Robey
acquitted himself, and whether he left the theatre without
a stain on his artistic integrity. In my view it would be more
to the purpose to ask *how the audience acquitted themselves*, and
whether they helped or hindered Mr. Robey in the very
difficult task of shedding one kind of glory to take up another.
The answer is a good deal of Yes and a little of No. Whenever
the actor relaxed an inch, the audience took an ell. It came
about in this way. Mr. Robey walked on to the stage with the

disciplined intention of playing the part and not clowning it, of moving in Shakespeare's world and not in that which he has made so gloriously his own. But, alas, he was not word-perfect ! Now there are two ways in which an actor can be so handicapped ; the part may come to him in rushes culminating in stops, or he may lag just that painstaking fraction of a second behind which is so distressing to him and to everybody else. Mr. Robey is too good an artist not to have known that he must cover up his difficulty, and that the obvious way for him was to hold the audience with his eye and so gain time for the next line to percolate into memory. But the effect of that basilisk stare produced reaction beyond the audience-victim's control ; it laughed willy-nilly, whether there was anything to laugh at or not. Action and reaction being equal and opposite, not the Robey eyebrows, but the places where they were wont to be would go up and the actor find himself climbing into a meridian of nonsense not in Shakespeare's contemplation. And, I repeat, the audience took advantage of the relapses into Robeydom.

Then there is another thing. Many a time and oft Mr. Robey has made great play with archaic methods of pronunciation and delivery, and once or twice the other night he appeared wilfully to use the same mock-serious intonations. But I am convinced that these were merely expedients suggested by extreme nervousness and used to cover the extremity of not knowing where the next line was coming from, and I am quite certain that in a fortnight's time Mr. Robey will be giving one of the best Falstaffs within living memory. It is in him to do so, but the audience must do its part. He has the authentic geniality of the old fribble, the genuine twinkle which kindles as easily as a taper that has been lighted many times. He is an English gentleman in ruins. (One appalling echo of the halls, the tasteless skit upon effeminacy has probably already been discarded.) Or shall

I put it that the new Falstaff is about to be and can be all
this, if the audience will let him. Or refrain from letting him,
in the Shakespeare sense. He has still to amend one or two
impermissible and calculated occasions. These are when
the actor slyly evokes his former self, the mask of Falstaff
is dropped, the audience leaps at the gleeful discrepancy,
and the ruin of the play impends. These stolen seconds—for
they are no more than seconds—are a threat to the illusion
the actor has laboured to create, and they must be resisted.
If they are not I throw up my brief, and it is on this understanding that this experiment, magnificently successful as to
nine-tenths, has my blessing. It would be ungracious to omit
to say how deftly, solicitously, and Shakespeareanly Lady
Tree, in the very small part of Mistress Quickly, stood about
ready to render Falstaff first aid.

For the Defence is all about a young woman who in East
Africa shoots her husband's blackmailer. It is a play of
mopping and mowing, mopping when the young woman is
not in the dock, and mowing when she is. Miss Beatrix
Thomson does both admirably, though I should still like to
see her in some part in which she has not to be, emotionally
speaking, broken on the wheel. Mr. Matheson Lang, as the
defending counsel in love with his fair client, is perfectly in
his element like some noble fish prancing about the waters
of its private aquarium. Here, you say to yourself, is a K.C.
who if nobody asks his advice can burn wig and gown and
stride into any theatre and demand a leading part. He has a
magnificent moment in which he hears in full court, though
the news is privately conveyed, that his sweetheart's victim
was his own brother. Like the good actor that he is, Mr.
Lang does nothing here except throw into his cross-examin-
ing voice a nuance of gratitude to the witness for not blurting
out the news. Leaving great acting out of it and coming
down to acting—held by some misguided individuals to be

the higher branch of the profession !—I thought most in this production of Messrs. Derek Gorst, Walter Piers, and Aubrey Dexter. The last of these reproduced the frigid impertinence and indecent detachment of distinguished counsel implying merely by vocal colour that the witness under examination is not only a liar now, but was one in a past existence and will be in all that are to come. Mr. Dexter's playing trespasses so nearly on the province of a leading man's that I fear if he continues he will get no more secondary parts. This risk should only be taken by actors with large private means to fall back upon. Let me hope that in this respect Mr. Dexter is ambidextrous.

CHALLENGE TO LONDON

FROLIC WIND. A play by Richard Pryce, based on the Novel
by Richard Oke. Royalty Theatre, Wednesday, March 13,
1935.   [*March* 17, 1935]

IF TCHEHOV had written this play it would have been
called *The Four Sisters*. Lady Bernice Jeune (Miss Nina
Boucicault) has got to the time of life when, were her blood
less blue, she would be a " body " in the Scotch sense. Lady
Athaliah (Miss Henrietta Watson), the descendant of dragonsome dowagers, has rheumatism and lives at the bottom of
the garden in a tower upon whose mysterious contents she
turns the key. Lady Damaris (Miss Mabel Terry-Lewis)
is all that we conjure up in connection with châtelaines of
houses with names like Branches. " It would be awfully
kind of you to come down to Branches," said Lord Lambeth
to Bessie Alden in the Henry James story. " What is
Branches ? " Bessie asked, and Lord Lambeth, who had
quite a lot of castles, said : " It's a house in the country. I
think you might like it." These three ladies, with their
youngest sister Cleone (Miss Dorothy Holmes-Gore), preside
over Pagnell Bois in amity like that of china tea-cups which
have lived long together, a little chipped, a little stained,
and one permits oneself to say that one of them is a little
cracked. This is Lady Cleone, who when she was in the
forties fell in love with one of the grooms, a handsome rascal
instantly dismissed by Lady Athaliah to seek his fortune and

favours elsewhere. Lady Cleone has never quite recovered
from the shock, and though sometimes not noticeably odd,
at others resembles an antiquated Ophelia, daisy-chain and
singing mad. These ladies spend their time in the only way
that is open to them, that of entertaining. Entertaining
whom ? Now the houses of the great, unlike flats, insist on
being lived in, and for their owners to entertain each other
would be too cumbersome a game of general post. Their
guests, then, must be chosen from among those who have no
castles, and this includes prime ministers, painters, poets
(" When Lord Tennyson was here, the rose-garden was
reserved for his use alone ! ") and other prey of these lion-
huntresses whom, were there space, one thinks one could
acquit of vulgarity. One is made to feel that if any of the
Guermantes had visited England, Pagnell Bois is where
Proust would have had them stay.

I suppose a good hour is spent in establishing the characters of the four sisters and of Miss Jewell (Miss Veronica
Turleigh), the poor relation who arranges Lady Cleone's
patience cards backwards so that her games come out, Mr.
Charlecote (Sir Basil Bartlett), the young man whose painting is causing a stir, Mr. Roxborough (Mr. Stanley Lathbury), the talkative bore straight out of the pages of Peacock,
General Tresmand (Mr. Graveley Edwards), a mindless
martinet, Mrs. Murat-Blood (Miss Mignon O'Doherty),
who is on the committee of five mental institutes, and the
very important Miss Vulliamy (Miss Fabia Drake), an avid
spinster whose novel has been all about the right of country
girls to have their babies and go on living at home. (I seem
to spend my entire life reading novels by Miss Vulliamy and
wondering what their authors would do if they met a cow in
a lane.) But the hour during which the ground is prepared is
not too long, and though the action is cut up into little scenes
our interest is not frittered away. Nothing has happened, and

there is no sign that anything will happen, and it doesn't matter, and the only question we ask is whether the author can possibly keep his play going on his chosen level, that of a comedy say by Mr. Aldous Huxley, for an audience of the same calibre. But at the very end of the first act there is promise of action. The party is taking tea under the shade and patronage of the oldest cedar in the garden, and the mutter of thunder is echoing the well-bred chatter, when the butler announces Sir Lothar Smith (Mr. S. J. Warmington), the self-made millionaire. We know from the glint in Lady Athaliah's eye what is going to happen. Sir Lothar Smith is going to turn out to be Lot Smith, the dismissed groom; the dangerous cat will be out of the bag—for this has always been the closest of secrets—but for Lady Athaliah's watchfulness. Even so one delicate claw protrudes, instantly recognised for what it is by Miss Vulliamy, indulging a week-end tenderness for the young painter whose attentions are given to the underling Miss Jewell, and if Miss Vulliamy is not going to enjoy him herself, then, by all that's feminine, misery and shame shall come upon Pagnell Bois !

The second act is a ladies' battle conducted with the utmost elegance, though with hardly a hit above the belt. The third act has an immense surprise. Or perhaps one should say that the surprise will be immense for playgoers unskilled in the mysteries of the human brain and body, which in the theatre are usually made so strangely subservient to those of the heart. We learn now why repression has not wreaked upon Lady Athaliah the same mischief that it did upon Lady Cleone, and as this play's surprise is part of its value I shall not be more particular. The tidying-up at the end—whereby the little underling, who turns out to be the daughter of Lady Cleone and the ex-groom, is united to her lover, Miss Vulliamy repents, and the family is brilliantly exhorted by the Princess Rosencrantz-Guildenstern (Miss

Martita Hunt) to believe that if they were commoners they
would have nothing to be ashamed of—all this tidying is
infinitely better than your normal windings-up concerning
a cub and a chit and a tennis-racket.

Purists may hold that this is not a good play, and I say,
weighing my words, that it is the cause of the best evening
I have spent in the theatre at something not strictly a play
since either Mrs. Mayor's *The Pleasure Garden* or Mr. Huxley's
The World of Light. True lovers of Berlioz have been known to
say that with such sounds in their ears, pedagogues who call
his harmony " spotty and helpless " can take any one of his
chords and with it go hang themselves ! What is there in this
play to fill the mind of the true playgoer ? The answer is:
character-drawing of subtlety and persuasion—the sense that
these people, unchallengeably real, as in Proust, move and
exist in the plane to which they are accredited—dialogue of
such point, variety, new invention, and authenticity that
you begrudge the rustle of a programme making you miss a
word of it—delicate adjustments and revision of the main
situation which engross and satisfy the mind—and the main
situation itself, of moment in an age which recognised the
social enormity. The modern attitude which would describe
the seduction of a lady by her groom as " rather fun, my
sweet " destroys any play on the subject; here is one of the
many things Shepherd Market does not know. This is the
place to record that one or two of my colleagues have dismissed this piece as " Meredithian," as though that were a
term of disparagement. May I ask whether they prefer the
exchanges in Mr. Winter's popular success, whereby a man
says to a presumed lady: " What a bloody-minded woman
you are ! " and the lady is made to reply: " I think you're
bloody, too ! " ?

I shall make no bones about the acting and say straight
out that as a mosaic it is in a different class from anything

else to be seen in London. As the centre jewel of the pattern, Miss Watson is blazingly good; the riot is always just below the surface of that libidinous old eye. Miss Boucicault is old age, fussy and silvered. Miss Terry-Lewis conveys with a certain acerbity the tender grace of a day that is dead; she has that air of perfect breeding which the vulgar mistake for looking down one's nose. Miss Holmes-Gore has the enormously difficult task of keeping our sympathy for a wanderwit, elderly and grotesque; what she has of mind is, like her dress, younger than her sisters, and it is very clever of the actress to perceive this. Miss Drake rakes with the eye of a searchlight the repressions of that venomous duck, Miss Vulliamy. Miss Hunt gives a bravura display of luxury of mind, body, and estate. Miss Turleigh is like some spiritual tureen whose soup has grown as cold as chastity. Miss Renee de Vaux, as Mrs. Dawe in whose car Sir Lothar travels, bubbles like some vulgar organiser of charity balls. And last, my soul's delight, Miss O'Doherty, squats in that garden as though Heaven had planted her there with the cedar.

Perhaps the men are not quite so perfect. The two bores of Messrs. Lathbury and Edwards are a little too much like the real thing. But as the young artist Sir Basil Bartlett is at least a gentleman; we thank him for holding the breach against some other players who would have over-conveyed this impression. I admired the imperturbability of Mr. Douglas Payne's butler, while feeling certain that the footmen, Mr. Colin Gordon as James and Mr. Ian Aylmer as Charles, dead-heated in a race to tell the second chauffeur what they had seen in the tower. This brings me to Mr. Warmington, who is the hub of the play's intrigue, and must stay as motionless. Having nothing to do or say, he must just be, and I don't know anybody who is better at just being. He stands in the background, the pink of polite attention, and attending. A lesser artist would, we feel, have given only the appearance of heeding, dividing his character's mind between the shoals of past solecisms and the snags of the impending peerage. But Sir Lothar has accepted hospitality, and during his stay belongs to Pagnell Bois.

The production by Mr. John Wyse is exquisite, and we may attribute some over-elaboration to the ardours of a first essay. The changes of scene are marvellously contrived, as the scene-shifters must have operated half in the wings of this tiny theatre and half in the street. To conclude, this is a piece for all those highbrows who pretended to despise *Cavalcade*, and I hereby challenge them to keep it going for a fiftieth part of that play's run !

MR. PRIESTLEY AGAIN

CORNELIUS. A play by J. B. Priestley. Duchess Theatre, Wednesday, March 20, 1935.   [*March* 24, 1935]

> Dirty British coaster with a salt-caked smoke stack,
> Butting through the Channel in the mad March days
>   With a cargo of Tyne coal,
>   Road rails, pig lead,
> Firewood, ironware, and cheap tin trays.   —MASEFIELD.

AND, I suppose the poet would agree, romance in the keen eyes of the look-out man. Romance to us who consider him from the land romantically, though doubtless the poor devil would give his soul and oilskins for the glamorous haven of the East India Dock Road. If Mr. Masefield's poem is to mean anything beyond being a thing of beauty—a preposterous claim to be made for any poem—it is that romance is absolute whether its momentary envelope be the quinquireme, the galleon, or the coaster. Well, is it? We are all agreed that there is a certain magic about the pedlar taking the Golden Road to Samarkand; the world is not convinced, despite all that Mr. Wells has had to say on the subject, that there is equal magic in the bowler-hatted rush for the 8.30. The point is moot, and a play based on a moot point will always be a good play provided there is a good playwright behind it. I will not go so far as to say that no one is better qualified than I am to express an opinion on the subject-matter of Mr. Priestley's new piece. What I will shyly assert is that few dramatic critics can have had wider experience of that which Mr. Priestley portrays. Few of them can have spent ten years trying to sell calico to the poor Indian whose untutored mind suddenly conceived the notion of weaving its own dhootis. Few of them can have spent a subsequent two years endeavouring to sell notepaper to a neighbourhood with no taste for writing, and which through addiction to the penny illustrated paper had forgotten how to read. Success is the justification of more things than rebellions; it is the only possible saving-grace for commerce. To buy in a cheap market and sell in a dear one may be romance in the eyes of your bank-manager; to reverse the process must always be the most dismal occupation known to man, particularly when it occurs in connection with something which in itself is without interest. To fail as a publisher of good books, or as a producer of good plays, may be a catastrophe, but it is a catastrophe preceded by exhilaration. To go bankrupt on account of tarpaulins or wash-basins is disaster plus humiliation. I ask the reader to pardon the personal allusions contained in the foregoing; they have been set down merely to prove that the present critic perfectly understands and sympathises with what in his new play Mr. Priestley is talking about.

Cornelius was a partner in the firm of Briggs & Murrison, brokers in aluminium, a ghastly metal lacking both the sheen of silver and the seriousness of lead. The firm's difficulties had nothing to do with the decreasing demand for or inability to supply aluminium; all would have been well if somebody or something had not been monkeying with the exchange. But the monkeying had very definitely taken place, with the result that profits had become losses and even that most courteous of institutions, the London and Middlesex Bank, was sending letters nicely poised between the peremptory and the plain nasty. Now Murrison, the senior

partner, was away on a desperate trip after orders, and the
point was how long Cornelius could stave off the creditors by
telling them that Murrison would return with three bags
full. The creditors, however, were not to be promise-
crammed, and, like the King in *Hamlet*, had nothing with
this answer. The end of the first act found Cornelius arrang-
ing for a creditors' meeting, this act having proved wildly
entertaining with the rehearsal of what on paper might look
to be poorish material. But part of the business of playwriting is to draw marrow from the unyielding bone, and
there was not only fun but irony and even a little pathos in
the successive visits to this breaking concern of pedlars and
canvassers still more broke. One of them, an ex-officer,
manfully tried to sell typewriter-ribbons to an office bulging
with these materials, a supply which would not have
been in excess of its requirements if the business had not
fallen away. There's construction for you ! The fellow faint-
ing through lack of nutrition, Cornelius gave him what we
took to be a ten-shilling note, which magnanimity, together
with the habit of reading in office-hours books about the
Amazon, proved that he had a soul above business. But how
came Cornelius to be in the outer office and not in the inner
one where he would have been immune from importuners ?
Because the fire smoked and the firm, in arrears with its
rent, could not complain to the landlord. There's more
construction for you !

In the second act Cornelius called the firm's creditors together—a scene which I take to be one of the higher flights
of Mr. Priestley's creative imagination. Anyhow, there they
all were, looking hang-dog, fly-blown, and moth-eaten, each
after his kind. Like Valentin in *La Peau de Chagrin*, Cornelius
found himself compelled not only to salute these fellows but
to salute them deferentially. Now must he bend low before
that imbecile bank emissary, drop his eyes before his scornful

gaze, and submit to his crass and odious lecturing. Flights
of soul, Balzac goes on, may be known to the debtor whereas
nothing of the impulsive and the generous marks those who
live for and by money; a debt is a work of the imagination
that your creditor never understands. That Mr. Priestley
should know all this shows him to be a student of life arriving
at the same conclusion as Balzac through a different route.
In fairness let me say that his way of making Cornelius take
the bit between his teeth and bolt is entirely his own. After
a time the ardent young man, losing patience with tor-
mentors glueing their eyes to statements of indebtedness,
told them that unless Murrison, who was momentarily expected, returned with his bag bursting with orders, the
concern was hopelessly, irremediably bust ! And before this
there had been another fine outburst in which this fighter
said that trumpery and dismal though the business of huck-
stering aluminium was, while the concern had been afloat
he and his partner had tried to save it with the enthusiasm
and devotion of a lifeboat battling to save a drowning crew.
Then Murrison came, and it was seen that he was out of his
mind. The curtain for the third act rose on a breaking-up
scene in mood a trifle too reminiscent of another famous last
act. But the details were good. One by one the employees
took their leave—the old cashier upon whose circumscribed
mind the limited task had never palled, the office-boy who
like all his kind could endure the thought of work only in
connection with wireless or aeroplanes, the plain little typist
who offered her bespectacled self as balm to her staggered
employer, and the pretty one upon whom Cornelius began
to dote too late. All this was admirable.

Perhaps Mr. Priestley pushed his devotion to construction—a good and unusual fault—too far in making the
pretty typist's sweetheart turn out to be a young man who
had tried to swindle the firm. The swindle was in itself not

feasible, and I think it much more likely that Judy would have chosen a gay but not dishonest spark, probably wearing one of the new fuzzy coats, whose flashiness was the direct opposite of Cornelius's sober, unstartling worth.

Also I beseech Mr. Priestley at once and at whatever cost to alter his ending, for I hold that a fine play and an empty house are better than a ruined play and a full one. I was aghast when Cornelius began to handle the pistol with which his partner had committed suicide and to play with the notion of doing the same. Aghast when, because there was merry-making in the flat overhead, Cornelius cheered up, threw the ledger through the glass-door, and walked out mur-muring something about the Andes. Neither action was in the character as Mr. Ralph Richardson played it, though Mr. Priestley is sufficient of a craftsman to have " planted," as they say, both possibilities. He had attempted to make a case for the pistol ending by endowing Cornelius with a hankering after metaphysics, and a turn for arguing whether the person who annihilates himself can annihilate the will setting the action going. But Mr. Richardson is too genial and chubby to make a purely philosophical exit, and too English and phlegmatic to make a theatrical one. What Mr. Priestley should do is to make Cornelius switch off the office light, let himself out, and by the light which still burns in the passage allow us to see him lock the door behind him. He should leave it to us to realise that for a man of the Cornelius-Richardson temper the failure of one job is not the end of the world. Personally I felt that Cornelius would launch out into dramatic criticism, which is the modern equivalent of " go-ing for a soldier " ! I am not prepared to apportion the blame for the actual ending, by which I really mean that I am prepared. Mr. Priestley wrote the play for Mr. Richard-son, has seen it grow, and should have realised that his last three minutes, with their unmistakable reek of grease-paint, are on an altogether lower level of imagination. As this play stands, it has not the beauty of *Eden End*, but I am not at all sure that if the piece were to end with a dying fall—in Orsino's and not the pistol sense—it might not in retrospect acquire that quality. It is immensely ingenious throughout; it has great invention and, so far as I have been able to check it, no other departure from truth. One would perhaps say that while it is only goodish Priestley, it would be magnificent anybody else.

Mr. Richardson gave Cornelius a swell of soul rising to genuine passion, and making one ask what such a fellow should be doing in business. Perhaps the whole point of this play is that people should do the jobs for which they are fitted and not those for which they are unfitted, that the Corneliuses of all ages should command quinquireme, galleon, or coaster, bring it safe to port through the teeth of a howling gale, write a poem about it, or do anything except sit in an office haggling over the price of ivory or cinnamon or tin trays. If this is the point, then Mr. Richardson made it very finely. " Let him roar again ! " said Bully Bottom about the lion, and this is what one said to oneself after the two barks which the author has allowed his magnificent player.

I think that by accident I have perhaps hit here upon the reason for the over-theatrical ending. Mr. Priestley wanted his lion to roar again, and to throw the ledger through the window was roaring in action. What this really means is that he has got hold of an actor who is a little too big for his theatre, bigger though that theatre is than that of any other man now writing for the stage, Mr. Shaw always excepted. Cornelius wasted twenty years of life making out bills of lading and fiddling with blotting-paper, and I am not sure that Mr. Richardson is not a little wasted on him. I feel that just as Cornelius was too big for his office, so this player is too big for Cornelius. He is too big physically; what was wanted was some narrow-chested little fellow with a mind as stout as Cortez. The rest of the acting, on the plane of strict realism, was extremely effective. Mr. James Harcourt gave a natural and unforced picture of the old cashier, Mr. Raymond Huntley was really moving as the starving ex-officer, Mr. Harcourt Williams played the demented partner in a subtle key of reserved power, Miss Dorothy Hamilton contributed a delightful sketch of one of Villadom's most appalling females, and Mr. Tom Gill was excellent as the office-boy, though his hands, face, and collar were all too clean. Perhaps next to Mr. Richardson the honours of the evening should be accorded to Miss Ann Wilton for her very clever study of the repressed typist. This took a good deal of acting, whereas as Judy Miss Victoria Hopper had only to look pretty and be unaffected, which took no acting at all.

MR. WALPOLE'S WEIRD SISTERS

THE OLD LADIES. A play by Rodney Ackland. Adapted from the Novel by Hugh Walpole. New Theatre, Wednesday, April 3, 1935.   [*April* 7, 1935]

> It is when one loses health and the last flush of middle-age, when the eye begins to make conscious adjustment to small print, and stairs grow steeper, and desire infrequent, that one envisages the Compensation to come. Heaven, I feel sure, was invented by a miserable man. . . .   —NEGLECTED AUTHOR.

NEXT TO DEATH, old age is the most pitiful thing that can befall a man, though from the earliest times a deal of lamentable bosh has been written to the contrary. I have no doubt that the earliest Babylonian tablet is a sigh for that old age which should bring the inscriber nearer to the grave. Even as a schoolboy one saw through the chunnerings of Cicero. Wordsworth, telling a young lady that " old age, serene and bright, and lovely as a Lapland night," should lead her to her grave is a soothing-poetic ass, but still an ass. And who has not retched before the dodderings of Maeterlinck's Plus Vieil Aveugle ? Shakespeare was in two minds on the subject, as on most others. In one place age is the first item in his catalogue of weariest and most loathed worldly life. In another it is like a lusty winter, frosty but kindly. The second is the sentimental view taken by your Royal Academician presenting some incredibly-lined old salt grinning under a sou'-wester, with the title " Athwart the Westering Sun." The vein is in direct descent from a Nashe descanting upon the old wives a-sunning. I have spoken with some of these old salts and wives and found them to be snappy and sour; both kinds instinctively know the truth about old age, though mercifully the powers of reflection are denied them. But Coleridge knew, and knew that he knew, and so did Hardy, and so did young Rupert Brooke, who put the best possible face on the matter when he called old age the " unhoped serene," which of course is the poetical term for the hopeless and the querulous. Mr. Walpole, the mildest author who ever made one character itch to throttle another, takes the sensible and correct view. He sees old age as an *olla podrida* or *clamjamfrie* of all the horrors, physical, mental, and spiritual, a hodge-podge of every kind of failure and frustration. If his old ladies still had husbands they would, one feels, not be calling down blessings on their frosty pows but denuding them by the handful.

A two-fold point has been raised about this play, which is why I have ventured to clear the ground. First it has been asked whether Mr. Walpole's Furies are in Nature or Grand Guignol. Second, since two of them smell so horribly of mortality and the third reeks of the asylum, why make a novel or a play about them ? Perhaps these two questions can be answered together. We can, I think, dismiss Mrs. Amorest from the argument. She is a nice old thing in whom, by one of those miracles which Providence seems to provide as a matter of course, the milk of human kindness has not turned sour. Indeed, Mr. Walpole underlines the fact that Lucy is pure gold, since she has successfully stood the test of union with a man who could write poetic balderdash in the late W. G. Wills or, still worse, early Tennyson manner. A spouse who could patiently listen to a husband reciting chunks from five-act dramas called *Tintagel* and *The Slandered*

Queen is, we feel, immune from shock on this earth, and when she dies needs no passport through the Golden Gates.

The difficulty is with the other two. Miss Beringer, of course, exists and is to be met with in every seaside boarding-house from Scarborough to Torquay; the captain of Mr. Masefield's British coaster finds his sole distraction in turning his spyglass on them as they sit reading novels from the circulating libraries on the edge of Flamborough, Spurn, and Beachy Heads, the Bills of Selsey and Portland, and the Points of St. Catherine, Start, and Prawle. Indeed, it was one such who at Penny Contract in a hydro at Budleigh Salterton said to me when I had doubled Four Hearts: " We do not double in this establishment, my good sir. None of us likes to be doubled, and we have abandoned the practice." But that is by the way. Amy Beringer, with her constant hedging upon any subject so that she may in one and the same breath assert her individuality and then withdraw that assertion for fear of offending, is the real thing. With her passion for dogs she is as ludicrous and as pathetic as Miss Flite, and we may reflect if we like how much more severe, despite its apparent lenience, is the modern form of frustration. In Dickens' day antiquated virgins went " clean gyte " and potty; now, alas ! they retain their senses and plumb the more tragic depths of neurasthenia. Yes, I think that Miss Beringer's actuality is perfectly established.

Mrs. Payne presents a different problem. She is an ogress seething in shapeless flesh, and stewing in malignant juices of her own devising. In the words of Grandfather Smallweed to his life-companion, she is " a brimstone scorpion, a sweltering toad, a chattering, clattering, broomstick witch that ought to be burnt." Part of Mr. Walpole's description of her is: " She was not a cleanly old woman. Her splendid hair, as black now as forty years ago, was tumbled about her head carelessly, and stuck into it, askew, was a cheap black comb studded with glass diamonds. Her colour was swarthy, brown under the deep red of her cheeks, and there was a faint moustache on her upper lip. But she must have been handsome once, a fine bold girl in those years long ago." I agree. As presented at the New Theatre, Mrs. Payne might some forty years previously have rivalled it, at least in appearance, with Calvé's Carmen, and I have actually seen Ortruds and Brangänes who were quite as fearsome. Despite her dirt she has temperament, always a redeeming quality, since generosity and not meanness, Nature's riot and not cheese-paring, are at the heart of it. And despite her gluttony she has the passion for beauty. " What do you know of lust or desire for anything ? " she asks Lucy Amorest, and follows this up with a statement which places her in a category apart from the others: " If I were to know that I had only half an hour more to live, I would want the sensation of owning that beautiful thing." If the glutting of a passion at all costs is madness, then this woman is mad. But then Miss Beringer was equally resolved to leave no stone unturned to glut another passion, that of genteel respectability, and I see no reason why one character, because she is less familiar, should be claimed for the asylum more than the other. In my view it is the desiccated spinster, and not the overcharged gipsy who is sub-human. Note, too, Agatha Payne does not murder with intent, since in the novel Mr. Walpole makes her say to herself as she replaces the amber on the mantelpiece and realises what has happened to Miss Beringer: " I didn't mean that ! " She even says it twice. Yes, I think a case can be made out for the actuality of Agatha Payne.

But even granting that the three characters are, as we say, real, we have to answer the suggestion that pleasure may not properly be taken in exploring the ghoulish recesses of the human mind and nosing about death's antechambers.

A colleague has said that Mrs. Payne's " lust for the amber toy and her sadistic glee as she breaks the nerve of her victim are aspects of lunacy and perversions of life which are scarcely tragedy's concern." But why must a play about these things be a tragedy ? Why may it not be what the French call a *drame*, like *Thérèse Raquin*, a genus which is the half-way house between tragedy and Grand Guignol ? If the reader asks me what pleasure there is in watching the unfolding of such a story, I can only say that for me that pleasure exists though I cannot explain it any more than William Archer could explain the exhilaration to be derived from tragedy. Asked by a lady what was the good of the *Œdipus*, Archer " left the question in obscurity, as Dr. Johnson, to Boswell's regret, left the details of the future state." I agree with Archer in finding it impossible to explain why technical mastery, dramatic vitality, and all the rest of the catchwords can make a hideous thing lovely; there are people to whom a dunghill remains a dunghill even if Cézanne paints it. So I shall do what Archer did when he raised the question apropos the first English production of *Little Eyolf* in 1896, that is, bid intending playgoers " while the curtain is up, clear their minds of all possible deductions, implications and generalisations, and think only of the story, the character-development, the emotion —in a word, the drama." And I suggest that " drama " is as good a translation of the French word *drame* as we are likely to get.

If this notice appears to treat Mr. Ackland's play as though it were Mr. Walpole's, it is because while the curtain was up it did not occur to me to separate the two. And any adapter who wants better praise than that must look for it ! A great deal depended upon the production, and it shall be said forthwith that Mr. John Gielgud rose to it admirably, rose in fact to the extent of a whole flight of stairs. He presented the interior of the old house in Pontippy Square with a universal dovetailedness and a sort of a general oneness suggesting that he had served his apprenticeship not only to Mr. Curdle's dramatic unities but to Mr. Pecksniff's " idea of " an apartment house in a cathedral city. The design, showing the three rooms at once, involved windows giving on to three sides with a chimney-flue backing up to the neighbour's. This was not only ingenious but characteristic, and much more grateful to the eye than the usual pigeonhole or boot-cupboard method. Mr. Gielgud has presumably not known such rooms as those inhabited by the three old ladies, each of them wittily expressing its owner. But he has used his imagination to fine purpose, and perhaps theatrical lodgings have helped ! It was an inspired touch which made Mrs. Payne bedeck her picture-frames with tinsel obviously ravished from Lucy Amorest's Christmas-tree of the act before.

As for the acting, *palmam qui meruit ferat*. Only there would have to be three palms. As Lucy Amorest Miss Mary Jerrold resisted all temptation to over-sentimentalise. She had one grand moment when, gazing at the Christmas-tree, she said nothing and let us read her lonely thoughts. The part fitted this lovely actress like a Shetland shawl, and was so well played that one might easily take it for granted and forget to praise. As Miss Beringer Miss Jean Cadell ran the entire gamut of nervous disability, beginning with gossip and dyspepsia and ending in breakdown and dissolution. She, too, brought off a grand effect when she made paralysed flight down the stairs, a step every hundred years. It would be as difficult to dissociate this beautiful player from this part as to separate Mrs. Micawber from her gloves. As Agatha Payne Miss Edith Evans revelled in it with high Romany gusto. It was murmured by one or two that the actress was hardly terrifying enough and that Miss Thorndike would have played it to steelier purpose. Maybe; but I think that purpose would have been thinner-lipped, and I hold that what was wanted was not this quality, but the gormandising flame ignobly guttering; this, in my view, is what this great artist magnificently presented, and, in any case, the person to be frightened was not me, but Miss Beringer. She had many grand moments—when Agatha kept up that knocking on the wall, when she defied the dead woman's vengeful spirit, and always when she filled out the name " Lucy " with the high-breathing scorn of a being cast in bigger mould.

THAT NATIONAL THEATRE

[*April* 21, 1935]

I HAVE BEEN READING the brochure entitled *The Case for the National Theatre*. The case seems to me to be as well made out as any case can be which is put forward for something that nobody wants. The argument in support of this last statement goes by a Latin name; as my dictionary is on holiday I forget whether it is *ad hoc, hominem,* or *captandum,* but will swear it is *ad* something or other. The plain knock-down answer to any case for a National Theatre is that if we really wanted it we should already have it. Even if we wanted it subconsciously and the State, acting in a statesmanlike manner, were to realise its duty of fulfilling the nation's subconscious needs, we should have it. I have not read anywhere that crowds mobbed the Houses of Parliament shouting: " We want a British Museum ! " or " Give us a National Gallery ! " The State, realising that these things were good for the nation, gave them to the nation. Now, either the State deems a National Theatre desirable or it doesn't. The point is an academic one, and can hardly matter since it is obvious that in this respect the State is as adamant as Mrs. Micawber's family.

It now becomes necessary to define our categories, which are five in number. Category A :—Things which the Nation wants and is conscious of wanting, and which the State provides. Such things as Army and Navy and Air Force, justiciary, postal services, and the registrars of births and deaths. Category B:—Things which the Nation wants but is not conscious of wanting, but which the State provides. Such things as museums, picture galleries, parks, coast-guards, and boards of agriculture and fisheries. Category C:—Things which the Nation wants and is conscious of wanting, but which the State refuses to provide. Such things as hospitals and lifeboats and zoos. Category D:—Things which the Nation doesn't want, even subconsciously, and which the State refuses to provide. There are only two things in this category. One is a National Opera and the other is a National Theatre. For if these things were really wanted they would fall into the fifth and enormous Category E, of things which the Nation wants, and is conscious of wanting, and with the provision of which the State is not concerned. This category includes racecourses, greyhound and dirt tracks, totes, stadiums, swimming-baths, cricket-grounds, boxing-booths. The nation wants these, and it even insists that the chiefest of them should receive a kind of national and official recognition, while remaining indifferent to the technicalities of ownership. The national race-course is Epsom Downs on Derby Day. The national cricket-ground is Lord's. The national football field is Wembley Stadium. The national lawn-tennis court is Wimbledon. The national boxing-booth is the Albert Hall. These are the race-course, cricket-ground, football-field, lawn-tennis court, and boxing-booth of a people which wants them and insists upon having them.

And now to make the point that a National Theatre would have to be the theatre of a people, and not that very different thing, a people's theatre, which means slum dramas performed by unfashionable actors and dowdy actresses before ill-dressed audiences. A National Theatre must be something which is above class because it appeals to all classes, and to which everybody flocks as a matter of course. If—and I insist upon repeating this argument *ad* something which I forgot before, that is to say *nauseam*— the public wanted a National Theatre it would have it. But the public goes further than not wanting it; it would violently resist the notion that it has a subconscious need which it is the duty of the State to fulfil. In this we are totally unlike other countries.

My friend and colleague, Mr. A. E. Wilson, tells us in his newly published little book on the theatre that " the inhabitants of Garbage-sous-le-Pont, 560 kilometres from Paris, who don't know an opera from Camembert cheese, raise no protest against being taxed in order to support a grand opera in Paris." Now hear him on the English analogy:

> " Nobody cared when the Nation paid out enormous sums for a yard or so of canvas covered by the industrious Velazquez with a representation of a liberally unclothed and pink-looking lady for exhibition in the National Gallery. Nor would there be any sort of protest if it were proposed to endow every football club in the United Kingdom with a Government grant and to pay liberal pensions to all footballers over thirty. But directly it was decided to hand over a small subsidy to Covent Garden— which most Englishmen vaguely know is somehow connected with the foreign and outlandish fad of opera— such a howl of indignation went up that nothing in *Götterdämmerung* itself could equal in volume. The entire nation has been sore about it ever since."

This seems to me to put the case against a National Theatre into an entirely sufficient nutshell. Nobody wants it !

Let me now set forth the Objects of the National Theatre as proclaimed in the brochure. These are:

(1) To provide in the Capital of the Empire a theatre where the people may have continual opportunities of seeing the best drama past and present, produced with the utmost distinction, and played by actors of the highest merit.

(2) To maintain the efficiency and dignity of the art of acting by providing opportunities for its exercise in its highest classical departments.

(3) To keep the plays of Shakespeare in its repertory.

(4) To revive whatever is vital in British Drama.

(5) To prevent recent plays of merit from falling into oblivion.

(6) To produce new plays and to further the development of modern drama.

(7) To produce translations of representative works of foreign drama, ancient and modern.

(8) To stimulate the art of the theatre through every possible and suitable means.

Permit me to append my notes. (1) If a sufficient number of people wanted to see the best drama past and present, the opportunities would be provided even in the existing state of affairs. If there were any real demand for the plays of, say, Ben Jonson, that author would be a standing dish. I really see no reason why somebody living in Kettering or Penzance should subscribe for a performance of, say, *Volpone*, or any piece which when it is put on by private enterprise London does not dream of going near. If it is argued that the National Theatre should be a touring concern, then I say that the Old Vic, Sadler's Wells, and Stratford-on-Avon can provide all the play-houses necessary, while the interest on the £150,000 already in hand is sufficient for a London office, a secretary, a typist, and an office-boy, provided all three are willing to work. As somebody said the other day, to be saddled with a white elephant is no reason for building a marble stable to house him. (2) If an art has become so unattractive that it cannot keep up its own dignity, I see no reason why its dignity should be kept up for it. (3) The Old Vic is the answer here. (4) That which is vital does not need reviving; the need pre-supposes that the vitality is lost or impaired. (5) They don't ! If they fall into oblivion the merit is merely highbrow or coterie, and a universal theatre should exist solely for plays of universal appeal. (6) No good new play ever fails to be produced. If it is a *really* good play it may begin in a hole, but it ends by reaching all the corners of the earth. (7) About the best of a poor lot of reasons ! (8) See my note on (4).

On the other hand these eight objects perfectly cover The National Theatre Which Nobody Wants. However, the appeal is launched. It is an appeal for money, to be exact for £350,000, and the method to be adopted is as follows. First, donations. In a reasonably governed State a knighthood would be given to anybody subscribing £1,000, whereupon the trick would be immediately accomplished. (An extra 350 knights prancing about would do no harm to anybody.) In the absence of any such bait I compute the results of the donations at £3,614 0s. 2d. Then I understand that there is to be a Matinée which with luck may double this amount. Also people are invited to buy stamps to put on to letters, which I suppose will bring in a few more hundreds. Altogether something under £10,000 will be collected, and one of the most influential General Committees which has ever been got together in this country will thereupon sit down and fold its hands for another twenty-five years. The whole thing is absurd. £350,000 is less than the few millionaires of my acquaintance habitually squander on their racehorses, yachts, and grouse moors. Has anybody asked the theatre managers of London whether they would be willing for the next ten years to give the proceeds of one special performance, say on St. George's Day? That would be forty matinées a year, or four hundred in ten years. Would the managers consent? Would the actors give their services on that day? Both are foregone conclusions, though I may be permitted to hint darkly that there is more than one way of concluding. What about a flag day a year for ten years throughout the country?

And now, after this column of destructive criticism, for a piece of the constructive sort! The Prince of Wales, broadcasting on April 12 an appeal on behalf of King George's Jubilee Trust, said: " I have discovered that nothing would give their Majesties the King and Queen so much pleasure as a fund to be devoted to the welfare of the rising generation, and I can think of no cause which should make so national an appeal." May I suggest that the welfare of the rising generation is as much mental and spiritual as physical, and that one of the best reasons for establishing a National Theatre is to give the youth of the country a playhouse alternative to the foolish and degrading influence of the American film? The Prince further said that the trustees of the fund also had in mind an indoor programme " to help towards club premises, workshops, and gymnasiums." May I suggest that in any indoor programme the mind as well as the body should be cared for? Were I a member of the Executive Committee I should respectfully pray and beseech the trustees of the Jubilee Fund, when it shall have been collected, to allot a small portion of it to a National Theatre, where seats would be specially reserved at special prices for the youth of the country, for whom the Fund is intended.

Why have I gone to the trouble of making this suggestion? Because I am at least as keen as anybody else in England on a National Theatre, though I see no good in writing highbrow guff about it and then whimpering for donations on the old soup-kitchen scale. I believe in going and getting the money, and if nobody will go and you can't get it, then I believe in chucking the thing and getting Parliament to sanction the use of the cash in hand in any manner decided on by a committee consisting of the Prime Minister, Miss Lilian Braithwaite and me ! The reader may think he has detected a note of sour grapes because the name of the present writer does not appear in the list of the general committee. I have to say that an invitation was extended to the dramatic critic of this paper by virtue of his office, and was declined on the ground that to become a member of any general committee is to enter into a conspiracy of inactivity. But I added that, while I would have nothing whatever to do with any general committee, I would be delighted to join the executive committee and to work. (I had contemplated undertaking a lecture-and-appeal-tour of this country, though I am not an idle man, and for expenses only—not my kind of expenses, but ordinary ones !) It was conveyed to me with diplomatic tact that that was not the sort of committee-man required. When I am old and grey and full of sleep I shall hope to renew the offer. For, of course, the question of the National Theatre will still be on the carpet, and, so far as I can see, it will remain there *ad*—as the Roman wit said—*infinitum*.

DUET IN TWILIGHT

CLOSE QUARTERS. A play by Gilbert Lennox. Adapted from
the German of W. O. Somin. Embassy Theatre, Tuesday,
June 25, 1935.

LOVE LAUGHS——. A musical comedy, by Clifford Grey
and Greatrex Newman. Music by Noel Gay. Hippodrome,
Thursday, June 27, 1935.   [*June* 30, 1935]

THIS IS THE SORT of piece which one should see twice to
enable one to decide how fair the author has played. The
curtain goes up on an empty working-class flat. Presently
Liesa Bergmann, wife of a Socialist agitator, Gustav Bergmann, enters, in obvious distress. She goes at once into the
back room and changes her dress, to which she appears to
have taken a violent dislike, after which she sets about getting
her husband's supper. Then Bergmann enters, obviously a
little exhilarated. He excuses this on the ground that the
speech he has made at that evening's meeting has been so
successful as to call for celebrating. He has been in great
form, has told his traditional enemy, the Minister in power,
exactly where he gets off, threatening even to do him in,
has been congratulated by his chiefs, and, in short, everything in the political garden has been lovely. If Liesa is a
good girl and she has some beer in the flat, they can go on
celebrating. She has, and they do. But Liesa is still a naughty
girl for having let him go out that evening without his
woollen gloves. However, he cannot be cross with her for long,
seeing that he has great news—the promise of advancement

which will enable them to move into a better flat. Liesa
is overjoyed and they fall to dancing to the strains of the
wireless, which are interrupted to announce the murder
óf the Minister. There is no more dancing that night, Liesa
shows unaccountable anxiety to get into the new apartment,
and Bergmann nervously confesses that that evening he has
come home not by way of the streets, but through the little
wood in which the Minister's house is situated. In fact he
must have passed it very near the hour of the murder.

The second act shows the couple in their new apartment
and much more worried than the business of shifting a few
pots and pans justifies. Bergmann now sees the folly of that
rhetorical threat to kill. The make of pistol that was used is
given in the papers, and it is the same make of weapon which
Bergmann normally carries. Liesa says that she can swear
to the fact that on the evening in question he had not the
weapon with him, but Bergmann asks what use such testimony would be coming from a wife. It seems that the police
have made an arrest, at which Liesa shows much delight.
But Bergmann answers that the evidence is so sketchy that
even the police don't seem to think that the man is guilty,
and Liesa asks what that matters since it will save her
husband. But throughout Liesa is singularly unhelpful, since
her excessive solicitude for her husband merely deepens the
hole he believes himself to be in. The act ends with the man
going out to pass the night in the streets rather than endure
any more of his wife's morbid comforting.

It is during the second interval that one feels the necessity
for seeing this play twice. Obviously husband or wife is the
murderer, and half of our attention is taken up with examining Bergmann's behaviour in view of the possibility that he is
the criminal. On the other hand, Liesa's agitated entrance
suggests that she is the murderer, always provided the play
is not just a thriller, when that agitation would be a perfectly

proper red-herring. But up to now we do not know whether
the play is thriller or psychological drama; and the fact that
we have been attending to Gustav means that we have not
been in a position to give more than three-quarters of our
mind to the question of Liesa's consistency. This is not
enough for a certificate to this play's watertightness. In fact,
I think it would be improved if the audience, instead of
strongly suspecting Liesa, should know that she is the guilty
party; it would be sufficient if she showed the revolver. For,
of course, it is Liesa who has done the deed, and in the third
act she confesses how, the Minister being a voluptuary, she
had yielded to him to secure her husband's advancement—
it appears that in political cricket the captain of one side can
dictate the batting order of the other—and how later she was
blackmailed into becoming his spy. This is a scene of magnificent tension equally divided between the wretched woman
making the confession and the man listening to it. Liesa also
confesses to using her husband's pistol and to wearing his
gloves, one of which she cannot now find. At this point the
wireless announces the discovery of a glove, whereupon
Bergmann kills Liesa and then himself. I think that the last-
second news before the curtain falls that the glove found by
the police is a lady's glove is a mistake. This play does not
need pointing with what will loosely be called tragic irony.
It is what the French call *drame* and, given the acting, is
strong enough to stand as a simple, straightforward drama.

Miss Flora Robson must not take it amiss if, for three-
quarters of the evening, we could not take our eyes off her
partner, Mr. Oscar Homolka. This for two reasons. Because,
whereas Miss Robson's brilliant talent is familiar Mr.
Homolka is a newcomer, and because while the woman's
part is almost entirely on one note, finely sustained by Miss
Robson and moving us deeply in the confession scene, the
man's covers a considerable range. The first thing to be said

about Mr. Homolka is that he is naturally an actor. As an Austrian he is as much superior to any English player of equivalent talent as the porters at Boulogne exceed their colleagues at Folkestone. Some other day I shall develop the thesis that there is more acting to be seen on a single French railway platform than in all the theatres of London. Like all foreign actors, Mr. Homolka regards the body as the natural means of expression, unlike your English player, who holds that the body's function is to conceal thought. " Lass diesen Händedruck dir sagen Was unaussprechlich ist ! " says Goethe, speaking for a race which is only too glad to let the pressure of the hand convey the inexpressible. How often have we not seen some inexpressive He exert that pressure, put his left hand on another's right shoulder, vouchsafe him a fish-like glare, and dumbly turn to fiddle with the decanter !

Mr. Homolka follows a different tradition. Anything that he has to express is expressed with his whole body. The nape of his neck, the toes inside his boots, the very hairs on the back of his hands *act*. Instead of the well-bred monotone with which your Englishman confronts life, death, and the drawing-room mantelpiece, Mr. Homolka has a hundred varieties of tone and pitch, gesture, and facial expression, with which to put before us his mercurial, commonplace, well-meaning little demagogue. He uses so much power when you are not particularly expecting it that in the great scene in the third act, when your London actor might be wondering whether he should not let himself go, he has no need to use any, but simply sits there letting us see on his face what is happening in his mind. As a piece of character acting the performance is superb; whatever horrors are heaped on the little man's head he never becomes a figure of calm and classic tragedy, but remains the quick, high-strung oddity he was in the beginning. Schumann, if my memory serves me, has a piano piece with the words " Mit

Humor " at the head of it, and that is how our visitor acts.

Though, Casabianca-like, I stayed to the bitter end of *Love Laughs*, honesty compels me to state that I missed a little of the beginning and therefore cannot tell how bitter that may have been ! By the way, one might conceivably ask whether Casabianca was ever late on parade. But let that pass. Starting from the third scene I think I may say that I have never been more aghast at the thought that such things can be and deliriously succeed. It is, one must suppose, characteristic of the English nation that it should regard the improvement of prison conditions as a huge joke and then take seriously the musical comedy built upon that joke. Ransacking my brains for something favourable, that is, for some encomium to be blazoned on the outside of this theatre, I can only suggest that this piece about convicts who successfully laugh at locksmiths is at least free from the mawkishness of Galsworthy's *Escape*. Mr. Syd Walker is a good comedian but has, alas, no material ! Mr. Laddie Cliff dances a little, but the show is really Miss Renee Houston, upon whose wit a music-hall training has put a scalpel's edge. Miss Houston does not so much act in musical comedy as prey upon it and upon its devotees, since there is not one single aspect of this kind of entertainment which she does not scarify and hold up to ridicule. Is luminous imbecility wanted ? She will welter in inanity and present a countenance as pretty as a bedspread and as blank as a mattress. Had any other of our musical-comedy actresses been present they must have died of shame ! Is there question of a leading lady in a straight play ? This little mischief at once acquires so much poise that it nearly chokes her, while through excess of elegance her vocal cords refuse their office. Shall Garbo and Shirley Temple suffer the searchlight of common sense ? It is turned on. In plain English Miss Houston saves a show that, without her, must have foundered twenty times.

J'ACCUSE

CLOSE QUARTERS. A play by Gilbert Lennox. Adapted from the German of W. O. Somin. Haymarket Theatre, Wednesday, July 17, 1935. [*July* 21, 1935]

J'accuse ! On Wednesday of last week I was taken to dinner at a fashionable restaurant and to supper at a smart grill-room. Between the two meals I attended the first night of *Close Quarters* at the Haymarket Theatre. I discovered to my amazement that none of the intellectuals, fashionables, or merely wealthy people who had crowded those dinner tables had gone on to this play. And later I found that none of the intellectuals, fashionables, or merely wealthy people thronging those supper tables had come on from this play. Therefore I accuse the intellectuals, fashionables, and merely wealthy of London of taking no interest in the true theatre, in a good play, and in what I hold to be the finest acting I have seen in London since Bernhardt's visit to Ealing round about 1906.

J'accuse ! I accuse all those intellectuals or so-called high-brows who, while sneering at entertainments like *Cavalcade*, do not actively support the type of theatrical representation which they pretend to prefer. I accuse the fashionable crowd. Are there no intervals at the Haymarket play at which frocks can be displayed ? As for the wealthy, I would merely ask whether the seats at this theatre are not as expensive as those of other theatres. And whether three-thousand-guinea motor-cars may not prance and curvet as ostentatiously in the

Haymarket as in any other thoroughfare. It was, of course, explained to me at my supper-party that the intellectuals, fashionables, and wealthy were all going to see this play in due course. To which I retort that it is not in due course that they go to the first night of a Cochran revue or a Leslie Henson musical comedy or a Noel Coward première. In such cases the here and now is regarded as the important thing. Let not the reader get me wrong, as in films the peccant thug always pleads to the double-crossed gangster. I look forward to Cochran, Coward, and Henson first nights with the liveliest expectation and in almost complete certainty of enjoying myself. What I am objecting to is the application of the here-and-now fetish to enterprises which stand in no need of that fetish. All the world knows that in six weeks' time they will still be running. This being so, the impresarios concerned do not need reassuring. Now the irony of it is that a manager who puts on a good play with magnificent acting and for whose first night the public does not roll up stands in every need of reassurance. How is he to know unless the public tells him through his box-office that support will be forthcoming in due course ? Hamlet, protesting that he lacked advancement and told that it was only a matter of due course, said: " Ay, sir, but ' while the grass grows '— the proverb is something musty." What the management of a good play wants is not advancement but advance-bookings ! While the grass grows, the steed starves. While the intellectuals, fashionables, and merely wealthy are mutely deciding to visit a good play, the manager, unapprised of the good intention, finds himself obliged to take the play off. Let me tear to ribbons the last shred of well-meaning excuse, that playgoers did not know about the present good play. They know about the Cochran and Coward and Henson premières and through exactly the same medium which, in the last fortnight, has shouted as loud as newsprint knows the

supreme excellence of the performance at the Embassy
Theatre, now transferred to the Haymarket.

J'accuse ! I accuse the entire Aryan race of not knowing
good acting when it sees it. Or with greater malignity I
accuse it of knowing good acting and fighting shy of it.
Therefore I appeal to non-Aryans, in other words, to the
temperamental people in this country who know and relish
displays of temperament on the stage, which is all that first-
class acting ever was or ever can be. A player may have
stage presence, technique, and even intellectuality; but if
he has not the player's temperament he is nothing; and both
Miss Flora Robson and Mr. Oscar Homolka possess the
player's temperament abundantly, lavishly, riotously. They
possess so much that on Wednesday some of it was transferred
to the audience, which at the end stood up and cheered.
I therefore appeal to the non-Aryans whose characteristic is
temperament, as opposed to the Aryans whose note is good
form, not to miss this opportunity. I am told—and have even
gone the direct way to being told, which is asking !—that
at this theatre there are 140 gallery seats at 2*s.*, 100 upper
circle seats at 3*s.* 6*d.*, 145 upper circle seats at 4*s.* 9*d.*, and
232 pit stalls at 5*s.* 9*d.* As evidence of genuineness, as con-
fidence tricksters say, I am prepared in so far as 100 seats
are concerned—since age brings prudence with it—to refund
the price of a seat in case the playgoer has been totally disappointed, or that portion of the price of which he thinks
he has been cheated. Only such playgoer must be non-
Aryan, for I should expect an Aryan to demand not 5*s.* 9*d.*
but 11*s.* 6*d.*, being the cost not only of his personal disappoint-
ment but of his wife's also !

The acting, in my opinion, is truly grand. At Swiss Cottage Miss Robson was a little over-partnered; she has now
brought more guns into action, and returns salvo for salvo.
There is no courtesy question of the English or the Austrian

troops firing first: they blaze away together and at point-
blank range. Not a word merely, but a whole history could
be given to Miss Irene Hentschel's production. There is no
means of knowing how much producing this deliberate
artist has done; here is a case where one can only judge by
results. The most acute critic cannot determine whether a
producer has ordered this or that to be done, or this or that
left undone. All one can safely say is that here is a play of
which each situation has been keyed up and made taut to
the point of maximum effectiveness, and so that all the other
people concerned in the drama, though we only hear of
them, are as much present in our consciousness as though
they had appeared on the stage before us. The jockey cannot come without the horse, and it is only modern cant
which pretends that a producer can take the place of sufficing
players. But let us consider one scene, the great scene of the
confession in the third act, in which three weeks ago I
foolishly said that Mr. Homolka does nothing. Watching the
performance again the other evening I perceived that the
actor does a very great deal. For one thing, on his face he
writes the whole tragedy of *Othello*, while his outburst about
the seducer who has died too easily has all the fury with
which a Shakespearean actor should speak the lines:

> *O, that the slave had forty thousand lives !*
> *One is too poor, too weak for my revenge.*

Then consider the marvellous play of that right hand, true
in nature as in art. True in nature because in moments of
great tension when the mind is taking in momentous news
there is always one small fragment of it which will watch,
with great particularity and detachment, say the antics of
a fly on the window-pane. Similarly Mr. Homolka observes
the articulation of his fingers. But the manœuvre is also true
in art, because it points the tragedy where it belongs. Every

Player King and Queen in *Hamlet* must have experienced the mortification of realising that we are not listening to their talk of Phoebus' cart and Tellus' orbèd ground. Every Hamlet who is worth Neptune's salt-wash knows that in this scene our eyes are not fixed upon him but elsewhere; the whole point of the mimic play is the moment when the light shall break upon the guilty Claudius that the game is up. It is *his* face that we watch.

Momentous though the confession is to the woman making it, the point of the scene is its effect upon the man to whom the confession is made. The position from the point of view of the actress is that her long and very difficult speech, requiring every virtuosity in delivery of which she is capable, comes to its focal point only in the hand of the actor listening to it. How great, then, are the artistry and self-sacrifice of an actress realising that the better she plays the scene, the more must our attention be drawn away from her and concentrated upon her partner ! With a lesser artist than Miss Robson and with a less subtle producer than Miss Hentschel, this would not be allowed to happen. Can we not see what at rehearsals would normally take place ? What pipes and timbrels ? What wild ecstasy ? In less high-flown English, what hysteria and threats of withdrawal from the piece ! To secure that this should not happen must not Mr. Homolka have been invited to imitate Dr. Johnson, withdraw his attention from Miss Robson, and think not upon his fingers but upon Tom Thumb ? But then, these are not normal players. And if playgoing London were sane, it would be flocking to see them !

A BABEL IN ONE TONGUE

YOSHE KALB. A play by Maurice Schwartz. Adapted
from the Novel by I. J. Singer. His Majesty's Theatre,
Monday, September 9, 1935.

THE HOUSE OF BORGIA. A play by Clifford Bax. Embassy
Theatre, Thursday, September 12, 1935.

[*September* 15, 1935]

BEING HONEST with oneself, and therefore with other
people, is sometimes a plaguey business. How comes it that
while almost every one of my colleagues has been plunged
into seething maelstroms and palpitating vortices of emotion
by the Yiddish Art Theatre Company, my interest on my
first visit the other night wobbled between the tepid and the
lukewarm? Am I less sensitive to acting? Am I slower in
the linguistic uptake? It cannot, I think, be the second,
since in a London paper I read: " So effective is the acting
that the story can be followed with no understanding of
Yiddish." And in a Manchester one I find: " The tragic
allegory of the story tells itself." Perhaps I had better
straightway make confession of a limitation which appears
to be peculiar to me alone. All my life through, I have never
been able to make anything of any play or any acting in an
unknown tongue. Even when the tongue is semi-known I
find myself at as nearly the same loss as makes no matter.
I have a quarter-understanding of German, and I suppose
I know *Hamlet* as well as most playgoers. Now, take Hamlet's
first soliloquy whose points are the melting of the flesh, the

canon 'gainst self-slaughter, the unprofitable uses of the world, the unweeded-garden simile, the comparison of the two kings, the first husband's gentleness, the increase of appetite, the frailty of woman, the beast that wants discourse of reason, the wicked speed of the second marriage. But let a German actor get going over this course and I am utterly unable to tell which hurdle he is at, even though I virtually know the speech by heart. How, then, if I can't follow a known speech in *Hamlet*, am I to follow the unknown orations of *Yoshe Kalb* ?

" Of course," people hasten to argue, " you can't expect to understand all that is said. But you've got eyes, and shouldn't have any difficulty with the story ! " That's where we differ. I have every difficulty with the story. In vain do I mug up the plot beforehand. I have not arrived at the sixth scene before I am completely lost. It is all very well for the synopsis to tell me that " Nachumtche's mother, repelled by the vulgarity and noise of the Nyesheve court, is filled with misgiving about her son's future." How can I, without striking matches, know whether she is repelling or misgiving ? Then take the second scene in Act Two, which is said by the synopsis to run like this:

" At the sexton's house hard by the cemetery. Konoh has finished his repast and is reciting at top speed grace after meals. This does not prevent him from transacting business with the smuggler, Yankel, who pays him for permitting him to hide contraband in the cemetery. Konoh is called away to a burial, whereupon Yankel, who has been having trysts with a half-witted girl in the cemetery, arranges for another tryst that night. He leaves, and soon Yoshe Kalb comes home. But when Zivya again makes love to him he runs out of the house. Presently Abush the Butcher, leading a committee in search of sinners, arrives and observes Zivya closely. She is found to be big with child and is dragged off to the rabbinical court."

Watching all this with owlish intensity, I come to the conclusion that it is all about some moneylender whose bill has been found to be too big with interest !

Later, when, still according to the programme, the court decrees that marriage of two orphans in a graveyard is an effective remedy for plague—well, frankly, neither the striking of matches nor the light of guesswork saves me. The pleasure of the evening, such as it is, resides therefore in the play's visual aspect. And I don't like beards ! It would be pure cant to say that I am enraptured at the sight of a score of Yiddish W. G. Graces wearing miniature top-hats like Chirgwin. Nor am I beglamoured when they join hands in a ring, and dance something that looks like the old nursery " Here we go round the Mulberry Bush " punctuated by cries of " Mazeltoff ! "—whatever that may mean—like a Highlander indulging in his Fling. On such occasions I feel as an Eskimo might do on looking at modern French painting. The trouble is that my love of the theatre is such that the inability to understand what is going on throws my mind into a state of exasperation where it resembles a distorting mirror. I become as jealous of my colleagues, to whom all is crystal clear, as a deaf man at a concert who sees everybody around him applauding.

Sobering down, one realises that some of the stage scenes are masterly, that the lighting has purpose and imagination behind it, and that here is a lot of corking good acting. How corking that acting is, it is, of course, impossible for me to divine, let alone pronounce. Mr. Maurice Schwartz has presence, voice, power, authority, and looks rather like the picture of Devrient as Lear. He shows, too, that in the course of an evening he can grow old and reduce the swelling voice not to the whimper of incompetent purveyors of senility, but to the shell of a voice that has been big. He obviously has great humour, and I should guess him to be a first-class comedian. How far he is a tragedian I just don't know, for his aspect never begins to frighten or move me, and in his heart-attacks, or whatever they are, I seem to see merely a good actor acting. One thing puzzled me throughout the evening. Why does not Mr. Schwartz, who is said to be a first-class English-speaking Shakespearean actor, give us some Shakespeare in English and so provide the opportunity to judge him ? The answer, of course, is the difference between the average English critic and the trout. The trout is shy of a fly it has never seen before, whereas your English critic rises at the unknown like anything.

Only two things are wrong with *The House of Borgia*, (*a*) the style in which it is written, and (*b*) the style in which it is acted. Hardly anything could be better than the general plan of it, for here you have a Pope upsetting all notions as to the celibacy of the priesthood by flaunting in Cæsar and Lucrezia Borgia as fine a pair of brats as ever took the quinquecento stage. Pope Alexander VI shows himself to be a compunctionable murderer. His only way of providing for his daughter's dowry is to murder somebody, which he does not in the least want to do as he gave up poisoning quite a time ago and has no desire to return to the nasty habit. Indeed he is quite fretful about it, and Mr. Bax has wittily looked upon him as though he were a church dignitary out of the *Bab Ballads*. Cæsar has more guts, and in this case the chip may be said to be better than the block. The play contains a lot of strangling; there is plenty of action, with a minimum of philosophising. And lastly, there is a Lucrezia who would not know prussic acid if she smelled it. Yes, thank you, I am aware that the poison the Borgias used was probably Heavy Water, that discovery of which

the twentieth century is so proud ! On the other hand, has
not the Borgia poison-cabinet with a dozen poisons still in
it just been sold at a public auction ? So we will let prussic
acid stand.

From the foregoing it can be seen that here is a capital
drama whose best author would probably be John Ford.
But that means the Phœnix Society on Sunday evening.
The other way is Mr. Rafael Sabatini's, with Mr. Lang in
full Florentine fig. In other words, if you cannot get great
poetry dished up with it, the next best thing is good modern
hurly-burly with a big stage and lots of crowds. What will
not quite do is Mr. Bax's small stage and kid-gloved Muse.
For the present play is dainty, and whatever the Borgias
and the year 1500 were, I do not think they were that !
And then, most of the acting at the Embassy will not do.
Mr. Reginald Tate's Cæsar prattles of insensate ambition
instead of mouthing it, and looks too much of a weakling,
with the result that the play which must be carried on his
shoulders gradually sinks to ground. Even less satisfactory
are Cæsar's two mistresses, who appear to hail from Peckham
and Peckham Rye respectively. Their failure to suggest
period is quite glitteringly complete. When will English
actresses learn to keep still in costume and stop plucking at
their flounces as though they were continually walking over
mud ? When will they realise that the sixteenth century,
having put on its beautiful clothes, thought no more of them
than we do of our own ? The fatal thing in period-acting is
for the player to be period-conscious. Miss Iris Baker as the
flower-like Lucrezia is better, though even she is a little too
like Goldilocks in the nursery rhyme. On the other hand,
Mr. Russell Thorndike's Pope is conceived and acted with
admirable whimsey, for there the old villain sits concocting
murder with the expression of a small boy caught stealing the
jam. His death scene shows that Mr. Thorndike remembers

Irving, for it is like dissolution and quite frightening; it must be a long time since any English actor has made an audience imagine that it is looking on the dew of death. The best performance is that of Mr. Alan Wheatley, who looks and behaves like Machiavelli and without pulling any faces. The actor just stands still, and something within does the rest. But when all is said and done, no acting could really save this little piece whose scope should make the welkin ring, whereas Mr. Bax has only made it tinkle.

IBSEN'S YOUNG PRETENDER

PEER GYNT. Revival of Ibsen's Play. Old Vic Theatre, Monday, September 23, 1935.

RIVALS ! A musical version of Sheridan's Comedy by J. R. Monsell. Music by J. R. Monsell, Herbert Hughes, Irvin Hinchcliffe, and Leigh Henry. Embassy Theatre, Thursday, September 26, 1935.

CLOSING AT SUNRISE. A play by Richard Carruthers. Royalty Theatre, Tuesday, September 24, 1935.

[September 29, 1935]

WOULD IT BE a fair thing to say of Mr. Shaw that his likes are other people's dislikes ? Peer Gynt, said the author of *The Quintessence of Ibsenism*, " selfish rascal as he is, is not unlovable," and I fancy that in the opinion of most people Peer is just not lovable. The point is an essential one if we are to believe with Mr. Shaw that Peer has " the same effect on the imagination that Hamlet, Faust, and Mozart's Don Juan have had," and with William Archer that his adventures give us pleasure like those of Sindbad, Gil Blas, Tom Jones, and Huckleberry Finn. At once another difficulty presents itself. If Peer belongs to Mr. Shaw's category, the play must be a great tragedy ; if the piece belongs to Archer's, then Peer is a rapscallion or ballad-hero like Tyl Eulenspiegel. No character can breathe both atmospheres. At least, I don't think he can, though pundits will doubtless send me postcards with proof to the contrary. For one spectator, at any rate, the cat of Peer's unlikeableness is out of the bag as soon as he starts driving his mother to the gates of Heaven. This may be good poetry, but it is pretty poor filial affection. And poetry, as we know, covers a multitude of sins. A charming touch which nobody ever seems to notice is that, once his mother is dead, Peer can't even wait for the funeral ! " See mother buried with honour ! " is the lovable fellow's way of getting out of the boring ceremony. Of course every actor wants to play Peer, because he is in the middle of the stage all the time and never stops talking, and the definition of your born actor is one who would go crazy about a part in which a man gobbled his grandmother if he had plenty to spout between mouthfuls.

When the second part begins I suggest that the hero's unlikeableness may be transferred to the play itself, which to my mind becomes sovereignly unseeable and unbearable, especially when, as in the present revival, all that is seeable and hearable has been omitted. It is noteworthy that both Ase and Peer were wearing glove-fingers, and I suggest that it was in cutting the play that they cut themselves, for such cutting surely never has been or can be again. Obviously a lot of the speechifying had to go, and a good job too ! For not even Shakespeare Pandulphing or expounding the Salic law is poorer music than any possible Englishing of Peer's later tirades. Among the cuts are the Sphinx scene, the Madhouse scene, the scene in which Peer drowns the cook to save himself, the Funeral scene with the Priest's magnificent speech, and most astonishing of all the extraordinarily important Onion speech. Perhaps it would be hypocritical to complain of the disappearance of the Lean Person ! By the way, didn't Mr. Shaw promise us that in the twentieth century the Lean Person, the Strange Passenger, the Button Moulder, and the Boyg would be as familiar as the witches in *Macbeth*, the ghost in *Hamlet*, Mephistopheles, and the

Statue in *Don Juan* ? Is it possible that Mr. Shaw was mistaken ? Anyhow, I will lay 100 to 1 that he cannot stop a
passer-by and obtain accurate information as to who, what,
when, where or why a Boyg is. I doubt very much whether
the Old Vic audience was better informed, and it all comes
back to a remark I once heard at this theatre. " Who's the
bloke in the coffin ? " asked one Shakespeare enthusiast when
at the beginning of *Richard III* the body of Henry VI was
brought in. His mate replied : " Blowed if I know ! " Reading *Peer Gynt* is easier, since the Boyg has a footnote referring
you to an explanatory appendix. But, alas, the appendix that
every playgoer carries with him is not William Archer's, so,
perhaps, it will be enough if we call Mr. Leo Genn's adum-
bration the broth of a Boyg and leave it at that. One rather
liked Mr. Ion Swinley's Button Moulder, a character which
for once in a way was not wearisome. Hereabouts one noted
the great importance of words in the theatre. To the English
the word " button-moulder " is one of comic significance
like " golosh," " carpet slipper," and other words in
despite of which *Hedda Gabler* continues to be a masterpiece.
Here the mind was full of overtones and comparisons, the
Button Moulder and his talk of Peer lacking a loop being set
over against Lear's " Prithee, undo this button ! " and all
the talk of loop'd and window'd raggedness. Compare, too,
Lear's madness with the whispered remark of a friend, " I
don't agree with the Button Moulder. I think Peer's loopy
enough ! "

No ; if *Peer Gynt* is a world tragedy, it should stand some
sort of comparison with *Lear*, and the fact remains that, for
one playgoer at least, the lightest word of that aged king
banishes Ibsen's supposed tragedy into the limbo where
lesser works have sway. The fact that the Button Moulder
is also a buttonholer is a reason for continuing with him for
a bit longer. I have never been able to see that the soul

which has committed weighty sin should preserve its individuality, whereas another which has disciplined itself to pettifogging misdemeanour should go back to the common stockpot. I am reminded of a prisoner who, when counsel asked the jury to reflect on the awful fate awaiting his client if he were found guilty of dancing with clogs on his wife's face, murmured to the warder: " Gloomy beggar, ain't he ! " The description seems to me to fit the Button Moulder exactly. Ibsen also.

Mr. William Devlin's performance of Peer marks a step in the progress of one who is going to be a very good actor. It was technically admirable throughout, though owing to the excisions the actor was playing under a considerable handicap, like that of a batsman who should be deprived of his bat and given no bowling to hit. Nevertheless, this young actor managed very skilfully to suggest the essence of Peer, and he also survived Peer's last-act ulster. But I should have liked to see him try a fall with the travelling cap and ear-flaps to which other Peers have found themselves condemned. He was beautifully seconded by Miss Florence Kahn, who as Ase spiritualised the death scene into something finely imaginative almost to the point of being jocund about dying, which I understand is the highbrow thing to be. Miss Vivienne Bennett's Solveig was sweet and in tune, but about a young lady's Anitra nothing shall be said. Clemency forbids. The always ingenious and often felicitous new translation by Mr. Ellis Roberts is sometimes better than Archer's, though in what way:

> *Thanks for each cuddle and smack,*
> *For all that you were when alive !*

is an improvement on:

> *For all of your days I thank you,*
> *For beatings and lullabies !*

eludes me. Every translator of this play is faced with the
difficulty of following what Archer calls the rub-a-dub
rhythm, which he alleges to be capable of " poignantly
pathetic as well as buoyantly humorous expression." That
is doubtless the reason why Mr. Roberts's metre seems to
vary between the pantomime jingle and the heroic couplets
of Mr. Billy Bennett.

In principle the musicalising of masterpieces like *The Rivals*
is indefensible; it deranges the conveniences, as Mrs. Malaprop might say. Especially when comic opera is the form.
Who wants to see a version of *Macbeth* with the witches
hopping, skipping, and jumping to a lilt of " Three Little
Maids from School " ? But adapters are a race apart, and can
no more be kept from adapting other people's property than
a pickpocket can be kept from picking and stealing. There
are no exceptions; everyone in this kind is as headstrong as
an allegory on the banks of the Nile. One came, then, to scoff,
but owing to the tact of this particular adapter remained to
enjoy a pretty entertainment which nowhere transgresses
the spirit of Sheridan's play. A good deal of the dialogue
remains spoken, and there has been no tampering with such
things as " amiable ladder of ropes " and " a deal of snug
lying in the Abbey." There is a fair amount of recitative, and
perhaps the composer has not yet lived who can reconcile
us to a musical rendering of " Hath she been in health and
spirit down in Devon ? " Here the dreadful thought crosses
one's mind that Faulkland, to whom these words fall, is about
to rollick in the immemorial and baritone Devonshire
manner. But Mr. Monsell, doubtless reflecting that rollicking
is not in Faulkland's character, mercifully refrains. Instead
he, or somebody else, gives him a gem of melancholy which
might be by Giordano. For there are four composers, though
I imagine that whoever has written Faulkland's little song is
also responsible for the quartet at the end of the second act

and for the Finale. If, however, the essence of collaboration is to be unable to tell one from t'other, then these four have collaborated perfectly.

The piece is nicely sung and acted. Mr. Bruce Carfax, who plays Captain Absolute, has come on enormously both as actor and singer. Mr. Norman Williams is heard to great effect as Sir Anthony, and Mr. Frederick Ranalow subdues himself with grace and finish to the comparatively small part of Sir Lucius O'Trigger. Miss Elsie French makes a brave but rather thin shot at Mrs. Malaprop, a character which gives one the impression of being essentially well in flesh. Mr. Grahame Clifford makes a riotous Bob Acres and looks exactly like a picture by Zoffany. The young ladies are a little crowded out of this production, but Lydia Languish, Lucy, and Julia Melville find reasonable representatives in Mesdames Winifred Campbell, Betty French, and Kathleen Burgis.

If things can be described by their opposites, it should be enough to say that *Closing at Sunrise* is all that M. Paul Morand's *Ouvert la Nuit* is not. Nine-tenths of the play is about the humours of a coffee-stall; the remainder concerns a gang of forgers. Mr. Anthony Ireland discovers suavity in a dinner-jacket, and Mr. Frederick Cooper is always about to become a character of importance but isn't allowed to. Mr. Mark Daly as the bar-tender is extremely funny. Miss Shirley Houston, making a first appearance in the West End, is about three times better than most West End actresses at their last appearance. This being so, I look forward to seeing Mesdames Billie, Renee, and Shirley in Tchehov's *Three Sisters*. Theatre-managers have had odder notions, and will have them again.

OTWAY PRESERVED

THE SOLDIER'S FORTUNE. Revival of Thomas Otway's
Comedy. Ambassadors Theatre, Tuesday, October 1,
1935.

PLEASE TEACHER ! A musical comedy by K. R. G. Browne,
R. P. Weston, and Bert Lee. Music by Jack Waller and
Joseph Tunbridge. Hippodrome, Wednesday, October 2,
1935. [*October* 6, 1935]

"WOT 'AVE YOU GOT THERE, MATE?" asked one
Tommy of another carrying a sandbag. And received the
reply: "'Arf of blinkin' France, and 'ad to walk the other 'arf
to fetch it !" In the matter of these Restoration comedies half
the cant in the world has to be cleared away, even if we have
to walk the other half to find a place in which to dump it.
Anybody who should think he had rendered this bawdy old
comedy inoffensive to modern ears would be deceiving himself. "Have you heard the argument? Is there no offence
in't?" asked Claudius of Hamlet. To which that young man
returned his famous reply about the galled jade. Of course
there is offence in *The Soldier's Fortune*, and it is alike in con-
veying that offence and enjoying its conveyance that the skill
of this play's actors and audience lies. For not to offend
would be to miss its whole point, while not to revel in the
offence would be clumsy playgoing ! The oldest of theatrical
chestnuts is the one about a street tout offering to Lady
Gorgius Midas the synopsis of Dumas's *Dam o' Cameleers* and

being repulsed with the words: " We have come to see the acting. We have no desire to understand the play ! " It would be the height of playgoing hypocrisy to pretend that one went to the theatre to enjoy Otway's wit and not the subject of it. Otway was no near-knuckler; he dealt in the knuckle itself. One understands that a well-known farinaceous sweet, according to the suburb in which it is encountered, is dubbed blanc-mange, mould, or even shape. The English language has scores of periphrases for the one name which Desdemona would not speak, and which Othello had called her. But Otway does not go round about, and we are to suppose that his Sir Jolly Jumble would hardly know what you meant by such refinements as " courtesan " or even " harlot." One word resounds throughout this piece, which might be described as a fantasia on Otway's trumpet. Solvers of crossword puzzles will have no difficulty in descrying the word here buried; it is three letters too long for the one which actually Otway dins into our ears.

The plot is of an intricacy which suggests that Restoration audiences must have attended more intently than modern ones. The kernel of it is this. Sir Davy Dunce, a snuffy, elderly husband, is allowed to think that he has caused his wife's lover to be murdered, and that his only chance of evading the consequences is to put the body, in which there is faint hope of life, into his wife's bed, draw the curtains, and leave it to the lady's ministrations. The whole imbroglio has been devised by Sir Jolly Jumble, a Peeping Tom whose heart is like the old lecher's in *Lear*, a small spark, all the rest on's body cold. It should be said straight away that the revival is justified and saved by Mr. Roy Byford's Jumble. There is a gusto about this actor for which Lamb would have claimed, as he did for Munden, the quality of ennoblement. As with the older actor's tub of butter, so Lady Dunce's four-poster contemplated by Mr. Byford amounts to a

Platonic Idea. It would be wrong to imagine that Otway's fun is wholly indecent. Take that scene in which Fourbin, the valet, primes a footpad called Bloody-Bones in the matter of the pretended murder. Fourbin begins:

" War, friend and shining honour has been our province, till rusty peace reduced us to this base obscurity. Ah, Bloody-Bones ! ah, when thou and I commanded that party at the siege of Philipsburg, where, in the face of the army, we took the impenetrable half-moon ! "

The playgoer of that day would know what was meant by " half-moon," a military phrase to be familiar later on in the mouths of My Uncle Toby and Corporal Trim. But Bloody-Bones does not know his cue and replies: " Half-moon, sir ! by your favour 'twas a whole moon ! " Fourbin then asks Sir Davy if he thinks his rival Beaugard has a heart. Sir Davy has the reply: " Oh, like a lion ! he fears neither God, man, nor devil." Whereupon Bloody-Bones, bettering instruction, says: " I'll bring it to you for your breakfast tomorrow. Did you never eat a man's heart, sir ? " To produce its proper effect this should be uttered in the tone in which the driver of the coach turned to little David Copperfield and asked him whether he was a breeder of Suffolk punches. The dialogue continues:

SIR DAVY: Eat a man's heart, friend ?

FOURBIN: Ay ay, a man's heart, sir; it makes absolutely the best ragout in the world: I have eaten forty of 'em in my time without bread.

SIR DAVY: O Lord, a man's heart ! my humble service to you both, gentlemen.

BLOODY-BONES: Why, your Algerine pirates eat nothing else at sea; they have them always potted up like venison: your well-grown Dutchman's heart makes an excellent dish with oil and pepper.

SIR DAVY: O Lord, O Lord ! friend, friend, a word with you : how much must you and your companion have to do this business ?

FOURBIN: What, and bring you the heart home to your house ?

SIR DAVY: No, no, keeping the heart for your own eating.

What great fun it all is ! Sir Davy is asked two hundred pounds, and replies: " Two hundred pounds ! why, I'll have a physician shall kill a whole family for half the money ! "

But the whole piece is full of permissible joking as well as impermissible. There is many a good phrase like Sir Davy's determination to " crack the frame of nature and sally out like Tamberlane upon the Trojan horse." And here and there a well-placed word like Lady Dunce's " I tell thee, Sylvia, I was never married to that *engine* we have been talking of." There is one little matter to intrigue the pedants. " Curse on my fatal beauty ! " says Lady Dunce, and the two points which arise are whether this is the first time the figure was used, and whether, when he made Archibald Grosvenor say, " A curse on my fatal beauty, for I am sick of conquests ! " Gilbert was consciously cribbing. The play is very well put on at the Ambassadors. Indeed, I am not sure whether with regard to one character the dressing is not a little too sumptuous, Courtine's clothes being much too tidy for his own description of them, and Mr. Anthony Quayle being too well in flesh for one of whom his mistress says: " Considering he eats but once a week, the man is well enough." Mr. Baliol Holloway as Beaugard sets the piece in the right key from his first words and keeps it there through-out the evening. Mr. Lawrence Baskcomb and Mr. Franklyn Kelsey extract all possible fun out of Fourbin and Bloody-Bones. And, as it is unnecessary again to praise Mr. Byford's

Sir Jolly, this brings me to Mr. Huntley Wright's Sir Davy Dunce. In many ways this is a first-class performance, animated and ludicrous, and full of the sting of cuckoldry. But there are odd phrases which suggest that Otway did not intend the old man to be pure butt, and at moments we thought that Mr. Wright was going to treat the part as Mr. O. B. Clarence would treat it. Whether this would run the play out of gear cannot be determined unless one saw it; one can only say that the hints of such a reading are of value. As for the ladies, Miss Lesley Wareing as Sylvia does very prettily, and Miss Athene Seyler is exactly the actress for Lady Dunce. She revels in the salacious salad and invariably chooses the right word to roll on the tongue. Miss Seyler keeps it up to the end and informs the whole character with a perfect sense of its profound enormity. To sum up, Mr. Carroll is to be congratulated upon his unsqueamish revival of a comedy every word of which is calculated to bring the blush of shame to the cheek of modesty!

It would, I think, be possible to feel much more uncomfortable about Messrs. Browne, Weston and Lee's *Please Teacher!* than about Mr. Otway's *Please Soldier!* The principal scene is one in which Mr. Bobby Howes and Mr. Wylie Watson pretend to sleepwalk in the dormitory of a girls' school. There is also something about a will hidden in one of four busts of Napoleon with which this school is endowed. I dare say the story has other convolutions. But recounting the plots of musical comedies has never been a strong point with me, and it is too late to start now. There is a scene in which the dormitory merges into a wood rather like a nightmare version of the scene in *Dear Brutus*, though there the resemblance ends. Whatever the plot, it affords enormous satisfaction to those connoisseurs who know where in these matters inanity ends and anity begins. About Mr. Howes I find it difficult to be both honest and fair. To my way of

thinking, he has none of the buffoonery which makes a
Henson, a Nervo, or a Naughton. To me he is not *droll,* and
the entertainment he provides comes from the contrast
between boyish mind and oldish countenance. Whence I
must deduce that as Mr. Howes gets older he will more
nearly attain oddity. Occasionally he wrings a smile out of
me, as when, garbed in an enormous nightgown, he holds
out the skirts of it and says: " With a trifle more breeze
Shamrock might win ! " But even here the fun is less in the
joker than in the joke itself. Now for a confession. In my
apprentice days C. E. Montague wrote to me: " You must
never say an actress lacks charm; she may charm other
people." So I think it must be with comedians. Mr. Howes
is not funny to me; it is only fair to say that an overwhelming
majority of his audience finds him irresistible. Making the
best of both worlds, I shall therefore say that Mr. Howes
has immense charm and no fun ! The same sort of thing
applies to Mr. Watson, who with the same kind of material
seems to me infinitely less riotous than Mr. Eddie Gray in
the music-hall. Mr. Watson falls between two stools, for he
appears unable to make up his mind between hilarity and
gloom. I shall, therefore, say that his performance strikes me
as being not uproarious but downroarious.

Twin towers of strength are Miss Vera Pearce and Miss
Bertha Belmore, part of whose skill consists in their common
power of navigation, of keeping out of each other's way, like
two battleships in a narrow strait. Woe betide anybody who
gets in Miss Pearce's way, as in that delicious dance in which
Mr. Howes goes down before her lightest gesture, like an
indifferent boxer at a tap from Joe Louis. Miss Belmore plays
the schoolmistress as though she were ten thousand of
Shakespeare's Volumnias rolled into one, and well earns the
evening's best witticism. The various characters have been
boasting of their old schools, one even claiming to be an Old

Carthusian. Whereupon somebody points to Miss Belmore and says, " As for her, she's an Old Carthorsian ! " To judge by the audience, the most appreciated item in the entertainment is the chorus, than which there can be nothing prettier between Dan and Beersheba. There is a much admired number in which these young ladies in nightdresses deposit their candles on the dormitory floor and then hop over them. In another place six of them provide on six 'cellos the accompaniment to Tschaikowsky's familiar Piano Concerto, the solo part whereof is banged out by somebody in the orchestra, and presently melt into the slow movement of the Sonata Pathétique of Beethoven ! Both feats and the way in which they are received should finally dispel the notion that the English are not musical !

A NOTE ON FOREIGN ACTING

Two Share a Dwelling. A play by Alice Campbell. St. James's Theatre, Tuesday, October 8, 1935.

The Black Eye. A play by James Bridie. Shaftesbury Theatre, Friday, October 11, 1935. [*October* 13, 1935]

Two points strike me very forcibly in connection with this production. The first is that the fact of having to play in a strange language imposes upon foreign actresses a certain similarity which it is quite possible that they do not possess in their own country. Take a typical Bergner-sentence such as, " Why must you *know* all these *peeple* ? " The strong accent on the word " know " and the lengthening of the vowel in " peeple " is not so much Bergner as it is German or, if you like, Austrian. To this matter of stresses must be added that of inflection, which with every German or, if you like, Austrian actress, rises or falls in exactly the same way. What I am getting at is that if you were to hear Miss Bergner, Miss Mannheim, and Miss Grete Mosheim, the newcomer, on the stage and all behind screens, and get them to say the sentence in turn, it would be very difficult to tell instantly which actress was speaking I know that this will be disputed, and I have before me the Awful Warning of the musical critics who pretend that from the first bar of the well-known Tschaikowsky Piano Concerto—or even from the first four bars! —they could blindly deduce Orloff, Moiseiwitsch, or me ! However, I still maintain that the same thing would not apply to English actresses speaking the same sentence in English. Put Miss Edith Evans, Miss Flora Robson, and Miss Athene

Seyler behind screens, and you could not possibly fail to tell t'other from which even before the sentence was well begun.

Another odd thing about these German or, if you like, Austrian actresses is the similarity of their voices, which have all the same pitch. It cannot, I think, be contended that there is the same difference between the voices of our three visitors that there was between those of, say, Ellen Terry, Olga Nethersole, and Janet Achurch. Whoever could mistake Mrs. Campbell, however arch, for Miss Irene Vanbrugh at her most sombre? Who would not instantly know Miss Thorndike's lightest word from Miss Tempest's heaviest? Then, again, our visitors all look alike, and I swear that, so far as I am concerned, if Miss Bergner, Miss Mosheim, and Miss Mannheim were to appear in the same play they would —at least as to the first two—have to wear different-coloured ribbons to distinguish them. Or shall I put it that, while they are as like as peas in a pod, English actresses playing in their native tongue are each a different vegetable?

The second point with which I have been struck—and I sympathise with those who wish it had been lightning!— is the appalling indifference with which I regard the dramatic strains and stresses to which our German or, if you like, Austrian heroines are subject. The heroine of the present play is a little girl who in her youth was brought up in the Austrian Tyrol. There is no earthly reason for this except to explain why the actress cannot speak English. Here in parenthesis let me suggest a halt in these lame explanations which take in nobody. When next some actress arrives on our shores with a strong Choctaw accent, let it not be explained that in her infancy the character she impersonates was kidnapped by Cherokee Indians. Let us just accept the foreign intonation as we do the Cockney of some native stars.

The young woman in this piece is a pathological case who is so virginal that, we are told in all seriousness, as a child

MN

she goes into the garden to bite the heads off growing mush-rooms. When I was a schoolboy I learned a Latin proverb to the effect that though you expel Nature with a fork she will have her own way in the end. This play tells us, though Sir Joshua Reynolds would not have believed it, that in-nocence can be too great a burden on the growing child who will be compelled by Nature to find some horrid way of restoring the balance. Or you might put it algebraically: Excess of virginity plus Erotomania equals Normality. The thing about which I feel compunction is simply this, that my interest the other evening was centred wholly in the moment at which Lilia Verrick was going to execute her volte-face. I felt no concern for her, and cannot say that I liked her more when she was Miss Jekyll or less when she was Miss Hyde. Now let us put back the clock a little and imagine what we should have felt if some twenty or thirty years ago one of Mrs. Kendal's firm matrons had suddenly turned into a frenzied mænad. Imagine the elder Miss Blossom, her advances rejected, restoring the balance of Nature by what Hamlet calls " honeying and making love over the nasty sty." Could we have borne it ? Must not the roof of the theatre have fallen in ? Nowadays we think nothing whatever of the pathological case presented and are not concerned for the victim. We say that such things are " too amusing," and coldly analyse the virtuosity of the player instead of being moved by the plight. Indeed, there are the cynically-minded who are inclined to ask whether plight is the right word.

And yet I don't know ! I imagine that if Miss Mosheim were an actress of, say, Miss Robson's calibre, we should have come out of the theatre the other evening not liking to look each other in the eyes. The whole point about a really first-class actress is the agonised tension with which you contem-plate her distresses. You cannot bear, let alone beteem, that the winds of heaven should visit her face too roughly. A tragic actress should make you feel that her characters have tragic souls; Miss Mosheim makes you think that Lilia is a sonsy little creature, and that it is really too bad that she should be a case for the doctors. I do not think you can have a heroine whose mental development was obviously arrested at the age of six. It all, you see, works in a circle, for unless you have this heroine you cannot have *Two Share a Dwelling*. And I should think that on Tuesday evening many more than two shared this opinion. Such entertainment as the evening afforded was provided by Mr. Wyndham Goldie, who played the difficult part of the husband with great skill and discretion, by Mr. Peter Gawthorne as a retired Major and active bounder, by Mr. Henry Hewitt as the suavest of blackmailers, and by Mr. Robert Eddison as a footman who footed featly.

Harum-scarúmque cano is becoming more and more Mr. Bridie's motto. His new comedy is all over the place. It begins with the old hero-as-captain-of-his-soul theme, and the devil take the consequences. Young George Windlestraw, a Glaswegian romantic, is all for the untrammelled life, holding the inability to pass his accountant's exams as a valid excuse for despising those who do. Particularly his elder brother Johnnie, the slave of office routine. At this point we ask ourselves whether we are to have Hankin's *The Return of the Prodigal* all over again. Now the father, an amusing variant of Galsworthy's Mr. Barthwick, meets with an accident, and an examination of the books shows that the Windlestraw fortunes are tottering, while at one moment embezzlement is mooted. Is this an echo of *The Voysey Inheritance*? And can it be that Glasgow has begun to think what the Manchester school of playwrights thought at the beginning of the century? Anyhow, George takes off his coat both literally and metaphorically, and everything points to a Deadly Serious Evening with Epikhodov—for George is a master-bungler—as central figure. Then Mr. Bridie launches out upon what at first sight looks like divagation. George takes to free-lance journalism and presently falls in with a riotous ex-convict rejoicing in the name of Samuel Samuels, from whom he wins £250 at roulette. Hereabouts we reflect that great dramatists—see Tchehov and Shaw *passim*—may divagate, but not as Mr. Bridie divagates; that while their excursions are cosmic his are trumpery, which is a very different thing from last-trumpery. Never was reflection less well founded ! For the trumpery is Mr. Bridie's hand of trumps; it is the decorations which are the play ! The hero now puts his luck-gotten gains on a horse which wins at 33 to 1, the family fortunes are retrieved, the father, mother, and their brood are promised a happy issue out of all their afflictions, and George and Johnnie return from a fight in the garden with their heads bloody but unbowed.

How cross Walkley, who doted on consistency, would have been with this farrago ! How poor a playgoing stomach—to put forward another view—would that man have who objected to a scene out of *Charley's Aunt* because it followed upon the heels of one from *Hedda Gabler* ! My own view is that as craftsmanship this play is beneath criticism, while as entertainment it is above adulation. Or may I put it that round about ten o'clock one gave up Mr. Bridie and then gave oneself up to Mr. Bridie's fun ?

Acting honours were fairly divided. First and foremost I shall place Mr. Ralph Roberts, who, as the ex-convict in bibulous mood, scored a success at which an old-timer of the music-halls would not have sniffed. Next, and on the spiritual count, comes Mr. Stephen Haggard, who could play George in his sleep, and in the early part of this piece, owing to the jejuneness of the character at this time of day, very nearly played him in mine ! (As a Scotch hobbledehoy he is wildly incredible !) Third place is honourably won by Mr. Denys Blakelock as Johnnie, who, at ten-twenty precisely, broke into the Gaelic for half a dozen words, and the one and only time of the evening. Fourth prize goes to Mr. Frank Pettingell for an inaugural and highly comic party who, in so far as he had nothing whatever to do with this or any other play, was own brother to the same author's Sleeping Clergyman. Fifth, if indeed not higher up, comes Mr. Morland Graham as the admirable Windlestraw *père*. In the last two instances only did the Scotch speech stand where it did. The ladies are not included in the foregoing placings. Here Miss Jean Cadell, correct in accent as in everything else, was " out by herself." If, early on, she disappointed a little, it was only because, to vary the metaphor, she was holding her punch. In the play's concluding rounds she let this go, and her dry and beautifully timed humour reduced us all to helpless merriment. Of the others, Miss Joan White seemed most alive, Mesdames Jill Esmond and Cathleen Lacey being drearily provided and breathing not Glasgow but Cheltenham.

I cannot overlook Mr. Bridie's attempt to establish a new technique, whereby the characters come out of the picture-frame and blab to the audience what they have already conveyed and implied within that frame. This ruinous innovation—loose thinkers will say it is the old Shakespearean soliloquy, which it is not, the difference being that between self-communing and a communication—is desultory and half-hearted, like everything else in this playwright's conception of playwriting. Fortunately at taking his hand from every kind of plough, experimental as well as dramatic, Mr. Bridie is a past-master, and this means that we need not bother with his new trick. Except to say that it too heavily handicaps Mr. Haggard, who is never allowed off the stage whether the curtain is up or down. The dialogue is plentifully sprinkled with wit, sometimes relevant and sometimes not, making the piece as gay as the confetti-strewn floor of a taxi-cab after somebody else's wedding.

TWO GENTLEMEN IN VERONA

Romeo and Juliet. Revival of Shakespeare's Tragedy. New Theatre, Thursday, October 17, 1935.

Espionage. A play by Walter Hackett. Apollo Theatre, Wednesday, October 16, 1935.   [*October* 20, 1935]

Thursday evening was all that an evening in the theatre should be—exciting, moving, provocative. Here in conjunction were the flower of Shakespeare's young genius and the best of young English acting talent. The producer was our leading Shakespearean actor, and the scenery and costumes were by the artists who had attained fame through the productions of *Richard of Bordeaux* and *Hamlet*. In other words, Mr. Gielgud had once more invested him in his Motley and given these young ladies leave to speak his mind. Let me begin with a word or two about the production, normally tucked away at the end. The difficulty of producing plays written for the Elizabethan and transferred to the picture stage must always be resolved by compromise, which means that good and bad must go hand in hand. The good point about this production is that it enabled that fiery-footed steed which is this tragedy to gallop sufficiently apace. Now, though the acquisition of speed has been a triumph, it has entailed certain sacrifices. For Mr. Gielgud's, and consequently Motleys', method is a combination of the Elizabethan and modern stages, with Juliet's bedroom and balcony a permanent part of the setting. That people might walk beneath it the thing was supported on posts, so that it looked rather like a hotel-lift which has got stuck half way up to the mezzanine floor. The device also precluded the full use of the stage, so that the action seemed to take place not so much in Verona as in a corner of it. I fault the lighting, too, in that gone were the sun and warmth of Italy and the whole thing appeared to happen at night, the tomb scene being the cheerfullest of all ! The costumes were charming, even if the football jerseys of the rival factions reminded us less of Montague and Capulet than of Wanderers and Wolves. Elsewhere Motley have rightly differed from Dickens's Flora, who could not conceive any connection between Mantua and mantua-making. In the theatre there is every connection, and Motley have caught the spirit of the place and time, brilliantly for example in Romeo's case, though in Juliet's oddly reminiscent of the pre-Raphaelite way of looking at Ellen Terry.

The ball, whose masks were those of hoopoes, puffins, and other outrageously-billed birds, brought up a very nice point. It had been more than whispered that presently Mr. Gielgud, who plays Mercutio, and Mr. Laurence Olivier, who plays Romeo, are to change rôles. At first sight this suggested a line much in vogue: " Just think what Toucan do ! " But Thursday night's experience persuaded one to the contrary. Am I in the foyer going to chip bits off my invention for the benefit of other critics ? Why should Mr. Gielgud pilfer his bright heaven for the benefit of another's Romeo ? This means that Mr. Gielgud had produced all of *Romeo and Juliet* except half the title part ! If not he was more than human, though in any case it was probably not humanly possible at one fell swoop to denude Mr. Olivier of his modernity and turn to-day's clipped speech into a passionate feeling for verse. Mr. Olivier's Romeo suffered enormously from the fact that the spoken poetry of the part eluded him.

In his delivery he brought off a twofold inexpertness which approached virtuosity—that of gabbling all the words in a line and uttering each line as a staccato whole cut off from its fellows. In his early scenes this Romeo appeared to have no apprehension of, let alone joy in, the words he was speaking, though this may have been due to first-night nervousness, since he improved greatly later on. But throughout one wanted over and over again to stop the performance and tell the actor that he couldn't, just couldn't, rush this or that passage. If ecstasy is present in this play it must be at the meeting in the Friar's cell, where Romeo's words hang on the air like grace-notes:

> *Ah, Juliet, if the measure of thy joy*
> *Be heap'd like mine, and that thy skill be more*
> *To blazon it, then sweeten with thy breath*
> *This neighbour air, and let rich music's tongue*
> *Unfold the imagined happiness that both*
> *Receive in either by this dear encounter.*

This is music and must be spoken as music. Again, what is the use of Shakespeare writing such an image as: " The white wonder of dear Juliet's hand " if Romeo is not himself blasted with the beauty of it ? Never mind Shakespeare's precepts; his verse must be recited line upon line, here a little hurry and there a little dwell. Apart from the speaking there was poetry and to spare. This Romeo looked every inch a lover, and a lover fey and foredoomed. The actor's facial expression was varied and mobile, his bearing noble, his play of arm imaginative, and his smaller gestures were infinitely touching. Note, for example, how lovingly he fingered first the props of Juliet's balcony and at the last her bier. For once in a way the tide of this young man's passion was presented at the flood, and his grief was agonisingly done. " Is it e'en so ? Then I defy you, stars ! " is a line which has defied many actors. Mr. Olivier's way with this was to say it tonelessly, and it is a very moving way. Taking the performance by and large, I have no hesitation in saying that this is the most moving Romeo I have seen. It also explains that something displeasing which I have hitherto found in Mr. Olivier's acting—the discrepancy between the romantic manner and such ridiculous things as cuff-links and moustaches. Now that these trivia have been shorn away and the natural player stands forth, lo and behold he is very good !

Mercutio is always a problem, for the reason that the Queen Mab speech, obviously inserted to satisfy an actor's demand, is not in keeping with that arch-materialist. In my opinion the way to play the part is to go all out for the sensualist, treat the speech as a cadenza and in the way a fiddler will plonk one of his own into the middle of somebody else's concerto, bow, decline an encore, and then get back into the character ! Mr. Gielgud reverses the process and builds his Mercutio out of the Queen Mab speech which, of course, he delivers exquisitely. This means a new death scene and saying " A plague o' both your houses ! " with a smile which is all a benison. Not good Shakespeare, perhaps, but very beautiful Gielgud. In these circumstances Mercutio is not our old friend but a Frenchified version, say Théodore de Banville's :

> *Jeune homme sans mélancolie,*
> *Blond comme un soleil d'Italie,*
> *Garde bien ta belle folie !*

I agree that the last line chimes with Shakespeare since both Mercutio and Adolphe Gaïffe keep their lovely riot in the sense that in the drama and the poem neither lives long enough to lose it. Miss Peggy Ashcroft's Juliet has been

greatly praised. Certainly the eager and touching childishness of the early part could not be bettered, so that we prepared to be greatly moved. Personally, I found the performance heartrending until it came to the part where the heart
should be rent. And then nothing happened, though all the
appurtenances of grief, the burying of the head in the Nurse's
bosom and so forth were present. When Juliet lifted her head,
her face was seen to be duly ravaged, but she continued to
the end with the same quality of ravagement, which as a
piece of acting spells monotony. In my view Miss Ashcroft
implied Juliet without playing her. That is to say, she did
not move me nearly so much as any of the children who
have played in *Mädchen in Uniform*. But then it is very difficult indeed, perhaps impossible, for any Mädchen to put on
Shakespeare's uniform. Mr. Granville-Barker dismisses as
" parroted nonsense " the saying that no actress can play
Juliet till she is too old to look her. Let this acute observer
produce an actress past or present to support him ! According to a great critic of the 'eighties, Ellen Terry herself failed
not only to conjure up the horrors of the charnel house but
to make the scene impressive. In my judgment Miss Ashcroft succeeded in the first half, only to fade away later. On
the other hand, the success so far as it went was complete.

I have not space to enumerate the admirable supporting
cast, and can only congratulate Mr. Gielgud upon a production triumphant everywhere despite the fact that Romeo
cannot speak his part, Juliet cannot act more than half of
hers, and Mercutio is topsy-turvy. To crown all, remains
the Nurse, knocking the balance of the play into a cocked
hat, just as would happen if the Porter were the centre of
Macbeth. Miss Evans rules the entire roost. Obviously of the
German-Flemish school, this is Agatha Payne metamor-
phosed into good instead of bad angel. It is a grand performance, and her pathos should teach young playgoers what

pathos was in my young days. One felt that whenever such
grief is heard in the theatre, Mrs. Stirling's heart will hear
it and beat, though it has lain for a century dead.

In a heated moment Mr. Pickwick objected to Mr. Blotton
of Aldgate's " vile and calumnious " mode of criticism. Mr.
Blotton retorted that Mr. Pickwick was a humbug but, it
will be remembered, after a short-lived hubbub, declared
that he used the word in a Pickwickian sense. Mr. Walter
Hackett, as all the world knows, alluded in a heated moment
to the work of this paper's dramatic critic as " offensive,"
but, after hubbub of shorter duration than any in theatrical
annals, handsomely pleaded the licence of a good Pickwickian. I am not sure that the handsomeness of Mr.
Hackett's generous admission is not rather annoying ! A
man whose life has been saved naturally resents his obligation towards his life-saver, since in the future all pleasant
impulses towards him will be discounted. Of course, people
will say: " Agate has now just got to like Hackett's new
play ! " But suppose I do like it ? Am I not to be believed ?
I can only assure readers that if *Espionage* had not been a
vast improvement upon *Hyde Park Corner* I should have
heaped coals of fire on the author's devoted head, and
trusted in their power to burn !

Now I genuinely hold this play to be in every way better
than its predecessor, and in saying this am not influenced
by the fact that the voice that breathed o'er Eden has
" nothing on " the wafts of goodwill that have passed between theatre and newspaper office. Preserving critical
integrity, I shall not claim to be able to follow the plot into
its ultimate coigns, merely claiming that they are those of
vantage and not disadvantage. The first act is a corker, and
readers will note my wideawakeness in the perception that
whereas the draught in the railway-carriage fritters the
blinds, the passengers are able to put their heads out of

window without a hair stirring. Perhaps one or two of Mr. Hackett's jokes are a trifle elementary, as when somebody mistakes the German word " Danke " for the English " donkey." Nor is his philosophy unexceptionable. " If the Conference succeeds," says the Foreign Minister, " the result will be a lasting peace ! " Against which we have Clemenceau's assertion that the world-agreement of 1918 could only result in a just and lasting war ! But these be small matters, and neither do I object to the fact that whereas to everybody else the floor of the railway carriage is terra firma, Miss Marion Lorne's progress and station thereon are a matter of titter and totter. That is what is expected of a leading lady, and in this piece Miss Lorne leads most amusingly. If it be alleged—and I have alleged it myself ! —that this delightful actress's performance is like the dots in a music score, meaning the same thing all over again, I shall retort that so were Lottie Venne's performances and those of many another distinguished comédienne. And if Mr. Hackett asks why I didn't think of that before, I beg to assure him that I shall just grovel. And in the art of grovelling I boldly claim to have no superior ! Messrs. Frank Cellier, J. H. Roberts, Eric Maturin, Cyril Smith, Edwin Styles, and Leonard Upton contribute in their several degrees to the success of a very jolly evening.

WATERLOO MEETS ITS TCHEHOV

THE THREE SISTERS. Revival of Tchehov's Play. Old Vic Theatre, Tuesday, November 12, 1935.

MURDER GANG. A play by George Munro and Basil Dean. Embassy Theatre, Friday, November 15, 1935.

[*November* 17, 1935]

" Pray, Miss Eliza, are not the ——shire Militia removed from Meryton ? They must be a great loss to *your* family."
—Miss Bingley in *Pride and Prejudice*.

THERE IS MORE innocent fun in this play, as in all of this author's, than the casual theatre-goer might imagine. Indeed if, like Bunthorne, you are fond of touch-and-go jocularity, Tchehov is the shop for it. Now is there or is there not an overtone in the phrase " touch-and-go " ? Might it not be the title of a play by C. L. Anthony ? The speculation here is admittedly abstruse, but it occurs to me that *The Three Sisters* is a purely arbitrary title and that Tchehov would have been just as pleased to name his piece *Call It a Lifetime*. Between you and me, reader, I have always suspected this dramatist of being the lightest of his kind, the C. L. Antonovich of Russia ! Tchebutykin, the doctor in this play, knows from the newspapers that there was such a person as Dobrolyubov: " But what he wrote I can't say ! " My idle fancy is that he wrote *serious* Russian plays, the kind of thing which those who have never seen any Tchehov imagine Tchehov to have written.

A great work is known by its power to provoke parallels, even unhappy ones. A gifted colleague has found a resemblance between these three sisters and their brother and the Brontë girls and Branwell. But surely the likeness is superficial? Tchehov's young women cry for Moscow as other people cry for the moon, whereas to the Brontës there was no horizon beyond Haworth's. In the end Tchehov's Andrey pushes a perambulator; Branwell ended by pushing open once too often the doors of the public-house. No! If a parallel is to be sought in English life or literature it can only be with the family of Mr. Bennet. It astonishes even me who make it, how little far is the cry here! Nobody at this time of day is going to rehearse the plot of *Pride and Prejudice*, though it would be rank intellectual snobbery to pretend that everybody remembers what Tchehov's play is about. Let me say, then, that one at least of the many things lying near its core is the havoc wrought in the sisters' hearts when the brigade leaves that small provincial Russian town. Alas! that Masha cannot follow her Vershinin as Lydia Bennet followed the ——shire Militia to Brighton! The reader will probably recall Mr. Bennet's reflection that at Brighton his daughter would be of less importance " even as a common flirt than she has been here—the officers will find women better worth their notice."

Perhaps some day Mr. Maurice Baring will write a fifth act transplanting Tchehov's three sisters to Moscow and showing us what happened to them in that land for which they had invented so many promises. But Masha's plight, though pitiful enough, is common; it is perhaps not too much to say that to the wife of any dull husband there comes at least once in her life knowledge of Masha's temptation if not surrender. There is greater pitifulness in Irina's case, since here the tragedy is wanton. Why, even in the name of all the old Russian gods, should she not be happy with her Baron in whom for the first time speaks the voice of the new Russia ? The young man has a quarrel forced upon him by a former comrade, a professional bully with the blood of two previous duels on his hands, and one of the most skilful things in this play is the way in which Tchehov brings together the passions of Vershinin and Solyony. Superficially nothing could be wider apart than the former's sentimento-philosophic hankerings and the latter's brutal ardours. But Tchehov knows and gives us to know that both affairs are merely the distractions of bored soldiers who in Moscow would not have looked at either girl.

Is it reading too much into the play to suggest that there is an essential difference between Irina and Masha, that whereas Irina will not easily love again, Masha with her hummings and cogitabundities is only Lydia and Kitty Bennet drawn to tragic scale, and will love the very next officer who has the wit to dress up his proposals metaphysically ? A very few weeks after the departure of the ——shire Militia, Elizabeth Bennet could hope that Kitty would presently be able to mention an officer not more than once a day " unless, by some cruel and malicious arrangement at the War Office, another regiment should be quartered in Meryton." I feel that if the Russian War Office had been similarly minded, Masha would not have been long in finding consolation, if only for the reason that she is wittier and therefore more volatile than Irina. Indeed in Masha I find a suspicion of Hedda Gabler, though declining to allow that red and whopping whale admission to the present track. Olga is the steadying point of the trio, never quite gay, yet never wholly sad. Of common everyday happiness Olga is to know nothing; she has overstood her market, and is not to marry, and she takes a brave view of what lies before her. Her name is serenity. It is in her that the play's dissonances are resolved, since to her is given the beautiful passage:

" Time will pass, and we shall go away for ever, and we shall be forgotten, our faces will be forgotten, our voices, and how many there were of us; but our sufferings will pass into joy for those who will live after us, happiness and peace will be established upon earth, and they will remember kindly and bless those who have lived before. . . ."

It is while this was being spoken that on Tuesday night the audience put away handkerchiefs used not more for tears than for controlling laughter. The Old Vic audience laughed its fill, and was also deeply moved, showing that it had " got " this play at first shock and sight. Whether an audience of West End fashionables would " get " it will never be known. For the first condition of " getting " a play is getting the audience together, and that one refuses to be got !

Mr. Henry Cass, producing with much skill and care, has scrupulously refrained from stealing any of Mr. Komisarjevsky's thunder. He should have stolen it ! We badly wanted those shadows dancing on the bedroom wall, and that dancing bear which, in the production at Barnes, so terrified Irina and frightened her still more when it turned out to be Solyony in mummer's guise. Solyony ought to be the most menacing personage. I suppose Tchehov knew his business best. But the explanation of why Solyony keeps on scenting his hands seems over-long delayed. Or perhaps the scent-bottle should be more obviously a scent-bottle. Or Mr. George Woodbridge should make more of it. Actually the actor gives the impression of unscrewing a fountain-pen and sprinkling the contents over himself, which may be highly Russian, but is not very understandable. I think, too, that Andrey's fiddle should not be as bridgeless as the noses in a Burne-Jones canvas. Media should not be mixed, and if Andrey is to carry an Expressionist fiddle he should when he sits down fall through an Expressionist chair. On the other hand, the scene in which the young soldiers say good-bye to the echo is most movingly done. This is one of the play's three strokes of surpassing genius, the others being the famous red-beard incident, and the blazing notion of that arbitrary fire which springs up from nowhere and is as irrelevant and motiveless as an earthquake would be in the middle oı *Hamlet*. It is almost as though Tchehov has said to himself: " Here are a lot of people intensely alive—let's see if they will go on living through something visitational, like flood or smallpox ! " and hits on a fire because it is something visible to an audience. The red glare on Skiddaw roused the burghers of Carlisle, and I think something of the same sort should be vouchsafed the burgesses of Waterloo Road. At Barnes we saw the flicker and the glow.

Mr. Ion Swinley is exactly right as Vershinin; one understands why his wife continually tries to commit suicide, and also why she has two children by him. As the young Baron who breaks with aristocratic tradition, Mr. William Devlin plays with much subtlety, and in the last act with much pathos. That the break is only a little one is shown by the dove-coloured frock-coat with the silk facings, still a mile away from to-day's Soviet tunic. The Baron resents having a footman to pull off his military boots; but I suspect that it is the same menial who brushes those civilian trousers. Nobody could fail in the part of the doctor, Tchebutykin, though it takes a clever actor to succeed as measurelessly as does Mr. Cecil Trouncer. Mr. Keneth Kent wheels Andrey's perambulator as to the manner born. Mr. Andrew Leigh as that cocky little dullard, Masha's husband, is excellent until he puts on the red beard, when he does not give sufficient signs of the struggle before compassion wins; he should be suppressing his own tears while trying to laugh away Masha's. As Andrey's vulgar little wife Miss Myrtle

Nn

Richardson is nearly as irritating as Natasha herself, which is inescapable in the case of an actress whose work one does not know. The ideal casting would be some exquisitely mannered actress, like Miss Fay Compton, who could not be Natasha except by acting; actually I suspect Miss Richardson of acting quite a lot. There has been a lot of suspecting in this article, which I finally suspect of being too long. This must be my excuse for saying nothing about those weeping willows, Miss Marie Ney, Miss Vivienne Bennett, and Miss Nancy Hornsby, who in the old-fashioned world of unlimited space would have a column all to themselves.

Let him that is without sin first cast a stone. Let him who has never gloated over a murder trial, read it twice, scorned the meagre report and pursued the ampler even to eleventh-hour lucubrations of the condemned—let such a one sneer at the crime-reporters in *Murder Gang* ! For oneself, one sat huddled in a corner, withers plentifully wrung, knowing that one had drained the dregs of every murder case since one was nine, and, with luck, would go on draining until one was ninety. Show me a man who does not like a " good " murder and I will show you a prig. If, said Stevenson, you told frequenters of alehouses about Germanicus and the eagles, or Regulus going back to Carthage, they would very likely fall asleep. But if you told them about Harry Pearce and Jem Belcher, about Nelson and the Nile, every one of them would lay down his pipe to listen. Given the right ale-house and the right narrator, I say that for the story of Thurtell, Hunt, and Probert somebody will proffer to turn off the wireless. Whenever I tell this story I never fail to end with the account of Probert's execution as found in the papers of Robert Surtees, who witnessed it. Probert was acquitted of this particular murder, but hanged for horse-stealing in the following year in company with two other horse-stealers and a burglar. Surtees writes: " The drop suddenly fell, and a thrill ran through the crowd as those four white-covered heads assumed the same sideway attitude as they were launched into eternity."

Now will any reader put his hand on his heart and swear that he would have been more thrilled by any possible account of the plot of the little play at Swiss Cottage than by the shuddersome image just evoked ? To appease malcontents let me just say that *Murder Gang* is all about the low tricks played by crime reporters to satisfy the low taste of those to whom the week's murder is Sunday's *bonne bouche*. There is a theory that every man who consents to the death penalty should be willing to pull the lever himself. Agreed ! On the same principle any reader of murder-cases should be willing to pinch photographs off mantelpieces and bribe warders for copies of last letters, or however it is done. Agreed ! It follows, then, that I must regard the crime-reporters in *Murder Gang* as a body of honourable men doing an extremely difficult (and honourable) job with virtuosity. I do. In the last act the leading sensation-monger turns maudlin and begins to drivel about good taste. Now whether the prig or the ordinary man is right in his attitude towards the murder appetite, it is incontestable that in its last act this play goes to pieces. But three-fourths of the evening have been exciting and admirable, and the whole thing is compellingly acted. Special mention in an enormous cast should be given to Mr. James Dale as the first dashing and subsequently maudlin reporter, Mr. Bernard Lee as any ordinary little murderer, Miss Barbara Couper as any murderer's ordinary little wife, Miss Sylvia Coleridge as any murderer's ordinary little doxy, and Miss Joan Hickson as the " local clairvoyant " whose assumptions of gentility set the house deliriously rocking.

HURLY WITHOUT BURLY

TIMON OF ATHENS. Revival of Shakespeare's Tragedy. Westminster Theatre, Tuesday, November 19, 1935.

THE INSIDE STAND. A farce by P. G. Wodehouse. Saville Theatre, Thursday, November 21, 1935.

[November 24, 1935]

"AH çA!" said Madame Perrichon, "est-ce que vous allez continuer comme ça?" This was at least one play-goer's unspoken thought during Acts Four and Five of this tragedy in which Shakespeare rises to a height unattained before or since in the art of saying the same thing over and over again. It is customary to compare this play with *Lear*, and to attribute the greater effect of the latter to the specta-tor's greater cause for sympathy. Lear—the argument runs—was a great baby, but then the fault was his second child-hood's. He threw away his kingdom, but at least he parcelled it out among his nearest and presumably dearest. And we are told that because there is something to be said for Lear and nothing at all for Timon, the failure of the Athenian piece is due to our greater impatience with its hero. To which I reply: " Garn ! "

Let us consider the two plays apart from the question of sympathy with their leading characters. I imagine that what strikes us in any such comparison is the richness of invention in the one play and the poverty in the other. In *Lear* the mind is continually embarrassed with choice of riches—the devotion of the Fool, Kent's loyalty, Edgar's enveloping sympathy, all that business of Gloster, the intricate sub-plot of Edmund, the fact that the vipers stinging the old man's bosom are his proper issue, the reconciliation with Cordelia. So tumbled and pell-mell are the *matters for interest* that merely in enumerating them you are forced to jumble the planes, since in the foregoing there are at least three—the plane of incident or what will happen next, the blood-thicker-than-water plane, and the plane of sheer sublimity which *Timon* nowhere reaches. On the last I place the fact that the hurt received by Lear is so great that he does not recover though cherished by at least three faithful souls. A man left to himself and going mad is not in the same case with the man losing his reason in the midst of friends; Timon solus in his cave can never rise to the height of Lear on his heath, alone and yet not alone. Grant, for argument's sake, that Timon's curses on humanity are the equivalent of Lear's. It may well be that his speech beginning: " O blessed breeding sun "—or that other beginning: " Common mother, thou—— " or any one of them, since they are all the same, is up to the level of Lear's " Defy lechery " speech. Now let us do a little sum. Take the " lechery " speech from *Lear* and what remains? Answer: The whole of the finest tragedy in the world less one speech. Take away Timon's tirades, which are all one tirade, and what remains? The answer is that nothing and nobody remains except the bright-armoured orations of that toy soldier, Alcibiades. No, I have not forgotten the churlish Apemantus. The point is that he spills himself and all he stands for at his first utterance and is of no further interest. And if the reader desires a simpler test still I will challenge him to lean back in his chair, close his eyes, think hard, and recall the name of any other character in this play.

To be brutal, the reason nobody admires *Timon* is that there is not enough in it to admire. Actually the play ends

with Timon's: " Uncover, dogs, and lap ! " Why does it
end here ? Because the play, as a play, is played out. We
have seen the man whose squandermania takes the form of
giving to the rich. We have seen the well-to-do respond with
their famous exhibition of ingratitude. And we have seen
Timon get in his slap in the face. The rest, which should be
silence, is interminable talk. Indeed, so little action and so
much talk remains that Shakespeare seems to have foreseen
the broadcast play ! You would miss nothing whatever if you
listened to Acts Four and Five in a darkened room, and I submit that to stay at home is not what one goes to the theatre
for ! Even so, the first thing in the unseen actor is a noble
and resounding voice enabling Timon's woes to come
through like the thunderings of a Wotan rather than the
whinneyings of a Beckmesser. On the stage the physical
counterpart is necessary. This brings up my old unending
war with the intellectuals, who will have it that subtlety of
interpretation can blind the spectator to, or make up to him
for, physical deficiency. I deny this. I deny that you can
have a chubby Hamlet, a plain Romeo, an insignificant
Othello, a little Lear. I know all about Garrick and Kean,
thank you, and patiently explain that their genius made the
spectator believe that Lear was not only every inch a king
but every inch of six foot as well ! Irving could have conceivably looked Timon, though his asceticism would have
been a stumbling-block in presenting this gormandiser—for
nobody doubts that Timon ate and drank as much as any
two of his guests—whose banquets were drawn to Fouquet's
scale which, Dumas tells us, outdid his royal master's. But
Irving's voice would have let him down in the second half,
and this was doubtless one of twenty good reasons for his
never attempting this play. " Realms and islands were as
plates dropped from his pocket," says Cleopatra about
Antony, and the point about Timon is that he must be big

enough to suggest that plates dropped from his banquets as they were islands and realms.

Now, Mr. Ernest Milton does not give this impression, his bodily aspect rather indicating that he would think a square meal grossly vulgar. This clever actor obviously knows what is in this part, though his offer to make the portion of Timon's servant equal to his fiancée's dowry has less of princely carelessness than of the meticulousness of the man who takes care to be in when the postman calls for the Christmas-box. He delivers the grace before hot water very well, after which and to the end of the scene he overmouths so much that no word can be distinguished. The second part of the play demands a great frame in ruins, and if that cannot be present then at least we must ask for a voice like the Albert Hall organ after the wrong boxer has been declared the winner. At the Westminster our ears, like our eyes, are unfilled. What signify the limbs, the thews, the stature, bulk, and big assemblance of an actor ? I say that in the absence of genius they amount to ninety per cent of one who attempts your heroic Shakespearean rôle, and that Timon, though an unpleasant hero, must be drawn to heroic size. He has a world of grievances to support, and should be drawn to Atlas-like proportions. To be practical, the part requires the torso of a heavyweight boxer, the voice of an Ainley, the drive of a Benson at his physical fittest, and lashings of temperament. It is a part for a great actor, as great acting was understood before little actors began to drag brains into it. In the absence of a Phelps, this play should be an opera by Moussorgsky, with Chaliapine in the title-rôle. It is a play of hurly-burly, and hurly without burly is no good.

As Apemantus, Mr. Harcourt Williams is churlish with difficulty, and, in my view, the best performances come from Mr. Richard Fleury, who makes a distinct character out of the Painter; from Mr. Torin Thatcher, whose speech as

Prisoner's Friend at the court-martial has a fine, warlike frenzy; and from that one of the Senators who stands up to Alcibiades. Mr. Nugent Monck's production is probably very satisfying to those who are up to this kind of thing. The dresses are like any haphazard section of any Three Arts Ball, Alcibiades being costumed like a Napoleonic general, and Timon's robes suggesting in the banquet scene this year's Paris model in bedgowns and for the cave scene some négligé of yester-year. Personally, I think that a masque should be jolly and not a piece of stylised junk hight " Baroque " or " Early Perpendicular." And last, let me confess that I am once again defeated by that music which insists on mirroring the spirit of a play. Timon bids the sun " draw from the earth rotten humidity," and Mr. Benjamin Britten bids a concatenation of bassoon, oboe, clarinet, and something that sounds like the tongs and the bones, echo this feat. A tiny orchestra of ladies accomplishes this *con mor-bidezza*, which presumably is what Mr. Britten desires. Whether the new Westminster is right in this, or whether the Old Vic does better to prelude *The Three Sisters* with Haydn's Gipsy Rondo, is matter for another Sunday. And another critic !

There's nowt so queer as evidence. I am prepared to swear that I saw the curtain rise on *The Inside Stand*, and on every act of it, and fall on all three of them. But I will also swear that when the players lined up for approval, there were at least five on whom I had not till that moment set eyes ! Perhaps this is only Mr. Wodehouse's way of making confusion worse confounded, for confused his piece certainly is. The " inside stand " is your burglar's indoor accomplice, and it would lick Pompey, as they say up in Lancashire, to know what crib is being cracked by who, and I don't mean whom ! In a cast of ten at least four are out-and-out criminals, while the rest appear to be detectives, actual or pretended, sub and even super rosa. The crib in question is a French country house whose magnificence the mistresses of Louis Quinze would have thought overdone. There is, of course, no more reason why we should expect Mr. Wodehouse to write a good farce than we should expect Mr. Douglas Furber to write an amusing novel, and perhaps the best lines in the play are those which on the stage go for little or nothing. For example, Mr. Ralph Lynn, encountering at his first entrance a bunch of Ghastly Young Things, has the line: " Are they all that age round here ? " Significant on the printed page, in the theatre of farce the line does not get a laugh. But there are times when Mr. Wodehouse catches the idiom of the theatre, and then the combined effect of the funny line and the comic actor is irresistible. Perhaps the best thing in the piece is when three people are so much agitated over a letter that not one of six trembling hands can hold it, and a foot has to be planted on the wretched thing before it can be read. This is really good theatre, proving that with a little more practice Mr. Wodehouse will be as good a playwright as he is a storyteller. I shall not pursue the hideous thought that the invention here is not Mr. Wodehouse's but his players'.

If one could make a pen-picture of Mr. Lynn's acting, there would be no need to go to the theatre. But one can't, so there is ! Mr. Ben Welden is a gangster with a childlike faith in the beauty of his profession. Mr. James Carew as an American Senator gives his famous impersonation of the Statue of Liberty, and Mr. Cameron Hall is excellent as a hen-pecked nonentity. As the hen in question Miss Aletha Orr crows lustily. As Mr. Lynn's enchantress, Miss Kathleen Kelly, a newcomer, presumably enchants the whole of him and some of us. As the featureless Miss Mossop, that renowned repertory actress, Miss Clare Harris, conceivably beguiles the time by thinking of other days and other playwrights.

Last, Miss Olive Blakeney as a " Dooshess " is allowed to begin brilliantly and then condemned to tail off like the squiggly poem in *Alice*. What a pity this gifted actress was ever permitted to wisecrack ! Anybody can crack more or less wisely; Miss Blakeney's success in this minor accomplishment is not going to blind me to the fact that we are losing and shall presently have lost a serious and clever actress.

THE FASHION IN ROMEOS

ROMEO AND JULIET. Revival of Shakespeare's Tragedy.
New Theatre, Thursday, November 28, 1935.

OUR OWN LIVES. A comedy by Gertrude Jennings.
Ambassadors Theatre, Wednesday, November 27, 1935.

DISTINGUISHED GATHERING. A play by James Parish. St.
Martin's Theatre, Tuesday, November 26, 1935.

[*December* 1, 1935]

"ROMEO'S HIMSELF AGAIN!" seemed to be the note
of the applause when Mr. Gielgud came on the other evening, while the roar greeting Mr. Olivier suggested that
Mercutio had regained his kingdom. Rivalry is always a
good thing for the theatre, and it is pleasant to reflect that
we do it better now and in England than it was done in
the past and in France. I refer to the famous row between
Mlle George and Rachel, which always amuses me, and with
which every reader may not be familiar. The older actress
went to call on Victor Hugo, and with tears in her eyes told
him how Rachel had snubbed her. She would not receive
George, and if George wanted Rachel to play at her benefit,
would she write to Rachel? George's indignation need not
be imagined, because Hugo has left an account of it which
I here translate and abridge: "I am as much a Queen of
the Theatre as Rachel. Like her, I have been a courtesan,
and the day will come when like me she will be a beggar.
Does the freak think I am going to wait upon her? Ah, but

no ! I suppose she has forgotten how she used to go round the cafés singing for coppers ? Now my fine lady gambles for stakes of ten thousand francs, but I say that the day may come when her shoes will be in holes and she will have less right to the name of Rachel than I have to George ! " There is a lot more, and George leaves Hugo vowing that rather than write to Rachel she will throw herself into the Seine. However, George did not throw herself into the river, but asked the great Samson to approach Rachel, who thereupon promised her patronage and assistance.

It was upon Sunday, May 27, 1849, that the battle royal took place. The piece chosen for the benefit was *Iphigénie en Aulide*, with George as Clytemnestre and Rachel as Eriphyle. The first two acts were, as George had probably foreseen and Rachel certainly hadn't, a triumph for Clytemnestre, the rôle permitting the setting star to outshine the rising one. It was a tragic duel, the older actress slowly but surely putting it across her young rival ! " I have never seen anything more terrible," wrote Jules Janin, " than those two serpents straining for an opening. One would have said that the younger actress was shaken to the depths at sight of this unquenchable verve, fire, pride, and majesty, and that the older actress meant once more, and for the last time, to regain the throne and sceptre which this chit had usurped."

Not only Rachel but her partisans lost their tempers, and George at her entry in the third act was hooted. The hint was not lost upon her supporters, who, when Rachel next came on, returned the compliment with interest. And here are two sentences which I refuse to translate. Fleischmann writes : " Le vent des grandes batailles romantiques balaya cette houle de têtes furieuses, vociférantes." And Auguste Vacquerie has this : " Tandis que Mlle George, escortée de la sympathie générale, s'épanouissait de plus en plus dans l'ampleur de sa beauté et de son talent, Mlle Rachel,

abandonnée, irritée, seule, se rétrécissait et disparaissait."
In other words, a good old 'un proved better than a good
young 'un. When the curtain went up at the end, there was
only one actress present, Rachel having turned tail and fled.
She did not appear in the after-piece, and Malibran's sister,
Pauline Viardot, finished off the evening.

If a thing may be described by its opposite, the foregoing
is a fair account of the state of affairs at the New Theatre,
where the clash of magnanimities is almost embarrassing,
Mr. Gielgud going to the length of not letting us see what
he thinks of Mr. Olivier's diction in the Queen Mab speech,
and Mr. Olivier tempering Mercutio's death agony to permit
us a glimpse of Romeo's contrition. It is the merest cant to
pretend that comparisons, on such an occasion, are odious.
They are inevitable, since two actors agreeing to fly at the
same part put themselves in the position of two golfers
engaging, not in a match by holes, but in a medal round,
the par of the course being the ideal performance of the
character. Now the par of Mercutio is pretty well known:
he is to Romeo what Grosvenor is to Bunthorne, a jolly,
sensual sort of fellow, who " takes life as it comes and death
when it comes." Incidentally Mercutio has to let off the
most elaborate set-piece in all of Shakespeare's poetical fireworks, and for myself I have never known any actor except
Frank Rodney who could both be the man and let off the
speech. Mr. Gielgud when he played this part gave us the
cascade, but failed at the bluff; there is plenty of honest
rock about Mr. Olivier's Mercutio, though he turns on the
poetry in the way that athletic young fellows turn on the
morning bath.

But the par of Romeo is something upon which the best
analysers of golf-courses have never agreed. Thus Hazlitt
says roundly: " Romeo is Hamlet in love," and Mr.
Granville-Barker says no less roundly: " Romeo is not a

younger Hamlet in love." All are agreed, however, that
Romeo is a mighty poetical fellow, which he could hardly
help being since he is the first tragic hero of a mighty poet.
Here, in the matter of comparison, there is cut-and-come-
again. Mr. Olivier's Romeo showed himself very much in
love but rather butchered the poetry, whereas Mr. Gielgud
carves the verse so exquisitely that you would say the shop
he kept was a *bonne-boucherie*. (If an Englishman may not
pun in French in what language may he pun?) Yet is this
Romeo ever really in love with anybody except himself? If
not, we must presume Mr. Gielgud to take the Hazlitt side
of the argument, and his Romeo to be, like Hamlet, in love
with love, its metaphysics and vocabulary, the passion rather
than the object of it. It is impossible to pin so delicate an
opinion to any word or look or gesture, though I have the feeling that this Romeo never warms up to Juliet till she is cold.
But the whole thing is a lovely exercise. Or you might put
it that the performance is better as absolute than as programme music. Miss Ashcroft's Juliet is gaining in depth
and power while losing nothing of childish fragrance, and
I fancy that Miss Evans does not run off with the play quite
so boisterously as she did. Alas, I still dislike the cramped
setting in which everything is sacrificed to that suspended
conjurer's box! Alternatively, it makes you think that the
tragedy happens in Verona's Birdcage Walk at midnight.

In *Our Own Lives* Mr. Baliol Holloway is an absent-minded
bookworm who forgets that he has a wife (Terry's Theatre,
1880). Miss Irene Vanbrugh is the wife who runs an hotel in
Venice (any Dodie Smith play, 1935). Miss Rosalyn Boulter
and Mr. Kenneth Villiers are the young people in love (any
Wind and Rain play, 1934, and still running). Lady Tree is
a Duchess (Tom Robertson's *Caste* period). Mr. Tristan
Rawson is the patient lover (pre-Menander). Miss Laura
Cowie, Mr. Lewis Stringer, and Miss Lesley Wareing are

comic Cockney reliefs (*Strange Orchestra* species). Miss Agnes Lauchlan is a Polytechnical female (*Madras House* school, 1910). Such are the ingredients of Miss Jennings's many-sided play. The story tells how eighteen-year-old Rosemary plots to bring her father and mother together again and happily fails. This has always been one of the more revolting devices for luring people into the theatre—revolting in its insincerity. For the author never tells you that when the interfering chit has succeeded she will at once go off and get married, leaving together two people who have long ago decided that all they want to see of each other is their backs. And has not the time come to leave this nauseabondic fudge to the films and Miss Shirley Temple? By the way, it is no good our young people thinking they will one day act like Miss Vanbrugh. They won't. It is only fair to say that on the first night the piece had a tremendous reception.

Distinguished Gathering sets forth how nine reputable people, hearing that the gaff is blown upon them in a book of memoirs, decide to murder the author, the idea having first occurred to the publisher who finds himself involved and has summoned the nine to dinner. Why not turn down the book? Because some other publisher would jump at it. Then why not get an injunction for libel? Because the author could publish in Paris. Anyhow the publisher is obsessed with the idea of murder and, as one has so often said before, a play has to be set going somehow. The ensuing complications are ingenious, and the piece is theatrically interesting throughout two of the three acts, though in the third it tails off with the simultaneous production of revolvers and the sensibilities, the police being held at bay so that one of the many murderers can climb into the cockpit of his aeroplane and immolate himself. On the whole, it is all not quite good enough, and I think Mr. Parish would have been better advised to gut it and transfer some of the lines and one character, the wanderwit played by Miss Joan Hickson, to some better-devised play. Or perhaps I should say that Mr. Parish has too much of a job to begin his play and too much of a job to end it, though in between it is good and exciting. Mr. Roland Culver is admirably nasty as the murderee, Mr. Oliver Johnston makes a first-class detective, Miss Barbara Couper as one of the murderers is coming along very nicely. Then there is Mr. Keith Toms, excellent as a footman who has too little to say, and Mr. Frank Vosper, even better as a publisher who has rather too much. But I frankly decline to believe in Miss Mabel Terry-Lewis as the head of a home for penitent drabs and confessing to a frisk or two on her own account. And why, pray, should this equivocal patronage send her in to dinner before an earl's daughter? Even in the best murdering circles precedence should still rule. Lady Macbeth's: " Stand not upon the order of your going ! " was said after the banquet and not before.

MACBETH IN MINIATURE

MACBETH. Revival of Shakespeare's Tragedy. Old Vic
Theatre, Tuesday, December 3, 1935. [*December* 8, 1935]

"Macbeth," for its boldness of sentiment, strength of versifica-
tion, variety of passions and preternatural beings, deserves to be
esteemed a first-rate tragedy, containing a number of beauties
never exceeded, with many blemishes very censurable; dangerous in representation to weak minds; unintelligible to
moderate conceptions in several places, upon perusal; therefore
chiefly calculated for sound understanding, and established
resolution of principles, either on the stage or in the study.
—FRANCIS GENTLEMAN. 1770.

FOR HIS PRODUCTION of my favourite tragedy Mr. Henry
Cass has had recourse to that highbrow method which I most
abhor, the window-cleaning school. Macbeth going to murder
Duncan, and his Lady going to tidy up afterwards, move
towards their design along a sill so precarious as to suggest
the sidelong step of your artist in washleather. It is thought
a good deal has dropped out of this play, notably Lady
Macbeth's baby; and I suggest that among the losses is Lady
Macbeth's cute notion in the matter of the royal bedroom.
The housekeeping arrangements have been in her hands,
Duncan has been " in unusual pleasure," we are not told
whether as a young man he was good at the rock-climbing,
and there was always the chance that the combination of
ledge and usquebaugh might do the trick, which would have
saved the worthy pair any amount of trouble ! But this
ON

revival has a graver fault. There can be no doubt that in
this play Lady Macbeth is the king-pin, and that if for any
reason the part is inadequately played this mighty drama
comes asunder. It is all a matter of scale, of our old friend
Relativity. Sir Thomas Browne has a passage about things
which, possibly of importance in their own setting, can be
so placed as to be of no moment, " like to mice in Africa."
I do not pretend to have got the quotation correct, but it
suggests what happens when a Goneril or a Lady Macbeth
are physically insufficient. Hazlitt writes: " A lady of the
name of Barnes has appeared in Desdemona at this theatre.
Her voice is powerful, her face is pretty, but her person is
too *petite* and undignified for tragedy. Her conception of the
part is good, and she gives to some of the scenes considerable
feeling and effect; but who shall represent the ' divine
Desdemona ' ? " This seems to me to apply quite perfectly
to Miss Vivienne Bennett's Lady Macbeth. What actress of
a round and dimpling countenance, of a height lacking the
necessary inches, and with no holding in tragic mien or
bearing—what shall a clever little player (who, by the way,
is an exquisite Desdemona) make of the " fiend-like queen " ?

Miss Bennett tried very hard, but it is or should be an
axiom of acting, as of war and business, that to do one's
best is half way to failure. The player probably knew she
could not look the part. Could she make up the weight by
diction and emphasis ? This, alas, only made matters worse,
for your authentic Lady Macbeth *is* the part so tremendously
that she is relieved from the necessity of doing very much
with it. Actually, of course, she must always be doing a great
deal, but the impression on the spectator will be that the
part is playing itself. Now we saw Miss Bennett striving to
play the part, and every line of the part, and every word of
every line, for all it and they were worth. Her delivery of:
" Thou'rt mad to say it ! " would have put the castle staff

wise long before the event. Then take the passage beginning: " Come, thick night ! " and ending: " To cry, ' Hold,
hold ! ' " Lady Macbeth is telling Heaven not to interfere,
whereas Miss Bennett, by shouting the last two words at
the top of her voice, transferred the horror from Heaven to
herself, as though she, Lady Macbeth, would prevent the
murder. Again, in the passage about the milking babe, she
put so much emphasis on the word " brains " as to suggest
a choice of injury to the child ! The sleep-walking scene had
little suggestion of somnambulism and none at all of poetry,
Lady Macbeth's frenzied efforts to get rid of the spot being
a highly realistic exposition of the difficulty of washing off
a real defilement, like that known to golfers who use pitch.
Whereas the stain is on the soul, so that the smear on the
hand becomes merely a symbol. Towering falcons may in
this play be killed by mousing owls, but not in the acting of
it. What, in short, we saw was a very clever young actress
flying—and flying very bravely—at a part of which she
comprehended every word, but not one word of which
suited her. And why, Mr. Cass, did you so handicap the
little lady by giving her a first-act head-dress of the trip-
perish " I'm No Angel " order ? For though you incarna-
dined it, you could not, I think, hope to imbrue ! To dis-
courage Miss Bennett is the last thing I should want. To
be a repertory actress must be to fail in some parts, since
the actress is not born who can, in one and the same season,
be wise, amazed, temperate, and furious, and play all leading
women to all leading men. Ellen Terry wisely said : " It is
no use an actress wasting her nervous energy on a battle
with her physical attributes. She had much better find a
way of employing them as allies." The passage occurs in
a lecture on Lady Macbeth.

If Lear is the most difficult character to act, Macbeth is
the most difficult to interpret. Everybody knows what to

make of Lear, but the difficulty is only in the making, whereas Macbeth is sent on to the stage with the enormous handicap of not knowing what to make of himself. There are those infernal Witches hanging round the neck of, and tipping the wink to, one who has already broached this business of murder to himself, while, in addition to the self-prompting and the metaphysical aid, there is the egging-on of his spouse. To see in *Macbeth*, as some do, no more than a welter of savage lusts is to reduce the central figure to the melodramatic Saturday-night stature of *Richard III*. The great point about Macbeth is that his lust for power is not savage enough. What he would highly, that would he holily; would not play false, and yet would wrongly win. The difference between Macbeth and the members of the audience is not that he is a murderer, but that they are not poets. Extraordinary sympathy should exist between them, and if we are not immensely sorry for Macbeth his battle is lost. Mr. Swinley, making no attempt to act any of this, appeared to have hypnotised himself into reciting it, now glumly, and now with show of animation, but always reciting. He made the oddest mistakes in the text. This Macbeth declared that present fears were *worse* than horrible imaginings, wanted to know who lay i' the *third* chamber, and said to the dagger: " Come, let me *grasp* thee ! " There was one awful moment, too, when Macbeth said: " What's he . . ." perceptibly hesitated, and so made us fear that he was going to slip into: " . . . that wishes so, my cousin Westmorland ? " and so fall to discussion of military rather than Cæsarean operations. Let us think these strange abuses of the text were but the initiate fear that wants hard use. Not, of course, presuming to dictate, but I suggest to Mr. Swinley that he should set about discovering the humanity in Macbeth, leaving the inhumanity to take care of itself. Also he might advantageously remember that as a poet Macbeth towers head and shoulders above everybody else in the play, and, indeed, in any other of the plays. For Mr. Swinley is a fine tragedian, though this part may not become him. His Macbeth is at least as inoffensive as that of Macklin, of which performance His Honour Judge Parry once wrote that it " had nothing about it to rouse the animosity of the theatre-goers, unless, indeed, it was his kilt." And we reflect that as Judge Parry never saw Macklin, we have to leave it to His Honour.

Mr. William Devlin's Banquo was a beauty, and as I am in the constructive mood, let me suggest to Miss Baylis that Macbeth and Banquo should repeat the Romeo-Mercutio exchange-of-parts business. Mr. Devlin does not have to talk to tell you what he is thinking, and Banquo's face while Lady Macbeth was paying her false compliments to Duncan was, as they say, a study. Throughout this performance Banquo's royalty of nature was admirably suggested, though here again I fault the producer for depriving the actor of the three lines:

> *And yet I would not sleep. Merciful powers,*
> *Restrain in me the cursed thoughts that nature*
> *Gives way to in repose !*

Shakespeare was careful to prove, and Banquo should be allowed to echo, that Macbeth's friend is not a galumphing innocent like Antonio the Merchant, but one whose royalty consists in knowing temptation and withstanding it ! Mr. Cass follows the namby-pamby modern method of having no Ghost in the Banquet Scene, a denial which has always seemed to me to be complete nonsense. When Shakespeare, or somebody acting for him, wrote: " The Ghost of Banquo enters and sits in Macbeth's place," he presumably meant it, unless we are to hold that whoever put the play together did not know the meaning of ten of the simplest words in the language. Did Shakespeare mean these ten low words which creep in one dull line ? Definitely. Very well then ! In comparison it is a trifling matter that Macduff should be deprived of his bonnet, though again Malcolm presumably knows what he is saying with his: " What, man ! ne'er pull your hat upon your brow ! " It is adding insult to injury to deprive Malcolm of the line just because Macduff isn't allowed a bonnet. Here I think the actors should take matters in their own hands, and that in future while Mr. Swinley lets in that " clutch," Mr. Leo Genn should secure that bonnet. Mr. Genn played Macduff very well, though the part is actor-proof; Macduff can never be a Macduffer. Mr. Cecil Trouncer, taking a lamentable view of Duncan, presented him as something between a toastmaster at a City banquet and a boxing M.C. at the Albert Hall. After a week I still shudder at a wilful and conscientiously perverse interpretation. Perhaps the best thing in the production was the lighting. At least it was this which prevented me from murmuring at the end: " Tout passe, tout lasse, tout Cass ! "

MARY QUITE CONTRARY

MARY TUDOR. A play by Wilfrid Grantham. Playhouse Theatre, Thursday, December 12, 1935.

[*December* 15, 1935]

How MANY WAYS are there of writing historical drama ? First, there is the Swan's way, with nobody alive at the end except the royal undertakers. Galsworthy has an interesting letter on the crushing superiority of the bird of Avon over all smaller fowles that maken the same kind of melodye but get it all wrong. In 1913 he had been reading a blank-verse drama by Mr. Drinkwater and he wrote: " It's not quite turtle. It's very good mock. That is the little trouble with this neo-classicism. A shadow looms over it all—a shadow that with all your earnest brooms you will never sweep off that path—the shadow of the Greeks and of the man Shakespeare. They have spoiled that form for you—spoiled it—spoiled it. For, try you never so bravely, you can but remind us that you are trying. There is a self-consciousness, a literary emanation from all this blank verse business in these days, which is, I think, my chief objection to it. Moreover, it wants the genius of a Shakespeare to override the chilliness of this form sufficiently to make one feel blood, not ink, in the veins of the characters." Mr. Drinkwater's way, then, is the way of dramatic platitudes promulgated in stained-glass attitudes. Next comes Mr. Clifford Bax's manner, which is the same thing uttered in a flageolet voice and with the jut of a witty-twinkling beard. I omit all consideration of the older dramas

of Browning, merely reflecting that they might have been
worse and by Mrs. Browning. And years ago I forswore
public mention of Tennyson's exploits, again merely reflecting that murders in cathedrals might be left to later and
lesser poets. Of course we still have with us the people who
insist on writing dramas about Lear's wife, Lady Macbeth's
father, Othello's mother, and Hamlet's aunt, and there is
the modern wit who cannot leave the story of Henry VIII
where Shakespeare and Fletcher left it. But, even so, we
are not yet at the end of our categories. There is Miss Gordon
Daviot's way, which means taking a Shakespeare play and
retailing its plot all over again in nice modern prose, but
without putting the sentiments quite so well. There is the
provincial or touring method in which a justly popular actor
burns cakes or signs a Charter, while a justly popular actress
romps around in a melodious farthingale. And, last, there
is the Wills method, whereby your good honest craftsman
takes a bird's-eye view of some fragrant historical anecdote
and bids the playgoer put that in his pipe and smoke it.

Something ought to emerge from the foregoing, and, I
think, does. The thing which emerges is that, barring Shakespeare, all that matters in a historical play is the story. Hans
Andersen, in the fairy-tale called " The Wild Swan," says
of its eleven princelings that " they wrote on golden tablets
with diamond pens, and could read either with a book or
without one; in short, it was easy to perceive that they were
princes." Shakespeare could write a first-class historical play
either with a plot or without one, which proves that he was
the very prince of historical dramatists. All the others, when
they have not got a whacking good yarn to tell, are lost,
though seldom when they have one. It is no discourtesy to
Mr. Drinkwater to say that the playwright has not lived
who could fail with a hero who gets himself murdered in a
box at the theatre. And perhaps nobody can ever again

expect to be presented with quite such a " sitter " as that
with which Wills was presented in Charles I, who goes about
the stage looking like a Van Dyk and finding resemblance
between traitors' eyes and those of Judas Iscariot.

The point, then, about *Mary Tudor* is less how the author has
written it than what sort of material he had to work on. I think
it can be said without fear of contradiction that Mr. Grantham
possesses all the passive virtues. He has sufficient literary
craftsmanship to get into a period and stay there. I do not
mean that he would use Natheless and Yclept (which sounds
like a newly discovered " Idyll of the King ") to denote the
Arthurian period, Halidoms for the Norman, Gadzookses for
the Plantagenet, and Marry-come-ups for the Tudor. He is
not oppressively archaic, and were bluff King Hal his
subject would not send him to Much Wenlock to harangue
the rustics on more wedlock ! No, Mr. Grantham just
postulates the period and then writes about it in an
English which, without being obstreperously in fashion,
is never imaginatively out of period. The Tudor queen
who bids her gossip come hot-foot i' the morn (see *Dorothy
o' the Hall*) bids me leave the theatre hot-foot there and
then. When in this play the Princess Elizabeth says to
her half-sister, Queen Mary: " I shall in all my best obey
you, madam ! " we hear something which could have been
said at any time from 1200 onwards, and it is merely a
happy coincidence that Shakespeare used the same words in
connection with another century and a different country.
This is not to say that Mr. Grantham writes like Shakespeare,
who was a poet, but to make the lesser claim that Mr.
Grantham writes as an Elizabethan might have written if he
had not been Shakespeare.

Here is not as mean a gift as the casual playgoer might
imagine. It depends upon the author's holding in the
English sense. When Mary tells Elizabeth that she has

stood between her and execution the younger woman
has the ordinary: " I am much beholden to Your
Majesty ! " or something of the sort. Let me warn Mr.
Grantham that when his play is made into a film Elizabeth's
gratitude will take the form of: " Gee, that was swell of you,
sister ! " and that no American will see anything wrong in
this. Technically, then, Mr. Grantham's work is very fine,
and that it is not large as well is because its scope is not so
big as most intending playgoers will want. For, taking the
subject by and large, what does the average playgoer want
to know about Queen Mary ? He has been taught to regard
this fiend-like queen as being, like Macbeth, bloody, bold,
and resolute. But obviously no playwright is going to drag
anybody into the theatre to explore a country he may be
presumed to know like the back of his hand.

Every experienced playgoer will have an inkling, then, that
he is to see a Mary bloody, of course, but timid and waver-
ing. This, indeed, is the play that Mr. Grantham has written,
except that he has burked the " bloody " part of the business,
the pretext for such burking being the fact that he drops
his curtain before the bonfires at Smithfield started. The
author, in other words, claims to have written the life of
Mrs. Beeton up to the time when she started her cookery
feats. But this just won't do. Long before Mrs. B. put pen
to paper one suspects her of culinary inclinations, and one
just doesn't believe that Mary up to September, 1555,
wouldn't have burnt a pudding. Besides, the facts are against
the playwright, protest he never so ! According to Froude,
who confined his tarradiddles to the Carlyles, Mary " was
determined that everyone who could be convicted [after the
Wyatt rebellion] should die," and eighty people were hanged
in London alone. Mr. Grantham shows us the crime, but
avoids the punishment. In February 1555, when Mary was
still buoyed up with her marriage and the hope of a child,

she started upon her orgy of persecution by signing the
death warrants of Bishop Hooper and Rogers, a Canon of
St. Paul's. In May of the same year she, of her own volition,
wrote a letter to Bishop Bonner ordering him to tighten up
his treatment of " such disordered persons as do lean to any
erroneous and heretical opinions; whom, if they cannot by
good admonition and fair means reform, they are willed to
deliver unto the ordinary, to be by him charitably travelled
withal, and removed, if it may be, from their naughty
opinions; or else, if they continue obstinate, to be ordered
according to the laws provided in that behalf."

As a result of this circular fifty persons, says Froude, were
burned at the stake in the three ensuing months. That is,
before the end of this play. One of the great points of Froude's
history of the reign is that Mary would have given her ears
to put Elizabeth out of the way, but dared not; Mr. Grantham makes out the opposite case. No, the present portrait
of Mary just won't do. Further, that unwritten law is broken
whereby whitewashers must not only go to work in the day-
light, but when they come across a nobbly bit of sepulture
be seen to cover it up with extraordinary brushfuls. If Mr.
Grantham wants to plead that Mary (a) was justified by her
religious convictions, or (b) didn't know what was going
on, he should (a) make her convictions one of his play's
rallying points, or (b) show us the horrors going on and Mary
ignorant of them. He must not pretend that until the end
of his play not a hair of anybody's head was singed, and that
Mary only took to bonfires at Smithfield to console her for
Philip's coldness. All this is not to say that the play is not
interesting. It is extremely interesting, with an interest for
which we are indebted occasionally to history but much
oftener to the author. His " bunking " has good dramatic
precedence in our own day, for did not Mr. Drinkwater
once treat us to a Mary Queen of Scots who had no desires

except for an "easy festival mind" and to walk her garden in the evenings in peace ? If this can be swallowed, so we may well accept a bloodless Mary Tudor alternating between her legacy of ill health and a passion for a handsome Spaniard, all very beautifully and often movingly played by Miss Flora Robson. Philip is wildly wrong. He begins by smelling April and May, degenerates into petty rages about not being called King, and except for a flirtation with Elizabeth nowhere gives any sign of the gross lecher and sensualist who would gorge himself to vomiting on bacon-fat. Mr. Marius Goring plays this odd version of Philip extremely well. But what a pity the author did not take his courage in both hands and show us the carnal Philip revolted by his " haggard bride, unlovable, yet with her parched heart thirsting for affection, flinging herself upon a man to whom love was an unmeaning word, except as the most brutal of passions."

The portrait of Elizabeth is altogether more probable and successful. Mr. Grantham has exactly caught that trick of logic-chopping which was the budding stateswoman's formula for saving her neck. Elizabeth did not want any jolly pardon; she had nothing to be pardoned for. On the other hand, if Mary could jolly well prove anything against her, she asked nothing better than the block. Would her gracious Sovereign stop talking nonsense, please, and get on with evidence not concocted by some village idiot ? Up that gum-tree, where Elizabeth so cleverly stuck her sister, Mary remained, and it must have been maddening. Miss Joyce Bland gives a brilliant and extremely understanding performance of the exasperating creature. It would be uncritical to omit mention of Miss May Agate's morose Wife of Windsor and Mr. Lawrence Anderson's Bishop Gardiner, who with his crenellated beard seems to have looked in from *Yoshe Kalb*. The piece is very tastefully mounted, and the tone of time lies thick on tambour and virginals.

LET US MEANDER

FRITZI. A musical play by Sydney Blow and Edward Royce. Music by Carl Tucker. Adelphi Theatre, Friday, December 20, 1935. [*December* 22, 1935]

"LET US HAVE NO MEANDERING!" said the old lady in *David Copperfield*, and on the whole I agree. But there are times when meandering is expedient and even unavoidable. Suppose, for example, that by some freak of fate you were bidden to cross a field and charged to take an hour over it. You would, I think, meander, and I shall not argue with the pernickety who desire to know how big was the field. There is the case of the journalist between whom and the foot of his column yawns an illimitable void, and I scorn the objection that the foot of the column limits it. Now let me narrow this down to the dramatic critic with nothing to say and the whole week to say it in. Nothing? Well, hardly anything! Let us, therefore, meander.

Few things are more tragic, or more comic, than those works of art which are born with the dust of oblivion in thick descent upon them. The still-born masterpiece has its peculiar pathos: the author has failed, and there's an end of it. The works I mean, and whose fate seems to me to be so ludicrously tragic, are those in which the author has aimed at posterity and missed it in his own day. Fishing recently in the second-hand boxes of the Charing Cross Road I hooked three out of the four volumes of the *Mémoires* of Ernest Legouvé, member of the French Academy. When this

worthy died I know not; it is difficult enough to discover
when, if ever, he was alive. Little is known of him except
that he was the collaborator of Scribe in *Adrienne Lecouvreur*,
that first-class second-rate play which is still so much better
than anything that anybody, except possibly Mr. Emlyn
Williams, is writing for the theatre to-day. (A perambulator
meandering in a field would relieve his boredom by taking
a pot-shot at a rabbit if he saw one; this must be my excuse
for casually pinking the entire British dramaturgy !) At one
moment in Scribe and Legouvé's play Adrienne recites La
Fontaine's fable of " Les Deux Pigeons," the piece chosen by
Sarah Bernhardt for her entrance examination for the Con-
servatoire. Hardly had she got to the end of the second line
when Auber, at the head of the jury, stopped her and told
her she was admitted. Mr. Maurice Baring has said of this
recitation: " When Sarah Bernhardt played Adrienne
Lecouvreur she used to recite the opening of that fable, and
one felt as one heard it that for the perfect utterance of
beautiful words this was the Pillars of Hercules of mortal
achievement, that it was impossible to speak verse more
beautifully." Dame Madge Kendal once said to me: " I
heard Sarah recite ' Les Deux Pigeons ' in a drawing-room.
I did not watch Sarah but the audience, and whatever it was
she made the pigeons say and do, the effect on the audience
was improper ! " The answer to that is that the effect of anything and everything on Dame Madge was improper ! Now,
what were we talking about ? Perhaps the next paragraph
will tell us.

Of Scribe and his quality sufficient is known to realise why
Heine, dying, said he had not enough breath left to hiss one
of M. Scribe's comedies. Legouvé talks a great deal about
Halévy who, with Hector Crémieux, wrote the words of
Orphée aux Enfers and with Henri Meilhac that famous *succès
de larmes, Frou-Frou,* and the operettes *La Belle Hélène, La*

Grande Duchesse de Gerolstein, Toto chez Tata and scores more, all in the genre of which our little piece so patiently waiting for notice is the legitimate successor. Returning, however, to that poor mutton, Legouvé, it is a strange irony that in the first of the volumes, discovered as I say in the Charing Cross Road, I should find him lamenting the faded glory of a personage with the altogether frightening name of Népomucène Lemercier. This individual was the friend of Napoleon, and, according to Talleyrand, the most brilliant chatterbox in Paris. Remembering what *Le Cid* had done for Corneille and *Andromaque* for Racine, the good Népomucène thought fit to burst upon the public with a drama which could only have been called *Agamemnon*. Lemercier wrote tragedies for thirty years. He tried a fall with Dante in a poem with the remarkable name of *La Panhypocrisiade* and with André Chénier in an astronomical, geological, natural-historical affair entitled *L'Atlantiade*. Where are these prodigious pieces now? Yet their author wrote nothing, according to his own confession, without asking himself what Corneille, Sophocles, and Shakespeare would have thought of it. He prefaces his struggle with the mighty spirit of Dante with the following remarkable address:

" Imperishable poet, where will you receive my letter? I address it to you in those unknown regions which immortality makes free to the sublime soul of genius. Imagination, that winged messenger, will bear my letter to you in the realms where my spirit soars. Show this poem, when you have read it down to its last line, to Michael Angelo, to Shakespeare, and even to Rabelais, and if its originality appears to them to consort with your gigantic invention, then ask what sort of a future they see for it. Perhaps they will behold twenty editions before a hundred years have rolled away."

Yet we must not be led by this fanfaronade entirely to despise the good Népomucène. He was paralysed down one side, and when he walked must hold himself together with his one good hand. In this condition he fought a sword duel. Like Byron, he must swim, box, and ride better than the physically perfect; his acts of courage and of passion were protests against Nature. It was Legouvé who persuaded Joséphine to marry Buonaparte. It was he who, at Malmaison, taught Napoleon the history of France. Later on the two quarrelled; one of the first Crosses of the Legion of Honour was sent by Napoleon to Lemercier, who refused it. In revenge the Emperor forbade the performance of his friend's plays; the friend said nothing. Driven from his house, he took silent refuge in a garret. And then one day, at the Tuileries, the Emperor perceived his old crony in a corner with the other members of the Institute. Napoleon, waving the crowd aside, went straight up to him and said : " *Eh bien*, Lemercier, when are you going to write a new tragedy ? " " I am waiting, Sire ! " replied the poet. Surely a magnificent remark to make in 1812 on the eve of the Russian campaign !

And now the dust of oblivion covers Lemercier, and Legouvé, and Scribe, and Meilhac, and Halévy, and even that little piece which, still marking time at the head of this essay, is—and here I drive home the peg of this article— the French operette's so well-intentioned successor. For I cannot think that *Fritzi* is immortal, and perhaps a six months' run is better than no run at all. And what about six weeks ? Yet there is a great deal of negative good to be said for the little piece. At least nobody croons and nobody tap-dances, and perhaps if there were a larger store of positive qualities to be celebrated I should not have meandered. But when I see entirely charming people trying to give us some-thing away from croon-and-tap vulgarity nothing on earth is going to induce me to blast it. Miss Rosalinde Fuller is to be remembered chiefly for her clever work in *The Un-known Warrior* and *Martine*, in the second of which she was particularly good. But it will not be claimed that either piece is a suitable training-ground for display of that saccharine termagancy which consists in lowering rebellious curls to the level of some interlocutor's middle waistcoat button and shaking them at it. Miss Fuller does her bright vivacious best, however, and the audience like her very much. But I protest against an assumed accent which says: " Forgeeve you ? Ach, no ! Thees cannot bee ! " That the character is French is no excuse for making her talk Viennese. And in any case why divagate from the pure Cockney of everybody else ?

One last saw Mr. Leslie French in *Comus*, in which high and poetic sphere one takes leave to think he should remain, except that there is hardly a living for an actor in Milton's Attendant Spirits. This well-graced player is to be excused, therefore, for flitting to another shore on whose

> *. . . Tawny Sands and Shelves*
> *Trip the pert Fairies and the dapper Elves.*

But there are dangers in such a transfer:

> *By the rushy-fringèd bank,*
> *Where grows the Willow and the Osier dank,*
> *My sliding Chariot stayes,*
> *Thick set with Agat, and the azurn sheen*
> *Of Turkis blew, and Emrauld green. . . .*

At the risk of thickly setting upon Mr. French, let me say that from the spirit of *Comus* to the high spirits of a musical-comedy buffoon is too vast a leap. Too vast, anyhow, for me, who would sooner cope with the Strid in Wharfedale. However, the audience likes him very much, and no more shall be said.

Pⁿ

The last time one saw Mr. Bruce Winston was in *The Alche-mist*, and there is justification for turning the representation of Sir Epicure Mammon into a sugar-daddy.

What is the piece about ? There can be no harm in saying that it concerns a kind of Wendy who keeps a kind of thieves' kitchen, and is a kind of French baroness, and ultimately falls in love with and presumably marries a kind of impresario about whom it would not be kind to say more. There is no harm in declaring the music to be pretty in a familiar way. Nor in alluding to the chorus if one grants that Mr. Cochran's Young Ladies cannot be everywhere. Neither can Mr. Cochran. Other producers must obviously be found, though I cannot think that one would ineluctably seek out Mr. John Wyse, the brilliant young intellectual whose production of *Frolic Wind* has probably been the year's best thing in the theatre. However, this frolic choice, which would make some managements windy, has been justified by its success, considering the material Mr. Wyse has had to work upon. That new brooms sweep clean does not mean that they will be allowed the clean sweep, and a dust-pan and brush were badly wanted for all the jokes in this play. But again the audience is fooled to the top of its delighted bent, and perhaps this is all that matters. On the first night it cheered as though the piece were a new Gilbert and Sullivan. Exactly. Music by Gilbert, words by Sullivan. Except that Sullivan would have been wittier !

DESIGN FOR PLAYGOING

To-night at 8.30. By Noel Coward. Phoenix Theatre, Thursday, January 9, 1936.   [*January* 12, 1936]

"They were nothing, sir, be they addressed to what they may!" said Dr. Johnson to a Clergyman who had asked whether it was not a fact that Dodd's sermons were addressed to the passions. One's first view of Mr. Coward's *Family Album* is that it is nothing whether it be addressed to our sense of the past, our feeling that *Bitter Sweet* should have a coda, or the author's hankering after a new genre. Yet let us be on our guard. That a genre is new means that it has not acquired proprieties to be stuck to or departed from. Its values are wobbly, and it is only when they have done wobbling that we can decide whether they possess value. The idea at the back of this new funning is to begin with some perfectly serious theme, strip it of its seriousness, and finally make a long nose at it. Death, it is generally admitted, is a serious subject, and Mr. Coward's comedietta seeks to show that underneath the sable hearse lies the subject for light verse. The paterfamilias whom this family has just buried was an old scoundrel. Very well, then, let's dry our eyes, sit up, and sing little songs about the old rapscallion! " To hell with our sick-making father!" is only the post-Waugh expression of a mood that was known before *Vile Bodies*. Nobody, I imagine, objects to that, since it has been more or less the theme of such respectable plays as *The Thunderbolt* and *The Truth about Blayds*. But it is getting to the point which is the difficulty. Death is still regarded by most people as an occasion for the exercise of such good taste as they have inherited or acquired. The line to be drawn is thin, which does not prevent Mr. Coward's jocosities from being perceptibly on one or the other side of it. For example, one of the daughters protests that it is " wrong to laugh with papa not yet cold in his grave," to which one of her brothers replies that since he has been dead four days the statement is without accuracy except as a figure of speech, while another sister is moved to remark that the cemetery is peculiarly bleak and wind-swept. I suggest that this is, to use a mild word, unfunny. On the other side of the line is the wholly admirable remark about the dead man's mistress who, at the funeral, was observed to be " grieving in her own way." As an indictment of English snobbery this is worthy of Wilde at his best. Permissible, too, is the remark of the youngest sister that papa would never again see a squirrel, rebuked by the eldest brother holding that such deprivation must be among Death's minor forfeits.

There is an unhappy breed of playgoer which, confronted with any play of manners, judges it entirely by the presence or absence of anachronisms. Personally I am not worried by these, and if Mr. Coward tells me that in 1860 the funeral drink was madeira, so be it. Nevertheless I feel bound to record the observation of a very distinguished lady who was heard to say tartly: " Madeira ? Nonsense ! We never drank anything except sherry and ham ! " On the whole *Family Album* misfires. On the other hand, it is proper to say that the audience took more kindly to this unhappy little prelude than to the evening's *pièce de résistance*, which it resisted with all its might. Resisted because, presumably, it wanted the home-chat and hay-fever of Chris and Barbara's terribly private lives, and not the post-mortem of a love-affair, which is what *The Astonished Heart* really amounts to. The audience had forgotten, or did not want to realise, that Mr. Coward has a serious vein, displayed as early as *The Vortex*, to which in this play he returns. Out for flippancy, it could not take to the author in pre-Waugh mood, writing seriously, away from his established line of success, and for the nonce entirely discarding Noelisms. Christian Faber is a psychiatrist married to Barbara and in love with Leonora. Barbara, sensing this, sits up for her husband, and at five o'clock in the morning a conversation takes place remarkable in its untheatricality. Barbara begins: " This isn't a scene—really it isn't, only I do want to talk to you. I've wanted to for a long while." No histrionics here. Presently Chris trots out the old, old formula: " You know about me loving you all the same, don't you—more than anybody in the world ? " To which Barbara has a plain: " Yes, of course, I do, but I'd rather you didn't go on about it just at the moment." If this isn't good husband-and-wife dialogue, then I have never listened to any married couple. Barbara invites Chris to go away with Leonora for a month or two to get the love-affair or whatever it is out of his system, because the battle between emotion and conscience—which, by the way, Mr. Coward calls intelligence—is doing him harm, and the battle has just got to be stopped. To which Chris replies:

" How can I put a stop to it ? It's there—it's there all the time—every moment of the day and night—it started so easily, so gaily—little more than a joke; there were no danger signals whatever. I felt just a few conscience pangs over you, but not seriously, the whole thing was so apart from us and all we mean to each other—my intelligence lied to me—my intelligence insisted that it was nothing, just a little emotional flutter that would probably loosen me up and do me a power of good; then suddenly I felt myself being swept away, and I started to struggle, but the tide was stronger than I knew; now I'm far from the land, darling—far from my life and you and safety—I'm struggling still, but the water's terribly deep and I'm frightened —I'm frightened."

Three-quarters of this is wholly admirable—I think it is the first time I have ever heard anybody in the theatre recognise that he has an intelligence and has been misled by it—though the simile of the tide and the deep water is an odd relapse into the worn-out counters of theatricality. But Mr. Coward very soon recovers. For the next sentence or two he is confessing in urgent and new-found words that jealousy of Leonora's past which is—to use the jargon of relapse—making both their lives a hell. The next scene shows the situation " from Leonora's angle." It is the mistress who tires first and who has on her nerves her lover's hateful habit of raking about in her past. Here is her tirade and its sequel:

> LEONORA: You've humiliated me and shamed me— you've dug up things that were once dear to me and made them look cheap and horrible. I can't even go back into my own memory now without finding you there jeering on every threshold—walking with me through the empty rooms—making them tawdry—shutting them off from me for ever. I hate you for that bitterly.
> CHRIS: Sentiment for the dead at the expense of the living—very interesting—quite magnificent !
> LEONORA: The dead at least have the sense to be quiet.
> CHRIS: Long live the dead !
> LEONORA: You are one of them now . . .

Leonora's " threshold " makes one a bit uneasy, and perhaps Mr. Coward will now go through this little play with a microscope and take out the very few passages of " literary " dialogue. But the last three sentences have something of the finality of a knell, and in the theatre are immensely effective.

Possibly if one were in hypercritical mood one would object that the final curtain buys its effectiveness at the cost of probability. Chris has thrown himself out of the window and now lies dying. To Leonora coming out of his bedroom is given the play's last line : " He didn't know me, he thought I was you, he said—' Baba—I'm not submerged any more——' and then he said·' Baba ' again—and then—then he died." This is immense theatre, but one does not quite see a wife, however *complaisante*, twiddling her thumbs in the drawing-room while her rival bends over her husband to catch his last words. Mr. Coward can easily forestall this. When Barbara is told by the doctor that there isn't much time, she should make the point that since her husband is asking for Leonora he must see her, even if at the supreme moment her place as a wife is usurped. And, of course, he will want to delete Barbara's " Is it all over ? " which is a strange piece of clumsiness for so fastidious a craftsman. One of the results of paring what would normally be a three-hour play into something under the hour is to impose upon the characters rather more than normal self-consciousness. But I am not at all sure that this fortuitousness does not result in good charac-terisation. Isn't it a criticism of life to-day that whereas formerly only the vulgar played to the gallery, now the smartest among us cannot get along without the help of the stalls ? Sleeping or waking, the world of which Mr. Coward writes is never without its audience. The last piece in the bill, *Red Peppers*, is a shorthand transcript of half an hour in the lives on the stage and in the dressing-room of two third-rate music-hall performers. This is magnificent fooling, in which Mr. Coward's wit, like the sword with which Sergeant Troy bedazzled Bathsheba, seems to be anywhere and everywhere.

It is too late to attempt more than the most perfunctory

compliments on the acting. Mr. Coward fails liberally in the
first piece, in which he is enjoined to sing with a voice
unfitted for the smallest opera. But his performance in the
middle item is a fine piece of taut, nervous acting with the
words of the part rightly reduced to a running commentary.
There is, you feel, more in this passion than in the handful of
words with which its victim explains it and himself. In both
pieces Miss Gertrude Lawrence runs the full gamut of her
sense and sensibility, with less reliance than of old upon
idiosyncrasy and more upon emotion acutely felt and imaginatively realised. She looks lovely throughout, and the
addition to her dignity is notable. When in the burlesque at
the end these two players joined hands, such shouts of laughter
went up that the Phoenix very nearly turned turtle. After
which I hope it is permitted to say that almost the best
acting of the evening came from Miss Alison Leggatt, whose
art now begins to reveal itself as an inexhaustible reservoir of
finely-controlled sanity. Mr. Alan Webb contributes three
character sketches of remarkable diversity. But the whole of
the select company is good enough to make one believe that
Mr. Coward has really selected it.

MR. COWARD'S RETURN MATCH

To-night at 8.30. By Noel Coward. Phoenix Theatre, Monday, January 13, 1936. [*January* 19, 1936]

In my view the scores in this match were as follows: First Series, 2 wows, 1 dud; Second Series, 1 wow, 1 semi-dud, 1 dud. But there, that is only the view of one spectator, who may easily have been mistaken. In his account of the Farr-Loughran boxing-match the other day, my favourite reporter wrote: " The verdict met with a reception that indicated derision mingled with disgust." Let contumely be my portion. I will not deny that in the general opinion Mr. Coward's Second Series was an easy winner.

Hands Across the Sea is lovely fooling. Lady Maureen Gilpin (Miss Lawrence) is an *étourdie*. Which, let me tell the purist lowering his head before a foreign word like a bull at a gate, is by no means the same thing as a featherbrain. A feather-brain is a nitwit; an *étourdie* is a young woman who has brains but chooses not to use them. (Postcard senders of the exact English equivalent will be suitably thanked and the home-bred word used henceforth as occasion serves.) Perhaps one might call Lady Maureen the gadabout *à la mode*, only happy when she is cluttering up airways in the course of which she invites all and sundry to visit her when in town. Nor is her London existence less inconsequent, since half a dozen times a day she nearly strangles herself with her own telephone cord. Her husband (Mr. Coward) is a naval com-mander who paces the deck with so airy a tread that Piggy's

heart would know it and beat were it earth in an earthy bed.
Who in the world's Piggy ?—some low-born reader may ask.
For it is low-born not to know that in Shepherd Market
Maureen becomes "Piggy," Doreen is obviously "Snuffles,"
and Noreen can only be "Tweet." Piggy is fussing tremendously because before the week is out her commander husband must put to sea, which numbing phrase calls up in her
mind visions of at least two years on the China station. But is
Piggy really fussed about it ? No ! Piggy can play the grass-
widow as prettily as anybody and looks forward to a semblance of weeds in a reality of crêpe-de-Chine:

Elle a des yeux retroussés vers les tempes,
  Un pied petit à tenir dans la main,
Le teint plus clair que le cuivre des lampes,
  Les ongles longs et rougis de carmin.

Par son treillis elle passe sa tête,
  Que l'hirondelle en volant vient toucher,
Et, chaque soir, aussi bien qu'un poète,
  Chante le saule et la fleur du pêcher.

Has not Gautier here perfectly described this actress and
this acting ? Are not these lines a pre-vision of " celle que
nous aimons " drawing from its sanctuary " un pied petit à
tenir dans la main " ? With the aid of jade scalpels, of
unguents, of shagreen pots and jasper pans Miss Lawrence
proceeds to the embellishment of " ongles longs et rougis de
carmin," and the curtain falls on our little lady saying, " I
must do my feet ! " In the meantime the playlet has taken a
turn nowhere indicated in the foregoing. A Mr. and Mrs.
Wadhurst (Mr. Alan Webb and Miss Alison Leggatt) have
dropped in from Malaya, having been mistaken for a Mr.
and Mrs. Rawlinson from Penang. A young man (Mr. Kenneth Carten) calls with some plans which may be from the

Admiralty. Or again they may not; nobody ever finds out. The Hon. Clare Wedderburn (Miss Everley Gregg) has been chattering her own nineteen to the dozen of another naval officer (Mr. Edwin Underdown) and an Army fellow (Mr. Anthony Pélissier) who, since everybody calls him " Bogey," can only be a Major Gosling. Presently we discover that the commander is putting to sea for a maximum of three days, an exile which Mr. Coward meets with the firmest set of shoulder. While all this is going on the telephone rings as incessantly as, in a later playlet, some lout's aunt is said to ride to hounds. What the Wadhursts make of it all we don't know. Nor they. Nor ever will. Every second of this admirable skit is not only perfect theatre but first-class satire.

That Mr. Coward himself is a little unhappy about *Fumed Oak* is proved by the sub-title, " an unpleasant comedy in two scenes." For may not unpleasantness exist less in the material than in the handling ? The story, which is the same that Mr. Maugham used in *The Breadwinner*, is at all times anybody's who cares to take it. This particular version tells how the head of a lower middle-class family, in bondage to his wife, daughter, and mother-in-law, finally rounds on and deserts them. Let it be admitted that they are an uncomfortable lot. We first meet them at breakfast, and Miss Lawrence, who in this piece puts on her thinking-cap and does some real acting, at once centres interest in Doris Gow, whose name in itself is a stroke of genius. All over South, North, East, and Far West London eight o'clock is the zero hour at which the Dorises impose silence upon husband and offspring, argue with their mothers, and with the tips of delicate fingers separate in a herring the eatable from the uneatable. We are, then, not altogether surprised that Henry Gow, after fifteen years of subjection, should suddenly decide to abandon Clapham for somewhere East of Suez. It is not the decision but the manner of it which finds us a little sceptical. Doris,

Elsie, and the unspeakable Mrs. Rockett may be all that Henry Gow's fancy paints them. But one cannot quite believe that he would say those things about Doris's prenuptial tendernesses, Elsie's adenoids, and the Rockett's rocketting with the lodger. These things are amusing to hear, but one feels that it is Mr. Coward who is saying them, that it is not in the Henrys of this world to be so devastatingly articulate, that in real life they either depart without a word or enforce argument with a butcher's cleaver. Again, one isn't quite happy about Mr. Coward's gibes at that respectability which is the ideal of Doris and the Rockett, and will be that of Elsie when she shall have got over her " pash " for the unseen Miss Pritchard. Is this straining after respectability any less genuine than Mayfair's strenuous flight from it ? The time is coming when Doris will rather see Elsie dead at her feet than in the arms of somebody's husband. But would not Mr. Coward's Mayfairies one and all choose death in preference to respectability, on the ground that it is less dreary ? In fact, one doesn't see that in point of sincerity there is a pin to choose between the two worlds, and it is odd that this escapes Mr. Coward. The fact that the play is a sneer makes it less than a work of art.

A complete dud, in my view, is the third item. In every revue there occurs a nostalgic interlude in which a young man and a young woman, gyrating with extreme rapidity, explain to each other in slow, dragging numbers that their mutual misery is due to their separate infidelities. *Shadow Play* is a revue-number interminably spun out. Simon (Mr. Coward) explains to Victoria (Miss Lawrence) that rapture cannot last, and we reflect that if Mr. Coward had remembered his Meredith he would have known that the art of life has less to do with cocktails than with " keeping the passion fresh." To tell your heart's idol that she will always be first, that your infidelities will only be minor, and that when she cannot help noticing these she is to hang on to the cliffs of Dover—Mr. Coward's figure, not mine !—all this seems to me to be cold-blooded to the point of meanness. Anyhow, I am not going to be spoofed into taking seriously Simon's attempt to stage an amatory comeback. It will be argued that the thing is not serious, but only a singing tragedy. Then why not engage singers to tackle Mr. Coward's sagging, defeatist little tunes ? The answer is that no singer would look at them, that they are for crooning, and that Mr. Coward and Miss Lawrence can do that sort of thing as badly as the next worst.

I do not suppose there has been any period in the history of culture when singing on the lighter stage was at as low an ebb as it is to-day. Can it be doubted that if actors or actresses danced, dressed, whistled, or even acted as badly as they sing, benches would be torn up and hurled at them ? But the public does not desire singing and would hate it if it got it ; what it wants is indeterminate mewings, the outpourings of homesick cats. If its chosen players can accompany their roof-noises with half-a-dozen steps a little more difficult than ordinary ballroom stuff but needing none of the arduous apprenticeship of the art of dancing proper—why then, everybody's happy. So be it. So far as I am concerned, *Shadow Play* is at the top of the slope leading to that crooning, shuffling morass which is the wireless after midnight. The acting throughout the evening was a feast of unreason and a flow of everything except soul. I should like to pay tribute here to the clever work accomplished in all six plays by Miss Leggatt and Mr. Webb, Miss Gregg and Miss Moya Nugent. I am a little unhappy about Mr. Pélissier, who is now at the cross-roads between his father's adorable buffoonery and his mother's exquisite grace. If I were he, I should let the buffoonery have it !

FULFILLING A PROMISE

AFTER OCTOBER. A play by Rodney Ackland. Arts Theatre, Friday, February 21, 1936.

THREE MEN ON A HORSE. A comedy by John Cecil Holm and George Abbott. Wyndham's Theatre, Tuesday, February 18, 1936.   [*February* 23, 1936]

IT WOULD BE INTERESTING to see this play performed by Russian actors before a Russian audience. It would be still more interesting to read the Russian dramatic critics next morning and find out whether they would say the same kind things about Mr. Ackland that we say about Tchehov. *After October* has not the momentum or the drive of the great Russian playwright, and it does not anywhere pretend to beauty. But it is all extraordinarily like that scene which occurs in every Tchehov play when everybody is talking nineteen to the dozen and nothing in particular is being mooted. There is the same atmosphere of melancholy, in the English case more apparent than actual, and the resemblance is stressed by the fact that everybody is a failure. Mr. Ackland's theme is gloom, his orchestration is as sparkling as Rossini's at his gayest, and Mr. A. R. Whatmore has produced in the spirit in which Sir Thomas Beecham conducts. In fact, were the score a musical one I should mark it *Adagio ma con Brio*. This may possibly be dog-Italian, but it comes from one dog-tired with laughing at this play. The story, such as it is, concerns the household of Mrs. Rhoda Monkhams

(Miss Mary Clare), a lady bereft of both husband and profession, since in palmier days she was an understudy at the Gaiety. Ill-luck has always pursued her. The principal having influenza on the first night, Rhoda had a chance of running her pagoda. But the principal was well enough to attend the dress rehearsal and on seeing Rhoda's performance screamed out: " I shall play to-morrow if I catch my death ! " And, as Rhoda says: " She did appear—and died of double pneumonia ! " Rhoda lives in these and other succulent memories not unmixed with dressing-room tittle-tattle on which the dust of ages lies thick. She remains a trouper at heart and, with the valour of her kind, is battling when the curtain goes up with a carpet-sweeper, an unbreakfasted family, reiterative duns, communications from owners of plain vans, and the laundry shrieking down the telephone. Her son Clive (Mr. Griffith Jones) is a playwright with a passion equally divided between the theatre and Frances (Miss Iris Baker), who is a manicurist, neurotic, and lodger or, as she would prefer to put it, Mrs. Monkhams's paying guest. Though Frances loves Clive she is accepting the roses and attentions of Brian (Mr. Whatmore), epitome of semi-public school, would-be pukka sahib, and sports addict, all of them hearty, good-natured, moneyed, and frantically boring to anybody outside their kind.

There is a younger daughter, Joan (Miss Ursula Marx), who is vaguely secretary to Alec (Mr. Geoffrey Denys), who is vaguely dipsomaniac. " Is Arabella Mr. Winkle's mistress ? " asked Mr. Beerbohm in his parody of George Moore on Dickens, and returned the answer: " If she is not, she has been, or at any rate she will be." The same applies to Joan and Alec. An older daughter of Mrs. Monkhams is Lou (Miss Leonora Corbett). Lou has been in the dancing business at Toulon, Toulouse, *que sais-je ?* and has married Armand (Mr. Godfrey Kenton), who is alluded to in the family as " Almond " and is now helping in a shop in Soho. Armand confesses that, outside his love for Lou, he is as much *désorienté* as if he were living among the Chinese. And with good reason, since in no country but this could he meet the Betty of Miss Merle Tottenham, a little drudge among whose forbears must have been Dick Swiveller's Marchioness. It would take a Dickens to tell us what the Marchioness would have thought of Greta Garbo's Anna Karenina, but Mr. Ackland does very well, and Miss Tottenham does even better. Two more characters remain. One is Marigold (Miss Gwladys Evan Morris), fat, forty, and frowsty as only Bloomsbury tea-parties know how. This is a Miss Mowcher with an over-developed mothering instinct thrown away on a scapegrace nephew who is continually in gaol. " Holiday-ing," is Marigold's euphemism for this state, and when asked how long it is to last she has fallen into the habit of reply-ing: " Three months ! " Last in the sad eventless category— for nothing happens to any of them—is Oliver (Mr. Peter Godfrey), who is our old friend Ulric Brendel all over again, existing on the crumbs of charity and the cud of a long, unpublished dramatic poem. It is typical of this play—and how like Tchehov !—that though the flat is Rhoda's it is frequently empty except for people unwelcome to Rhoda who have no business to be in it at all.

Rhoda has a contempt for Marigold because she has been seen to eat peanuts in Bond Street, and dislikes Oliver still more because he insists upon turning up at meal-times. Oliver and Marigold have only to meet to take an intense dislike to one another, and here is a passage which shows how when the dialogue is good enough in the theatre Time can stand still and Space go 'round and around until the talkers have had their say:

OLIVER: Do I inflict myself? One day they'll be proud to say that Oliver Nashwick came into their house. Look at it ! This bourgeois pretentiousness ! They've put on evening dresses. They've bought two bottles of wine. They're celebrating. Like a wedding of proletarians. Or a funeral. You think I'm rude, don't you ? Rude because I don't say " How do you do ? I'm delighted to meet you. Will you have two lumps or three, and was it the Monday or the Tuesday ? " D'you ever say what you mean ? D'you ever *know* what you mean ? D'you ever think ? Have you ever, for one moment, been honest with yourself ?

MARIGOLD : I knew you'd go on like this, directly I saw that beard !

OLIVER : Why is your gown such a phantasie ? (*walking round her*).

MARIGOLD (*sternly*) : It's a very beautiful dress.

OLIVER : Don't you mean to be ridiculous ? Please tell me. What were your parents ? Shopkeepers ? Bourgeois ?

MARIGOLD : No, indeed, they were not. They were the Ivenses of Buxton ! What were yours ?

OLIVER : My father was a buyer in a draper's shop and my mother an assistant who " lived in." She seduced him, and afterwards, I've heard, he entered the merchant service, where he saw a great deal of the world. I've never met him, but I often think of my father. I believe I should have liked him because he had an adventurous spirit. When my mother was left alone she became a servant. My life has been spent in kitchens listening to servants' gossip. . . . I've a finer brain than anyone living, and I dwell among servants. I am bitter, but I am not full of hatred. Perhaps one day I shall be. And that would be a pity because I have a great capacity for being gay.

It is possible that this does not read wittily, the reply to which is that if it did I should fear for it on the stage. Oliver's

lines are written for an actor who can act, and Mr. Godfrey
delivers them superbly. Marigold has little to say, but there
is a world of meaning in Miss Morris's: " They were the
Ivenses of Buxton ! " For it is the folds of Marigold's cheeks
and the flounces of her preposterous dress which make you
realise that the Ivenses, whether of Buxton or not, were
never, in point of fact, anybody. Now and again Mr. Ackland permits himself to be a little serious, and Clive has
this excellent passage:

> " Why is looking forward such a necessary thing ? I'll
> tell you why. It's a law of nature so that one shan't look
> too far forward. ' Something to look forward to ' is some-
> thing for one's mind to stop at, like a wall in time, between
> oneself and death and the rest of the unpleasant things
> lying in wait. When the wall is reached, one passes through
> it. And then quickly—so as to shut out any glimpse of the
> journey's end—up goes another wall. And I think one
> continues putting them up until one's dying day. Even
> very old people, I'm sure, erect little walls between them-
> selves and death, even if the walls are merely to-morrow's
> dinner or the visit of a grandchild."

But—says the reader—can I be certain of enjoying a play,
however well written, in which nothing happens ? The
answer is that it entirely depends upon what kind of playgoer the reader is. If he is the kind which refrains from visiting a play until he is bidden by the Board of Agriculture
and Fisheries or the Port of London Authority, I should
think that he may spend a very dull evening. If he has one
grain of playgoing sense to rub against another, he will be,
I venture to think, entranced. I was spellbound throughout
by a piece which it is nevertheless important not to rate too
highly; I should place it exactly half way between *Call It*

A Day and *Uncle Vanya*. It is dazzlingly acted; and flibberti-gibbet though Rhoda has been and still is, it is Miss Clare who plays luminous centre to the galaxy.

Everybody by this time knows the joke on which *Three Men on a Horse* is built. It is not a very good joke, and consists merely in the notion that an innocent with an unexplained prescience as to the day's racing results might be profitably exploited by a gang of crooks. No other point is made throughout the entire play, everything that is said and done springing from and being an elaboration of this idea. And now a personal anecdote must be permitted. I was entertained at luncheon the other day by two extremely distinguished pantomime-dames, one of whom is entirely made up of the milk of human generosity, while the other is a stickler for truth. The first was gallantly explaining away the failure of a certain comedian by saying that he had a bad part. Whereupon his friend replied: " Rot ! In pantomime the part is always as good as the comedian ! " Something of the sort is true of this play, which must always be as good or as bad as its actors. It lives and scores triumphantly by virtue of the performances of Mr. Romney Brent as the innocent and of Messrs. Bernard Nedell, Edmond Ryan, and David Burns as the three crooks. These are like the creepy-crawlies under a large flat stone, and I should guess it to be the largest and flattest stone in America. In league with the creepy-crawlies and future wife to one of them is a sweetie, wittily played by Miss Claire Carleton. Mr. Alex Yokel's direction of the piece is swift and sure, and the speed is tremendous, the jokes and laughs treading so hard on each other's heels that the resulting situation could only be described in terms of algebra, becoming more and more complicated as the evening wears on.

JANE IN THE THEATRE

PRIDE AND PREJUDICE. A play by Helen Jerome, from the
novel by Jane Austen. St. James's Theatre, Thursday,
February 27, 1936.

PROMISE. A play by Henry Bernstein; English adaptation
by H. M. Harwood. Shaftesbury Theatre, Wednesday,
February 26, 1936.

THE LADY FROM THE SEA. Revival of Ibsen's Play; translation by Isabelle M. Pagan. Playhouse Theatre, Monday
afternoon, February 24, 1936.   [*March* 1, 1936]

> Playgoers are not by nature readers. It is safe to say that the
> majority of a theatrical audience will not have read the novel.
> —A. B. WALKLEY.

BUT SURELY, O lamented shade, you were not thinking
of the audience at the St. James's Theatre ? The play you
were criticising was a dramatisation of *If Winter Comes*, which
not even its best admirers would place in the same category
with *Pride and Prejudice*. Nor perhaps should we assign such
a dramatisation to that stage on which Henry James made
his high but fatal bid. At this point I hear a sardonic chuckle
from the Reader Who Lies In Wait. But this time he has
waited in vain. I am aware that the title of the Great Circum-
locutionist's failure was *Guy Domville*, that *The High Bid*
happened at His Majesty's, and that the theatre at which
If Winter Comes was produced was, in fact, the St. James's !
Having landed ourselves in a mess, let us begin again. It

would be much safer to say, O Walkley, that he who dramatises a great work, be it *Pride and Prejudice*, *Madame Bovary*, or even *The Diary of a Nobody*, must proceed on the assumption that his audience does not know the book, though suspecting that it may have it by heart. In the case of the ignorant the rule needs only to be stated; when it is broken the knowing will be the first to perceive that the theatrical tub has lost the bottom on which it should be standing. Austen, Flaubert, Grossmith, and every other author, or their dramatisers, must in the theatre prove their case all over again. For my part, O great and mighty one, I shall assume that the audience at the St. James's on Thursday last had never read or had forgotten your essay entitled " Jane on the Stage."

Re-reading your essay when I got home after the play, I found myself wondering to what extent Miss Helen Jerome had read and remembered you. How else could she have miraculously done those things which you said one in her position ought to have done, and left undone those things she ought not to have done ? You complained that in Mr. and Mrs. Squire's version Mary Bennet's sententious commonplaces, so delicious in the book, went for nothing, and that her original *value* had been lost. Miss Jerome avoids this charge by losing Mary, who does not appear at all. You said that Lady Catherine de Bourgh was left without any preparation for the great dialogue with Elizabeth: " We lost the full bitterness of her defeat abroad because we knew nothing of her magnificence at home." Darcy, you told us, suffered because, since we were not taken to Hunsford, he had to do his wooing anywhere handy. Here Miss Jerome has killed two birds with one stone and the most beautiful skill, since she gives us a breath of Rosings and makes Lady Catherine invite Elizabeth and Darcy to stay with her, thus allowing to both the place and the breathing time of day in which to deploy themselves. This will annoy the Janeites, who will pretend that to confer upon Elizabeth the honour of a visit instead of that of a mere dinner is out of Lady Catherine's character. *Cela se peut*, and you, my dear A. B. W., will not ask that I should translate that !

Janeites will also complain that Elizabeth does not read Darcy's famous letter, either aloud or to herself, while we sit still throughout its six pages. Super-Janeites, indeed, or sticklers for the whole novel, will insist that Elizabeth reads, and we sit still, *twice*. The answer to the sticklers is that they must stay at home and be content to read the book, for the essence of stage-adaptation is transposition, and of good adaptation the smallest possible amount of transposition. In a word, if I may be allowed to call this great novel a reader's *sanctum sanctorum*, then the playgoer must be satisfied if the stage version amounts to a *sanctum*. Everybody must think that the present production amounts to this, and one wishes, *cher maître*, that you had been there to see it. And not only to see it, but to write about it. You would certainly have condoned the restoration of the Wickhams to favour, which besides being a theatrical tidying-up is a concession to the sentimental playgoer insisting that not only the mousey-pouseys but the roguey-pogueys will live on happily after the curtain has come down.

You would also, had you written again about this novel turned play, have developed a subject which, a column being no more than a column, you had to condense into a paragraph. You were outlining a disability attaching to this novel and not to, say, *Madame Bovary*. In Flaubert's work we see the characters objectively and through Flaubert's eyes; in Jane Austen's masterpiece we see everything and everybody through the eyes of Elizabeth Bennet. She is, as you say, " in the novel, and at the same time over it, for it is through her eyes that we see the other people, and her feelings about them that we share." In the theatre this disappears, and with it goes also the essential quality of the book. We still see Jane Austen's facts, but we no longer see them, as Jane Austen presented them, at one delicious remove. Given this invalidation, which must apply to all stage-versions of this story, it is hard to see how the play could have been better produced, better cast, or, with a minimum of exceptions, better acted.

Since each of us has his own mental pictures of these life-long friends, allowance must be made for individual preferences. (Let me interpolate here that no two opinions can be permissible about the justness and beauty of Mr. Rex Whistler's scenes and dresses.) Is Miss Celia Johnson too young a twenty, and would one like her a little staider of aspect? But then in an actress older and staider one might not get those eyes in which Mr. Bennet so clearly read the magnanimity of his " little Lizzie." In any case *that* quality is present in Miss Johnson's Elizabeth, together with the courage, the vivacity, and the common-sense. There was not a moment in the evening when I did not endorse Stevenson's: " Elizabeth Bennet has but to speak, and I am at her knees." But since everybody in the house was prostrated by the sheer loveliness of Miss Dorothy Hyson's Jane, even when she didn't speak, it was a grovelling evening! Resuming the erect position, one would opine that this planet will never see a better Mr. Bennet than Mr. Athole Stewart's, that Mr. John Teed was chivalrous as Bingley, and that Mr. Hugh Williams was unimaginably good as Mr. Darcy.

But the production abounds in good performances, and I can only just mention those of Messrs. Anthony Quayle and Deering Wells, Mesdames Viola Lyel, Leueen Mac-Grath, Margaret Emden, Gertrude Sterroll, and Joan Harben. Mrs. Bennet is an awful problem; a passive bore in the book, on the stage she can hardly avoid being an active one. I shall not say that my beloved Miss Barbara Everest gives a harassing performance till I have seen some actress give an unharassing one and remain Mrs. Bennet. But I think I should have cast Mr. Collins differently; I cannot agree with Mr. Lyonel Watts's cheerful interpretation, and in the mind's eye see here the black and oily exudations of Mr. Alistair Sim. I must choose some other occasion, too, for championing Miss Eva Moore, who appears to mistake Lady Catherine for Boadicea. In any case I implore her to join her flats and make it less obvious where that Roman nose begins.

Let me now dispose of M. Bernstein's play, which is a very adroit theatrical battlepiece on the subject, one is led to suppose, of being on with the new love before you are off with the old. Pretty thin material for a whole evening ? The reader who asks this has forgotten Balzac's *Le Contrat de Mariage*, in which the contract is nearly as long as the marriage ! In this piece M. Bernstein returns to the hammer-and-tongs school of French *drame*, where, some matter being in debate, the opponents fight it out with the persistence and reiteration of champions at table-tennis. Its one trace of modernity consists in a certain subtlety whereby while the drama is ostensibly concerned with the young people's mismanagement of their love-affairs, actually it centres in the mess made of married lives by their elders. The real interest of the evening consists in the war of styles magnificently waged by Miss Edna Best and Miss Madge Titheradge, doughty and respective champions of the quietist and the rampageous schools of acting. Miss Best is our finest exponent of what I should like to call back-bedroom martyrdom. With her Tessa in Miss Kennedy's play she became first in this country in what Keats so nearly called the *attic* breed of maidens overwrought, nymphs constant to a state partaking equally of glumness and spirituality.

When Duse first brought over the new style the highbrows cottoned on to it like anything. A leading English critic said that " acting can imitate only external things, gestures, accents, and looks. What makes it an art is the spirit that informs it, and is expressed through it." And a lot more about the actor who, attempting to express what is not in his own spirit, ceases to be an artist and becomes what the Greeks called a hypocrite, or one who presents effects divorced from causes. Duse, according to this critic, was not an old-fashioned actress but the new artist expressing her own soul. Another great critic said that Action, with Duse as with Rimbaud, " was a way of spoiling something." Of all this I should imagine that Miss Titheradge knows nothing. This magnificent technician would, I imagine, hold that a leading lady earned her money too easily by just walking on to the stage, pulling up the blinds of her soul, and doing nothing more about it except let the audience gaze. Miss Titheradge belongs to a school of acting which dates back as far as *Hamlet*, whose First Gravedigger insisted that an act hath three branches: to act, to do, and to perform. Whence it follows that an actor may be defined as a doer and a performer, not as a sitter and a be-er. There was never a minute on Wednesday night last when Miss Titheradge was not bringing off some bravura passage or other. She was the soloist of the concerto, and if the performance had a fault it was the inescapable one of too much brilliance, inescapable because the composer had willed it so.

Now comes a point not always too clearly perceived. Either you are a Duse or a Bernhardt; either you sit still and are, or move about and pretend. Neither actress can get away from her temperament and personality, and there is no more merit in belonging to the one kind than to the other. But I do suggest that to be a Duse takes a great deal less out of the actress than to be a Bernhardt. Moping—

ineffably, if you like, but still moping—can be done while
the actress is calculating her income-tax, whereas I defy
anybody to bring off simultaneously mental arithmetic and
any of the great tirades in *Phèdre*. Earlier on I gave a musical
illustration which shall be repeated here to clinch the
matter. The difference in difficulty between our two schools
is the difference between the first and the last movements of
the Moonlight Sonata. I will undertake to play the first
movement so nearly well that you will merely think a great
pianist is sickening for influenza. Whereas if I attempted
the last you would think that the great pianist had broken
all his fingers and sprained both wrists. That was the thing
to say, and it is said ! Mr. Ralph Richardson gave a lovely
and moving performance of an elderly husband. Or, rather,
it would have been lovely and moving had he not played
throughout like a pianist attacking the first bar of the
Moonlight Sonata knowing he had forgotten the second
and gaining time to think. The whole of this performance
was that first movement with the Funeral March from the
Opus 26 Sonata thrown in !

What was the tale the Colonel told the Adjutant ? Why, in
Ellida Wangel's story, did the second mate murder the captain in his cabin ? Why did Ibsen call his play *The Lady from
the Sea* when *The Gentleman from the Sea* was so much more
obvious a title ? Can there be anything less superficially
appetising than Ibsen's favourite outdoor set, a cromlech on
the top of a mountain ? Is not little Hilda Wangel the
nastiest piece of goods in the history of the ingénue ? Is she
not the equivalent of the bright young thing of Mrs. Lynn
Linton's period ? Did Ibsen when he first planned the play
round about 1884 foresee *The Master Builder* of 1892 ? Or is
the later Hilda just about the most skilful picking up of an
old thread that has ever happened ? Should this piece be
brought up to date by people wearing zip-fasteners and

looking at wrist-watches? Didn't Mr. Shaw bring Ellida, wobbling between Husband and Stranger, up to date when he made Candida say: "That's a good bid, Eugene!"? Why in *The Quintessence of Ibsenism* does he give this play the least space? Did the play, even when it was first produced, seem a compelling one? Has it lost much of its compulsion now that we know it to be part of the old Ibsen formula? Is it true that if you knock the chains off a prisoner he won't want to run away? Does this play want a Duse, and did we terribly care whether Miss Flora Robson's Ellida stopped at home with her husband, or ran away to sea with the Stranger, and ultimately settled down as pier-mistress at some Nordic Clacton? Can it be denied that Mr. Nicholas Hannen did very well with the spineless Wangel? Did not Miss Patricia Hayes as Hilda put up a clever performance? And who gave that ingenious young actor, Mr. Valentine Rooke, the wicked notion of presenting Ballested as the red-headed Corno di Bassetto of the 'nineties? I have, alas, no space in which to answer any of these questions.

A PLEA FOR A PLAY

RED NIGHT. A play by James Lansdale Hodson. Queen's Theatre, Wednesday, March 4, 1936.

DUSTY ERMINE. A play by Neil Grant. Comedy Theatre, Friday, March 6, 1936.

CHILDREN TO BLESS YOU ! A comedy by G. Sheila Donisthorpe. Ambassadors Theatre, Tuesday, March 3, 1936.
[*March* 8, 1936]

The Devil whispered behind the leaves, " It's pretty, but is it Art ? "
—RUDYARD KIPLING.

" IT'S UGLY, BUT IS IT ART ? " murmurs the highbrow behind his programme. There are, at the simplest, two kinds of modern war play. The first is a representation of the Great War as the soldiers who took part in it knew and remembered it, and the highbrow is perfectly within his rights who says: " I do not like this kind of war play, which neither moves nor excites nor amuses me." But he is not entitled to say: " This is a bad play because it does not belong to the kind of war play which I prefer." In such a case a critic's duty is simply to determine whether the play is good or bad in its kind. The other war play is the kind of thing Euripides turned out a thousand mythical years after a mythical war, or that Shakespeare turned out some two hundred years after Agincourt. This is the semi-poetical drama which Mr. Drinkwater is liable to produce at any moment, and that has been

turned out by Reginald Berkeley in *The White Château*, or
at least in the blank verse interludes thereof, by Mr. O'Casey
in the second act of *The Silver Tassie*, M. Paul Raynal in
The Unknown Warrior, and M. Obey in *Bataille de la Marne*.
Awe-inspiring, edifying, but, it will not be disputed, lacking
in that entertainment value for which ninety-nine out of
every hundred people go to the theatre. Nor will it be main-
tained that such plays give a realistic picture of the war as
the participators recall it, for it is not in my recollection
that the Trojan Women were Amazons, or that Dame Sybil
Thorndike, girding on her armour, leaped on to a warhorse
and with a ringing: " By the right, charge ! " bade troopers
follow her.

De minimis non curat high poetic war-drama, and I find
that about Mr. O'Casey's second act I wrote: " The whole
mind of the soldier under stress of war is not represented by
complaints about conditions and girdings at staff-officers."
An eminent colleague has written of *Red Night* that " its
pacific argument has the quality not of spiritual indignation
but of a long and grumbling discontent." I agree as to the
statement of fact. But I submit that the business of this kind
of play is to be vocal about the grumbling and shut up about
the spiritual indignation. *Red Night* is full of the soldiers
of 1914 as we remember them. It does in the theatre
what the painters of the Imperial War Museum did in their
cartoons. These gave you the facts, the bodies hanging on
the wire, the appearance of men ten days dead. They left
it to the spectator to conjure up his own spiritual indignation, and I submit that Mr. Hodson's work does the same.
In support of this I will adduce the fact that this play rings
true everywhere except in those passages in which the author
allows the implicit spiritual indignation to become explicit.
I just don't believe Private Hardcastle when, in discussing
the five-hours-old death of a comrade, he quotes to Private

Whitman the Omar quatrain beginning: " For some we loved, the loveliest and the best." Nor in the previous scene do I believe Hardcastle when, invited to give a toast in the estaminet, he says: " To those who died that we might live ! " There is a moment in this estaminet scene which might be made highly significant and is not. The man who is to die within five hours has started playing the piano— one of those Schumann Romances whose direct sentiment can move even the simplest. Strike up " The Long, Long Trail " or the Londonderry Air, and even the rowdiest canteen will abate its noise. In the present play the rapt expression of the soldiers' faces does very well until the melody reaches its development stage, when it is incontestable that actual soldiers would start shuffling their feet: only a minimum of what musicians fancy does them good ! The same, I suggest, applies to poets.

One is wrongly staggered twice in this play. Once is when Whitman says: " When spring comes the larks'll sing fit to burst their throats and the flowers and leaves'll come breaking through—just as if Nature were laughing at us." And again when the Cockney Summers says: " Nah, nah, you two stop at 'ome. This is a blinkin' workin' party, not a poets' corner. 'Ad enough o' you on that wirin' party when you did nothin' but argufy about Keats's ode to a bleedin' nightingale." No, reader, it is not the word " bleedin' " which shocks ! It is Mr. Hodson's odd notion that even privates from Oxford University would argue about Keats when on a wiring-party. Mr. Edmund Blunden has told us about reading poetry *behind the line*. Mr. Sherriff went as far as he safely could when he made Lieutenant Osborne pull a book out of his pocket after he had been warned for a raid; with the finest tact he arranged for that book to be *Alice in Wonderland*. No, Mr. Hodson fails whenever he departs from strict realism, just as in *The Conquering Hero*, that war play after the highbrow heart, Allan Monkhouse failed whenever he departed from spirituality. No man who is not a Shakespeare can get into the same play blunt Private Williams and that spirituality-monger, Henry.

On the other hand, there are moments when one is staggered by the extraordinary verisimilitude of the scene and the characters. I include the aspect of the trenches which, to one who was never in them, seem startlingly real, down to the nasty half-light and the feeling of an air strict and cold. Mr. Malleson has produced very well throughout, and the cast has been finely chosen. There is Mr. John Mills, whose Cockney sparrow is a remarkable study of Cockaigne. See him dictate a letter home, his cheeks blowing and his brow pale with unusual cerebration. As he paces the room his mind is a whirling chaos, determined only on three things—his *panache* as a soldier, his affection for his missus, and his defiance of that scrimshanker and lead-swinging philanderer, Alf Mottershead. This is the best acting in the play, though it is run pretty close by Mr. James Gibson's wee Scottie, a character antipathetic at the start but growing on you, and by Mr. George Carney's Hollinwood, the slow-moving, bullock-brained giant from Lancashire.

The quartet is completed by the Private Hardcastle of Mr. Robert Donat, to whom all honour is due for putting on this good play with a part for himself which he must know to be a poor one. Poor because actorish, and because that actorishness and insistence upon false values which are enjoined upon Mr. Donat just can't live with the photographic realism of his colleagues. Hardcastle does what Mr. Charles Morgan wants, but how poorly ! Mr. Bernard Lee, who plays Whitman and has exactly the same difficulties to face as Mr. Donat, comes out of them better, first because he is not so glamorous an actor, and second because he does not orate. Mr. Hodson has gallantly refused to break an

unwritten law of the theatre, which is that hearts shall not
be needlessly wrung. To kill off the cocksparrow Summe:
would be unbearable. But since to save more than two is to
overstretch the law, and McTaggart is also to live, the
ponderous Hollinwood, the trio's Porthos, must die. We
accept this. Conversely, we are not at all affected by the
holocaust of mouthers and speechifiers. As the proprietress
of the estaminet Miss Hélène Lara does very well in a short
grief-stricken scene; she waters the *vin rouge* with liberal
tears, an accomplishment which actresses unable to cry on
the stage tell me is a mean one. Like Sam Weller, these scorn
the action; but Miss Lara does not, and she sets the play
firmly in France. In conclusion, it only remains to say that
I came as near as manliness permits to dropping a few tears
of my own, and for the rest of the evening held my sides with
laughing. And I utterly decline to say that a play which
does these things is bad. *The Trojan Women*, when last I saw
it, did only one of them ! Let me plead for *Red Night*. If it
fails through lack of public support, I shall still be glad to have
seen it, and shall remember it. But it must not fail. The
public has only to see it to like it almost as much as *Journey's
End*, to which in some respects it is superior. If this play
fails, I see no reason why any film star should ever again
revert to the intelligent theatre. Readers of the *Sunday Times*,
it is up to you !

No plea is put forward for *Dusty Ermine*, which cannot fail.
Why cannot it fail ? Because it is utterly untrue to anything
in the heaven above, the earth beneath, or even in the water
under the earth. No fish would look at a plot as fishy as this
one. Walter Kent, a K.C. and descendant of a line of judges,
has a forger for a brother. But he has also a daughter and
a son. The daughter, wanting to be an opera-singer, raises
£2,000 from a married but undivorceable admirer, trots off
with him to Paris, carries out the minimum of her bargain,

and returns to Kensington's bosom without question asked. Later on this semi-yielding peach becomes the prickly pine-apple of morality. For her brother is also a forger, who has inherited his uncle's talent and while pretending to be a barrister sits in a back bedroom at his father's house forging away nineteen to the dozen. And again no question asked, except by the police. Whereupon Uncle Kent takes the blame on himself and goes to prison again. Wherefurtherupon Miss Kent, babbling of honour's green fields, proposes to hand brother Gilbert over to the police. But the boy poisons himself and the curtain comes down on the K.C. saying nothing whatever, which he has done throughout the play, and Miss Kent, who has by now become a prima donna, presumably wondering whether the B.B.C. who have taken to employing her are quite going to like this sort of thing.

Fortunately Mr. Grant has an eye for character and a knack of dialogue which enables him to put over what from another angle might be deemed a superb novelette. Mr. David Horne is excellent as the convict who appears to look upon stretches in the way in which Jack Worthing looked upon christenings—having stood one he can stand another. The part, *plus théâtral que le théâtre*, would be a gift to any-body, and Mr. Horne does not waste it. Miss Merle Totten-ham as a maidservant gives her usual gem. Mr. Frederick Piper's detective fills the house with a gloomy joy, and Mr. A. R. Whatmore is the saving background to everything and everybody. When this actor's spectacles come in at the door playwriting absurdity flies out at the window. Bung, too, in the middle of all this nonsense is a first-rate character out of a Priestley play, the uncomfortable daughter-in-law Janet, played by Miss Rosalind Atkinson with a breath-taking realism. This part devastates by contrast that of Miss Kent, through whose stilted evolutions Miss Leonora Corbett walks on the highest of heels. Mr. William Fox does everything
RN

possible with young Gilbert. But why, Mr. Grant, do you not avoid that name of all names ? Throughout the evening another shade hovers in the background, and we think how tunefully he would have set a libretto whose opening song could only be: " When the gentlemanly forger goes a-forging." While all this is going on Mr. Douglas Jefferies and Miss Winifred Evans, being given nothing to do as the parents, turn sorrowfully away and present us with their sobbing shoulder-blades. I predict that this play will run for red night after red night. The suburbs will flock to it, the provinces run special trains, and the red glare of Panton Street rouse the burghers of Carlisle.

The proper title of *Children to Bless You !* is *Spare the Rod*. It was all very well for Mrs. Lawrence to sink on to a sofa at the end and declare that she would never desert her second born who had just had a kettle of hot water spilled over him by a bit of foreign fluff. She should have prevented him from getting into hot water earlier on ! It was the same with all the children. Her eldest born embezzled. Her elder daughter painted her nails scarlet in the intervals of a little polite sinning. Her younger daughter was a noisy, screeching gawk. Really it is no good Mrs. Lawrence pretending to be a long-suffering progenitress of what a Victorian poet described as " clambering limbs and little hearts that err." She should have done a little clambering with the birch-rod. It is all very well when this sort of thing is done with wit and invention and credibility, as Mr. Rodney Ackland did it in *After October*. It is another pair of shoes when the intrigue turns on a much-divorced aunt who has an affair with the elder daughter's young man. This makes everything quite incredible. But then, Mr. Sydney Carroll may be right in his judgment. It may be that the public doesn't like wit, invention, and credibility, and will flock to something which is unwitty, uninventive, and incredible.

The casting is excellent. For an actress of accomplishment, to play Mrs. Lawrence is easier than falling off a sofa; Miss Mary Jerrold is an actress of great accomplishment who could not fall off a sofa if she tried. Miss Irene Browne, whisking her way through the piece as the aunt, and knowing herself to have an unbelievable part, exhibits that quickness which deceives the eye and makes you think she is not there. At least, the artist hopes and we hasten to believe. One thing shall be said to the credit of the uncouth cubs and gauche brownies of this play—that their enactors and enactresses at least abound in gracelessness. But do the young ladies abound too much? And do the young gentlemen, careless of the " a," devote themselves a trifle too wholeheartedly to bounding *tout court*?

AN EASTER GARLAND

THE HAPPY HYPOCRITE. A play by Clemence Dane and
Richard Addinsell. Based on Max Beerbohm's Story. His
Majesty's Theatre, Wednesday, April 8, 1936.

[*April* 12, 1936]

> For this is the happy ending dearest to the lover of the
> " wholesome " play—that known causes should not have their
> known effects; above all, that in last acts any leopards which
> gain the playgoer's regard should be left rigged out in snowy,
> curly lamb's-wool, and nice Ethiopians go off at the end as
> blonds with straight, tow-coloured hair.
>
> —C. E. MONTAGUE.

> No artist has ethical sympathies. An ethical sympathy in an
> artist is an unpardonable mannerism of style.
>
> —OSCAR WILDE.

OF LORD GEORGE HELL Mr. Beerbohm writes that
" many persons were inobnoxious to the magic of his title."
The lay mind will want to know the significance of the prefix
" in " ; one had left school many years before one realised that
" invaluable" did not mean " of no value." The point can only
be resolved by consulting (*a*) any dictionary, and (*b*) our
author's preciosity. " Obnoxious " can, my dictionary tells
me, be held to mean that which the public normally takes it
to mean. But to use the word as a synonym for " odious " or
" offensive " is to use it in a plebeian eggs-and-bacon sense ;
there is the higher Baconian sense of " subject " or " amen-
able." The writings of precious artists, like those of Bacon's

lawyers, are " tied and obnoxious to their particular laws."
The magic of Mr. Beerbohm's style is inobnoxious, that is to
say, unamenable to ostentation or display except in the
jewel-case sense. Long, when she contemplated adapting
this jewelled fairy-tale to the grandiosities essential to
popular entertainment in a large theatre, must Miss Dane
have pondered this. Can a drop-earring be pantographed
to chandelier-size without loss of exquisiteness? A man
might, if he were of a fearful heart, have staggered in this
attempt; Miss Dane's femininity has saved her. She has done
beautifully, and this is largely the result of having gone to
work something gingerly. Gingerly because Miss Dane, beyond transferring them from one medium to the other, has
laid no finger upon this play's Mortals. Or only a little
finger, and alas it is a mistaken one? This adapter should
have left Beau Brummell in the essay on Dandies; he is too
big for her present world. It is true that to eke out the evening she has added a couple of Immortals; but when it comes
to trafficking with Amor and Mercury it may be that Jill is as
good as her master. Purists may not approve of the addition,
and one or two were heard on Wednesday night to say that
perfection could only have been attained by dancing the
whole thing in the Russian manner, even at the sacrifice of
words. The question is a vexed and a vexatious one, and
some other opportunity must be found to discuss whether to
add or take from a masterpiece is the more noxious to it.

There are five scenes. The first shows Carlton House and
its habitués living up to the maxim propounded by Mr.
Burke that " Vice by losing all its grossness loses half its
evil." Habitués who, quarrelling over a pinch of snuff offered
and refused, know all that chastity of honour which, to
reverse another of Mr. Burke's sayings, feels a wound like
a stain. The second scene shows Garble's open-air theatre
and George Hell falling in love with Jenny Mere for the same

reason that Bunthorne fell in love with Patience: " The bitter-hearted one, who finds all else hollow, is pleased with thee ! " Straightway Hell begins to dream of Heaven, but it is not till the next scene, that of Mr. Æneas's shop in Bond Street, that the wicked nobleman discovers more innocent virtue in himself than the casual spectator has imagined. This is probably the best scene in the play, though the one which most delights the eye is the Motleys' setting for the wood in Kensington. This and the last scene, the garden of the cottage inhabited by the now happy pair, are the essence of decorative wit. The play by this time is moving as leisurely as the setting sun, and we do not want it to go faster; the pace gives the mind room for little rambles of its own, and when Jenny is asking her husband whether he will celebrate the mensiversary of their wedding with honey, little strawberries, and brown bread or with yellow raspberries, honey, and bread, it has leisure to reflect that even so simple a thing as rusticity is not so simple as to be of one kind only. It is another author's Lord Henry who, eyeing the gleam of a laburnum's honey-sweet and honey-coloured blossoms, remarks that " even the cardinal virtues cannot atone for half-cold entrées." The difference is that between the Doric and the Dorian lay. In the fresh wood and in the new pasture of these last two scenes the Motleys, rising to the height of fancy, have given Nature a mantle of delicious blues, tender greens, and quite impertinent pinks. The very air is wine-coloured, an emanation from Jenny's dewberry concoction.

The tale is as well told as it is set. Is it true ? No. Can leopards change their spots and Ethiops bleach ? No. Has rake ever reformed ? I remember no instance. Has any man, naughty or nice, at the height of his fame, plucked from the garish scene some new-kindled artist and with her sought alps and sanctuaries ? *Je ne me rappelle pas.* Nobody, as a sterner playwright has remarked, does such things ! But the point is that nobody writes them so well as Mr. Beerbohm. The only fly in the ointment is the musical one. Mr. Chesterton once told us of a great modern composer that he is a humbug who cannot even hum. Mr. Addinsell is in the same case, but for the opposite reason; he is too sincere and too serious a musician to permit himself the light intoxication that should accompany this book. His orchestration is exquisite, but the harp that Tara-lirra sings is a melancholy one, and in his hands Jubal's lyre jubilates but scantily. I think I never heard a glummer tune than that which brings down the first-act curtain, and lilt is something with which Mr. Addinsell would seem to be unacquainted. There were two ways of doing this score. One was to distil from the early nineteenth-century tale that sparkle which a Richard Strauss would impose upon a late eighteenth; Mr. Herbert Menges and Mr. Walter Leigh are both practised hands at this sort of thing, and there are others. Mr. William Walton, for example, could have done the thing extremely well in the *Façade* manner. Another way would have been to dig up Cimarosa or somebody. Better be gay before the event than sad after it. Mr. Addinsell's score, though clever, is in the lugubrious vein of his song in *The Good Companions*; it does not turn the corner.

The piece is extremely well acted. Mr. Ivor Novello plays Lord George Hell with great sincerity. His make-up for the first act is very effective and exactly strikes the note of " Caligula with a dash of Sir John Falstaff." He acts all the later part of the play with a disarming simplicity; to have such a profile and pretend not to know it would write him down an artist of little sensibility; it is a delightful performance throughout. Mr. Charles Lefeaux, condemned to a part which we wish away, speaks Brummell's lines with a rare clarity; it is a pity that all our stage dandies have not his bravery of speech. Mr. William Dewhurst's Garble is admirable, and very nearly the best performance is given by Mr. Stafford Hilliard as Mr. Æneas the mask-maker. Here, again, is English as it ought to be spoken, with a good sense of the value of good words. Not over-value, for Mr. Hilliard does not over-act. The Immortals of Mr. Marius Goring and Mr. Carl Harbord are witty and decorative, though if any of the gods had sung as one of them does I feel sure he would have been sent to Vulcan's smithy with instructions to mend his bellows. Miss Vivien Leigh as Jenny might have stepped out of a poem by Tom Moore. She is artless without artifice, and no simper mars this freshness and this charm. Miss Isabel Jeans's Gambogi is a fine piece of mockery and vengeful lustre; this clever player rightly permits herself one moment of feeling, the moment when La Gambogi tears off the hypocrite's mask and sees the same beauty beneath. Her admonition to Amor not to shoot since she is hurt already is well in our story-teller's vein, and one of Miss Dane's most ingenious additions. It will be interesting to see what reception awaits this production which, in my view, the non-musical may rate too highly and the musical not highly enough. In any case the authors and the management are to be thanked for making London so charming an Easter gift. It is seemly at this season not to be indoniferous. May the town prove not inobnoxious !

SERMONS IN SHIPS

BEES ON THE BOAT DECK. A farcical tragedy by J. B. Priestley. Lyric Theatre, Tuesday, May 5, 1936.

AH, WILDERNESS ! A comedy by Eugene O'Neill. Westminster Theatre, Monday, May 4, 1936.

RISE AND SHINE. A musical comedy. Drury Lane Theatre, Thursday, May 7, 1936.

[*May* 10, 1936]

THE ONLY DRAMATIC CRITIC of modern times who could have done justice to *Bees on the Boat Deck* was William Archer, and for two reasons. To Archer, being a Scot, a joke was a joke, and as such to be respected whether it was good or bad. And then there was his extraordinary fairness, and I desire above all things to be fair to Mr. Priestley. Oddly enough, while unwilling to wound I am not afraid to strike, and to do away with any notion of sycophancy or kow-towing I shall say straight out that I have never been so bored by a man of brains since Mr. Shaw's last political skiff went on the rocks. Now for some fairness, beginning with a story of Arnold Bennett. I once sent a book to Bennett with the inscription: " Because we both love the theatre." Quick came the tart reply: " You are wrong. I do not love the theatre ! " Yet he could not keep away from it, or stop writing for it. The same thing applies to Mr. Priestley who, in my opinion, is the most ill-used playwright in this

country. I never saw an egg with so much meat in it as
Dangerous Corner had of ingenuity and theatre-sense. *Eden End*
was a lovely play which set all the parrots in town squawk-
ing " Tchehov ! " as though the Russian had a monopoly of
the autumn of life and its mellow unfruitfulness. Neither play
had the success it deserved. Mr. Priestley took these comparative failures with comparative philosophy, was not un-
duly elated by the success of the pot-boiling little *Laburnum
Grove*, or cast down by the failure of *Cornelius*, a play rather
like a golf round in which there are no bad strokes though
nothing quite comes off.

What has been Mr. Priestley's difficulty ? Simply the old
one of finding some ground on which the play he wants to
write may come to terms with the play the man in the street
wants to see. Our author is not an idealist in the sense of
desiring to write for guilds and groups and movements; he
is a realist who, wanting his plays to make money, retains
sufficient artistic conscience to insist that they shall make
that money worthily. How, Mr. Priestley asks himself, shall
he set about it ? Obviously the first thing is to take a theme
in which most people are interested, but meaning something
better than the kidnapping of a baby or the romance of a
lawn-tennis star. What about this maniac world and the mess
it's getting into ? But everybody's business is nobody's business. So what about this country of ours and all the maniacs
who are driving it to destruction ? There is the Communist
with his red and ruinous tale of a tub. There is the Fascist
drawing a red, Bismarckian herring across the path of sane
progress. There are the peace-proclaiming armament-makers
whose busy factories work overtime like Hell with the lid on
—always, as any amateur Guy Fawkes knows, so much more
dangerous than Hell with the lid off ! Surely, argues Mr.
Priestley, everybody must be interested in a play having to
do with the peril in which we all stand. Never was idea so

mistaken. That beggared outcast, Wilkins Micawber, could still eat walnuts out of a paper bag on the top of the London coach. Whatever the state of national peril, the theatre is still to the individual playgoer his bag of walnuts and his coach; the only difference between Mr. Micawber and the playgoer is that the former is on a day's and the latter on an evening's outing. Mr. Priestley agrees to the extent of having foreseen this and arranged for it. Instead of convoking us to a dismal round-table conference, he has invited us to a party of japes and jinkeries on board a cargo-steamer laid up in an estuary of the River Trim. On board are the care-takers, formerly the ship's chief engineer and second officer, and presently there arrive duly accredited representatives of Communism and Fascism. Represented also are the arma-ment-maker in the person of a destructive scientist, the bloated capitalist, and the modern, unblushing girl. Each of these has his or her reason for wanting to blow up the ship: the Communist because it will be a smack at Capital; the Fascist because the Communist will get the blame; the capitalist to cheat the insurance company; the girl because it is exciting to see anything or anybody sent sky-high. On board also are a representative of the Little Man who takes all his opinions from the newspapers, and a nurse who is the echo and backwash of some lawsuit, unsavoury and un-disclosed.

Well, there is Mr. Priestley's play, and if it fails it is for a variety of reasons. The first reason again has to do with Mr. Micawber, who, we are told, sat on the coach, " the very picture of tranquil enjoyment, smiling at Mrs. Micawber's conversation." From this it is conclusive that whatever Mrs. Micawber was talking about, it was not her spouse's financial position. Similarly, it is to be argued that people in a time of national peril seek the tranquil enjoyment of smiling at subjects other than peril. The play, then, has a basis of

non-entertainment. Again, I find a discrepancy between the
mood and the man. Even if the theme is right this is the
wrong author for it. Mr. Shaw may stand on his head, but
his figure is still Blake-like and the voice that of Isaiah. Mr.
Priestley in the same attitude is less impressive, and between
you and me his scoldings do not amount to very much. The
two things which lend Mr. Shaw, even when inverted, his
peculiar authority are weight and wit; Mr. Priestley's
combination of heavy-handedness and jollity are not quite
the same thing. But a play may wholly fail as symbolism—
and indeed this allegory never really gets off the banks of the
Trim—and yet succeed as a play. Who, except professors and
the thin fondlers of wan beards, has ever cared tuppence
about Ibsen's symbolism? Or thought about it till he has
got home? What fun the best of the old man's plays are,
considered just as plays! Let us apply this test to Mr.
Priestley's tragic farce and ask to what extent, apart from
its underlying meaning, this is good playgoing fun. Here I
am afraid my vote is an adverse one. Where in the chief
engineer and second officer are the Captain Shotover and
Henry Straker, with their blinding wit, that another hand
would have given us? They are just not there, and Mr. Ralph
Richardson and Mr. Laurence Olivier, having nothing to act,
can only cover up poverty with fuss. And how poorly they
do it! Mr. Richardson is no more like a retired seaman than
he is like a retired postman, which is odd in view of his
magnificent naval-officer in *For Services Rendered*. The truth
is that Mr. Richardson's picture of anæmic middle-age is
uninteresting; the man should be both full-blooded and
introspective, and have the Conrad quality which Mr.
Richardson lacks. Mr. Olivier is even less happy, for his
second officer is no second officer at all, but a young gentleman from behind the counter of a bank or stores. That his
Bob Patch should know enough about an anchor to outline

it correctly on his forearm in semblance of a tattoo amazes me exceedingly. On the other hand, staggeringly sufficient performances come from Mr. Raymond Huntley, Mr. Richard Goolden, Mr. Allan Jeayes, and Mr. John Laurie. Miss Kay Hammond, whom normally I find delicious, takes a night off and for the nonce gives a staggeringly insufficient performance.

The conclusion of the whole matter? Simply that Mr. Priestley should go back to the mood of his first plays and write something in which he believes with all his heart and soul and mind. It's no good his trying to treat serious themes lightly. He hasn't the knack of it, any more than he has the knack of unashamed pot-boiling. I am convinced that some day he will write a magnificent, serious play. I do not think he will ever write a frothy comedy that is even approximately good. He is Yorkshire, and I am Lancashire, and frivolity is not in us.

Ah, Wilderness ! is a play of wit and charm about a young man who, taking his Swinburne too literally, finds himself in the position of that poet when confronted with Adah Menken. The limbs of the little Connecticut street-walker may be as melodies yet, but they are melodies to be unsung by him. So back he goes into the forgiving but astringent bosom of his family. There are many touches of fancy in this picture of restricted small-town life in 1906, and if mourning becomes Electra it is indisputable that a certain amount of fun-making becomes Mr. O'Neill. There is no need to see this play, though the playgoer who does see it will enjoy it immensely. It is a welcome change from those morbid masterpieces which have to be seen under the penalty of remaining mum at Bloomsbury parties. But perhaps there is no necessity to see these either, at least for those who do not enjoy the parties ! There is certainly an obligation upon all who have the theatre at heart to view the extremely good

acting put up by the Dublin Gate Theatre company. Mr.
Cyril Cusack as the boy plays extremely well, Mr. Harry
Hutchinson is in his most brilliant form, and I have sworn
never again to visit any play in which Miss Ann Penhallow
appears. For I cannot bring myself to imagine that after her
grand performance as the mother in this play she would not
tragically disappoint me.

The Drury Lane curtain rose and the audience shone. All
those shining lights which had frowned on *Cavalcade* were
there to smile on a show crammed with all that wit, story-
telling, sentiment, excitement, and sense of the present which
Mr. Coward's piece so notoriously lacked. Here was no
morbid return to the past, no maudlin echo of South Africa
and Northern France; here was no sordid railway station
with stretchers and stretcher-bearers, but a nice, new,
luxury affair. " Cows flash past the window " has written
another master. Here the station flashed past the train,
alleging motion. Cunning past man's thought !

Presently we attended a banquet, at which a ballerina
pirouetted on the very spot on which so many Macbeths have
been rooted to earth. At the end of the scene an autogiro
took some three minutes to rise some five feet, whether under
its own power or not I am unable to say, while Orion and the
Great Bear tumbled the skies at the rate of millions of miles
a second. One remembers seeing this sort of thing when one
was eight ! Being a Song and Dance show, there was no plot,
and such words as I heard held, for me, neither sense nor
sensibility. The acting ? Not wanted. Singing ? Uncalled for
in the sense of that art as I remember it. Dancing ? Yes, there
was plenty of what, I believe, is to-day's version of that once
graceful art. Mr. Jack Whiting, bending himself double, kept
himself from falling on his nose by waving hat, stick, and
coat tails aloft in the air behind him on the approved
autogiro principle. In way of relief, Miss Binnie Hale graced

the proceedings with her lovely presence, and now and again even condescended to take part in them. There is an exquisite cold glow upon this charming artist, setting her apart as though she were one of Hans Andersen's snow-maidens.

The rest was glamour, solid, expensive, " regardless " glamour. The kind of glamour which makes any Drury Lane show so much better than others equally good. Was it funny ? Not so that I personally noticed it. Nor yet, perhaps, so that anybody noticed it. For your smart Drury Lane audience has this in common with the gentleman in Matthew Prior's poem —it holds wit to be the bane of conversation. And laughs like anything to hear such quantities of whatever in these orgies takes the place of wit. The dresses are extremely handsome and the rowdy, luscious, and familiar tunes have been orchestrated much beyond their deserts. Alas ! that my ear refuses to take in more than a limited quantity of these subnormal racketings, however skilfully " arranged." It is the same with the glamour. I reach saturation point too easily, after which overplus of this commodity reduces me to a fakir-like state of insensibility, in which the opening of the heavens themselves would be viewed with an eye glazed like a breakfast tongue.

TRIUMPH FOR KOMISARJEVSKY

THE SEAGULL. Revival of Anton Tchehov's Play. New Theatre, Wednesday, May 20, 1936.   [*May* 24, 1936]

THIS WEEK has seen and heard two remarkable things, though I can only vouch personally for the second—a new and great Isolde and Komisarjevsky's endlessly beautiful production of *The Seagull*. I remember when I was a young man taking up a copy of the *Saturday Review* and reading the late J. F. Runciman on a performance of *Tristan* which ought to have been given at Covent Garden but was not, *Faust* being substituted. But did J. F. R. write about *Faust*? No, he wrote a long article explaining what *Tristan* was about, and why it ought to be played. In the same week, or near enough, the by no means late G. B. S. was telling readers of the same paper what was in Tchehov's plays and why they should be performed. Fortunately, we have changed all that. Most people know what Wagner's opera is about, and I shall not affront readers of the *Sunday Times* with any summary of *The Seagull*. On the other hand, one should not be in too much of a hurry to congratulate the age on its improving taste. Now that the blues have come into fashion, melancholy has gone out. I heard one vivacious lady say as we left the theatre: " My dear, I don't mind it being too dreary. The pre-wars used to like that sort of thing. But as technique isn't it quite too old-fashioned ? " Who knows that this lady was not right ? In Ibsen's day melancholia and duck-shooting went hand-in-hand. In Tchehov's, low spirits found their vent in potting at seagulls. To-day's bright spirits go out to supper and harness their blues to a wild mustang. But I still have no intention of recounting the plot of this masterpiece.

A writer in one of the old Badminton books describes three perfect moments which, in his view, athletics afford. Two of these are the off-drive at cricket and, at tennis, the laying of a chase " better than half a yard." But the perfect player brings up the perfect spectator, and the thrill of seeing the thing done, though different from the thrill of doing, is not necessarily less intense. Playwrights like Tchehov achieve an unending succession of drives and chases, bringing to the playgoer the same ecstasy that batsman and tennis player communicate to the pavilion and dedans. At such moments playwright, actor, and spectator are each in their several capacities at the height of being. A Sparkenbroke will tell you that such moments announce a transcendence; lesser people just feel that for the instant of such happenings the world has stood still. The best proof of these plays' superb merit is that the world does not stand still in the same place for two productions running or even for two evenings together. Every spectator must make his own choice of such moments, or rather he will have the choice forced upon him. On Wednesday evening I had this experience three times. The first was on the highest level, when Nina in Constantin's arms probed and lanced her misery by reciting the familiar phrases of his boyish play. The second was a stroke of pure comedy worthy of Henri Becque. Arcadina having re-won Trigorin after a Cleopatra-like bout of dissembling, flattery, shameless surrender, all dished up with the virtuosity of a big, splurgy actress, pulled herself together and offered to let her once-more-enslaved noodle stay with his chit for a day or two if he liked. The third moment was at the very end of the play. There was the noise like a pistol shot, which the doctor explained away.

Sn

Arcadina, frightened, was reminded of Constantin's earlier attempt to shoot himself. Covering her face with her hands, she said: " I feel quite faint." But Constantin had shot himself, and here you had a playwright deliberately refusing to end on a note of fuss, which is what any actress up to Arcadina's weight must make of the intimation. It was exactly like a lawn-tennis player refusing to win game, set, and match with a spectacular smash and preferring to put the ball quietly away.

This being a thundering good play, it is full of thundering good parts which can all be interpreted in almost any number of ways. Take Arcadina, for example. When Miss Miriam Lewes played this part she gave the fascinating creature a baleful, Strindbergian quality, largely because Miss Lewes is good in Strindberg. My gifted colleague, Mr. Morgan, wants Arcadina to have " that element of persuasive pity with which Tchehov enriched the character and made it credible." This is because Mr. Morgan cannot conceive femininity shorn of the finer aspects of womanhood. Now, in my view, Miss Edith Evans plays the character exactly right, for the reason that she puts nothing whatever into it that does not belong to it, however good an exponent she may be of those alien characteristics. If a baleful tigerishness were the thing, she had only to turn on a bit of Agatha Payne. But she didn't, and her pacing up and down the room had the right amount of bad temper, and no more. On the other hand, if an ethereal quality had been wanted, the actress had only to turn on Gwenny or some other housemaid in act of oblation. But this, again, would not have been Arcadina, who holds Constantin by the mere fact of being his mother and Trigorin by her sex. Reading the scene very carefully, I cannot find one single syllable of the Duse-like quality of ennoblement. Arcadina is a well-known actress; Trigorin is a well-known novelist. The liaison is notorious and a good advertisement for both. She has got used to him, at forty-three doesn't want the bother of looking for somebody else, and is not going to have her nose put out by a ninny who goes in for amateur theatricals. Her re-conquest of her lover is a sordid business, skilfully and conscientiously carried through, and as no actress is ever quite good enough to play a scene perfectly without feeling a bit of it, Arcadina towards the end takes on some show of sincerity. And then, what a witty piece of acting Miss Evans made it, taking the eye like a drawing of Sarah by Toulouse-Lautrec, and incidentally reproducing Sarah's coiffure, *circa* 1885, her frocks and collarettes *circa* 1895, and the saucy little skiffs and sloops which *circa* 1900 Sarah used for hats. A lovely performance of shimmer and sparkle, and quite rightly without one atom of heart to it ! Her behaviour at Constantin's play proves that this is right.

But one must be getting on. One is in a little difficulty about Mr. Gielgud's Trigorin, which was a shade too young and not raffish enough. Trigorin is worse than a second-rate novelist, he is a third-rate character ; and nobody who could look and listen to Nina as this actor did in the third act would have behaved towards her as he does towards the end of the play. It was an exquisite exhibition of sensitive Gielgudry. The actor wanted here was Mr. Clarke-Smith, who would have made a mouthful of Nina, just as the wolf did of Red Riding Hood ; Mr. Gielgud seemed rather to pine after her as Dante did after Beatrice. On the other hand, it is only fair to say that Tchehov had a handsome share in making a mess of a part which has never been convincingly played even in Russia. As Masha Miss Martita Hunt was an unholy joy. This exquisitely poised actress radiated glumness, hammered out a full-dress Hungarian rhapsody on a theme of Mrs. Gummidge, and rightly convulsed the house. I am convinced that in Russia the minor melancholics must be comic characters. Miss Hunt's tragic mask, wet with booby tears, made one cry with laughter. This is acting when you remember that Miss Hunt has an Arcadina up that clever sleeve of hers. Miss Peggy Ashcroft's performance of the earlier part of the piece was heartrending; she Sparkenbroke all hearts. But alas, when she came to the last scene there was not enough power in her to carry it through. This was just a child hit on the head by a bludgeon, and this Nina had not lived those two years which she recounted. Obviously she would have thrown herself into the lake instead of going off to play lead at Omsk or Tomsk, which is what she does. Perhaps the best acting of all came from Mr. Stephen Haggard, and at the time when he apparently did least. Throughout the whole of the last scene he held Nina in his arms, averted his head, gave the stage to his partner, and filled the house with the sense of the boy's pain.

THREE NOSES

THE LADY OF LA PAZ. A Play by Edith Ellis. From a Novel by Elinor Mordaunt. Criterion Theatre, Thursday, July 3, 1936. [*July* 6, 1936]

> Gather ye nosebuds while ye may !
> —Anon.

MR. EVELYN WAUGH's recently published volume of pathetic fallacies may or may not have won the Laburnum Chaplet, or whatever they call these wan guerdons. But it is excellent fun nevertheless, and I take leave to think that some of it fits my present subject perfectly. Here is a passage about a young lady's nose which I hope I may pilfer with profit:

> "The feature which, more than any other, endeared Millicent Blade to sentimental Anglo-Saxon manhood was her nose. It was not everybody's nose; many prefer one with greater body; it was not a nose to appeal to painters, for it was far too small and quite without shape, a mere dab of putty without apparent bone structure; a nose which made it impossible for its wearer to be haughty or imposing or astute. It would not have done for a governess or a 'cellist or even for a post-office clerk, but it suited Miss Blade's book perfectly, for it was a nose that pierced the thin surface crust to the English heart to its warm and pulpy core; a nose to take the thoughts of English manhood back to its schooldays, to the doughy-faced urchins on whom it had squandered its first affection, to memories of changing room and chapel and battered straw boaters."

Felicia and Ana both had such a nose. Or should one say
" such noses " ? Not, I submit, in this case, since, speaking
metaphorically, the buttons on these children's faces even
when put together hardly amounted to an organ of normal
magnitude. How right Pascal was about that inch less of
Cleopatra's nose and how much more it might have done for
the luckless Queen ! Might she not with it have got round the
other Cæsar, and so added, if not a better, at least a longer
page to History ? I agree that the more immediate point is
what all this has to do with the Lady of La Paz. Simply that
her granddaughters' spiritual noselessness got them into the
most moving accidents by flood and field, and finally won
them a couple of husbands, English and English-speaking,
with heads as well as hearts of unexceptionable pulp.

Felicia had the stickier time. Her father, a pure Spaniard,
who had married the Comtesse Victoria's daughter by one of
four husbands, betrothed Felicia to a chum of his, one
Vicente Alcantara, a black-avised hidalgo who planted coffee
in his grounds—the scene is Costa Rica—and the seeds of
hate in anybody who walked in them. He took his mistresses
from among the women working in the fields, and when,
ultimately, he was shot nobody was greatly surprised or
bothered much about bringing the crime home to anybody.
But before this happened there were terrific pratings about
family honour, and such Othello-like rumblings about keeping a corner in the thing he loved, that poor Felicia was
always riding, bare-headed and bare-backed, from her
prison of a home to her grandmother's birdcage of a drawing-
room, and in the most inconvenient thunderstorms ! At grave
risk to health, too, since confinement *chez elle* ended in confinement *chez grand'mère*. And then came the dawn of another
day in the person of a young American in whom Felicia's
nose had stirred memories of campus, flirtatious football, and
all that the films have taught us of American college life.

And while all this was happening was Ana idle ? Sakes, no ! She was fixing a quick change from convent cell to bridal suite, and just when the play was in danger of becoming gloomy threw over the à Beckets and the à Kempises and threw a wedding breakfast instead.

Miss Nova Pilbeam and Miss Janet Johnson played these fragrances inconceivably well. Perhaps I should say conceivably, since it was the very stuff of that screen which one of these little ladies adorns. The other is very, very pretty. Only I do not think that we should be asked to contribute such extreme pianistic virtuosity to Miss Johnson. " Hark at the child ! " said the Comtesse. " How passion-soaked is her Debussy ! " This while some obviously professional artist was pounding away off-stage, whereas Miss Johnson suggested that she might with diffidence and with one finger pick out the notes of " The Bluebells of Seville." As one of the two young men, Mr. Clement McCallin did all that was wanted throbbingly enough, though here again one missed the screen. When it comes to unrealities flesh and blood get terribly in the way. Incidentally, if Mr. McCallin is not an American there is a touch of genius in that low-geared accent. As the destroyer of youth in bloom Mr. Anthony Ireland was at his suavest and best. It is impossible for this actor to do anything without distinction; a wise Desdemona might prefer to be thugged by him to being hugged by men of grosser mould. Another performance of style was that of M. Paul Leyssac, whom one will want to see again when he has a part, instead of the pitiful mockery of one.

Miss Lilian Braithwaite ? Her Comtesse achieves one remarkable feat—that of making one playgoer think simultaneously of three such different people as Rudyard Kipling, Walter Pater, and Mr. Max Beerbohm. The Comtesse Victoria Rochecourt, who has enjoyed four husbands, might well say with the old soldier :

I've taken my fun where I've found it;
I've rogued an' I've ranged in my time;
I've 'ad my pickin' o' sweet'earts,
An' four o' the lot was prime.

Now consider the alleged age and the incontestable looks of this exquisite period-piece in grandmothers. " A marvellous woman ! For all the gamut of her experience, she is still lightly triumphant over time. All this has been to her, as to Mona Lisa, but as the sound of lyres and flutes, and lives only in the delicacy with which it has moulded the changing lineaments, and tinged the hair. Hers is the head upon which all the ends of the world are come, and the eyelids are not at all weary. . . ." No, reader ! Not quite Pater, but the incomparable Max comparing Sarah Bernhardt to Leonardo's model. And neither has a line for that nose, " tip-tilted like the petal of a flower." No nose in all the world till Lilian came ! But enough in this vein. How much does Miss Braithwaite illude us ? How much does she illude herself ? Is this a serious piece of acting, a proclaimed skit, or just a little joke among ourselves ? If it be guying, then it must be said that the actress guys with gusto. Anything more horrific, born of wit and malice aforethought, than that wedding " creation " it would be impossible to imagine. Yet the Comtesse appears to glory in this confection of charlotte russe topped with raspberry jelly. But is it the Comtesse glorying ? Or just Miss Braithwaite making fun of the absurd old thing ? With any interpretation it is a masterly jibe at " mutton dressed lamb fashion." But perhaps this would sound politer in French. Let it be said, then, that this delightful player keeps us infinitely entertained with her cartoons of *mouton habillé en agneau !* Which may, or may not, be the French equivalent of our English saying.

A PRINCIPLE AT STAKE

MADEMOISELLE. A play by Jacques Deval; adapted by
Audrey and Waveney Carten. Wyndham's Theatre,
Tuesday, September 15, 1936.

CERTAINLY, SIR ! A musical comedy by R. P. Weston and
Bert Lee. Music by Jack Waller and Joseph Tunbridge.
Hippodrome, Thursday, September 17, 1936.

GIRL UNKNOWN. A play by Ferencz Molnar; adapted by
Margaret Webster. New Theatre, Friday, September 18,
1936.   [*September* 20, 1936]

IS IT UNGRACIOUS, after spending an extraordinarily
happy evening in the theatre, to confess oneself a trifle
unhappy about the play ? So be it. Caviare is good, and
marmalade is good. The point is that one would not necessarily want to eat both on the same piece of toast. But just as
one is firm as to the sum of one's delight the other evening,
so one wants to be particular in cavilling. It is not true to say
that the caviare and the marmalade are spread on the same
piece of toast: courses of each are served alternately. Does
this matter ? One more remark and I promise that the
culinary metaphor shall be shelved. This is in the nature of
a confession. The other evening, at the end of a delicately
devised meal and having lit one's cigar, one realised that the
menu had offered treacle roly-poly, half a foot of which was
promptly sent in pursuit of the angels on horseback. Brillat-
Savarin may have turned in his grave; one slept as soundly
as a babe.

You see, one is not in one's private capacity a Brillat-Savarin, and one would not put the foregoing in a cookery book. But playwrights must not take these liberties, at least in so far as their works are to be judged by gastronomes. The wittiest play of recent years is *Hay Fever*. Recall how it begins:

> SOREL: I should like to be a fresh, open-air girl with a passion for games.
> SIMON: Thank God you're not.
> SOREL: It would be so soothing.
> SIMON: Not in this house.
> SOREL: Where's mother?
> SIMON: In the garden, practising.
> SOREL: Practising?
> SIMON: She's learning the names of the flowers by heart.

And a little later the sister says to the brother:

> " Abnormal, Simon—that's what we are. Abnormal. People stare in astonishment when we say what we consider perfectly ordinary things. I just remarked at Freda's lunch the other day how nice it would be if someone invented something to make all our faces go up like the Chinese, because I was so bored with them going down. And they all thought I was mad ! "

All this is exactly the key in which *Mademoiselle* starts, and if one quotes from the earlier play it is because, being known, quotation cannot harm it, whereas one is reluctant to take the bloom off a new and unknown play. The point is, or ought to be, established that on that first night the faces of Mr. Coward's audience were at this point on the up rather than the down grade. Laughter was in the air, and the jokes were rocketing. So with M. Deval's piece. The most moving play of recent times is undoubtedly *Children in Uniform*. What, now, would Mr. Coward have thought if somebody had proposed that Manuela should burst in on that week-end at Cookham with her tragic tale out of school? What would Mr. Coward have said if somebody had proposed to divide his play into two equal halves of merriment and misery? Might he not have babbled something about form? And I think I can tell him what would have happened—the laughter would have drowned the snivelling. The whole point about comic relief is that it must be strictly relief and that there shall not be too much of it. You can put the grave-diggers into *Hamlet* and the porter into *Macbeth*. But you could not put Sir Toby and his circle into *Lear*, because if you did the boat would break in two and only one half of it be left floating.

I feel very strongly that something of the same sort happens to *Mademoiselle*, which instead of being one perfect play is made up of two admirable halves which just don't fit. The story is simple. After the elaborate drawing of a French household as scatterbrained as *Hay Fever's* Blisses, we are introduced to the daughter and the fact that she is going to have a baby. She is also to be tied to a governess who is to keep her away from the men and so enable her to get married, in contradistinction to the English system which encourages girls to make friends of the opposite sex with the result that " the men retire to their stables and the women are left waving hockey-sticks." The serious part of the play centres in the governess, an abnormal creature who entertains a longing for a child at the same time as an aversion from men. This, of course, is an unconquerable impasse until Mademoiselle conceives the notion of a secret confinement for the daughter, after which the baby is to be given up to her, the governess. Later the girl is to be returned to her parents who, living in a world like a March wind blowing through a feather-bed factory, will hardly have noticed their daughter's absence, much less wondered at its cause. This is probably a very moving story. But if I had been the author I should have felt like saying to my audience: " If you have tears, please don't bother to shed them now; my comic pair are just coming on again ! " For I feel it in my bones that M. Deval's heart, when he wrote this play, was bound up with the comic side of it.

What, then, should have been done? It is no use crying over spilt milk, though there may be interest in speculating on safer ways of carrying the jug. If there had been a formal central intrigue—say that Christianne's seducer was only potential, and had been foiled by Mademoiselle's revelation, first that he was older than he looked and second had seduced Mademoiselle herself in some precedent heyday !— why, then, we should, I suggest, have had a flawless little comedy of bad manners. The alternative plan would have been to shear the play of its hilarities, and turn the production over to Miss Leontine Sagan, when I have no doubt that tears in plenty would have been wrung from it. Here ends this plaguey business of criticism by rule. All dramatic critics know and are fond of proclaiming that a house divided against itself cannot stand. But a play is not in quite the same case as a house. It can do something better than stand; it can jolly well run. It is a long time since the English theatre has seen anything so exhilarating as the acting of Mr. Cecil Parker and Miss Isabel Jeans. They take the thing at terrific speed. In this comedy M. Deval uses his wit as Sergeant Troy used his sword for the bedazzlement of Bathsheba, and one can do no better than to declare that both these players turn that blade into a two-handed one. Mr. Parker achieves a remarkable doubling of stolidity and finesse; Miss Jeans has never before quite so perfectly hit off the marriage of the preposterous and the logical.

Plonk into the middle of all this comes Miss Madge Titheradge's study of the old maid hungry for motherhood; this would be intensely moving if one did not feel the necessity for removing all of this sad imbroglio into another play in which this very gifted artist could have the audience's undivided attention. One hopes that this does not sound *grudging*; after all, one must not refuse a precious jewel because it is in the wrong setting ! One has never admired Miss Greer Garson more, though here again the divided quality of the play does her an injustice. As I read, Christianne is essentially a flibbertigibbet and the true daughter of her parents; it is emotion under stress which is alien to her nature. Watching Miss Garson I feel that that part of Christianne which is acting is her frivolity. What I am trying to say, perhaps, is that here is an actress up to Nora Helmer's weight, that the implication of high seriousness is implicit in everything Miss Garson does and says, and that consequently her presentation of Christianne is like an impersonation of a butterfly by a rather heavier member of the family. Whether one is right or wrong about this, the performance is one of great skill and interest.

The play has been brilliantly adapted by the Misses Carten, and is produced by Mr. Noel Coward with the result that not a moment of it drags. I think he will perhaps delete two sentences—one about Mademoiselle's religion, which an English audience cannot be expected to understand, and the other the pale echo of a joke made by Wilde's Lady Bracknell at the expense of Miss Prism. The décor by Mrs. Calthrop is of a loveliness which on the first night drew from the house an audible gasp. It is like ivory notepaper in a cedarwood box.

An august critic said in his notice of *Certainly, Sir !* that Mr. Mackenzie Ward, " himself a pleasant humorist, appears a trifle embarrassed by the thinness of his jokes."

But might it not be possible to hold that the jokes in this entertainment find themselves a trifle embarrassed by the thinness of the jesters ? The play needs a more solid backing than has been afforded its two principals, Mr. Robey and Miss Renee Houston. Alice, where art thou, indeed ! Vera, where art thou, and Bertha ditto, must have been in everybody's mind who remembered how vigorously and valiantly Mesdames Pearce and Belmore have supported better shows than this. Or should one say " bigger " ? Here again crops up the matter of discrepancy.

> *A little pot of jelly*
> *Best fits a little belly——*

wrote Herrick. The little pot of jelly which is this unpretentious piece is surely something lost in the cavernous maw of a huge theatre like the Hippodrome. One or two of the items, notably a ballet of musicians, performers on tinkling glass and brittle cymbal, and another on the subject of Nelson's days are exquisite enough to adorn the most recherché revue. But elsewhere the support is to seek. Mr. Robey does what he can, which is much. This is the place to say what meat and drink it is to see this greatest of buffoons still throning it in an age all for comforting sad-eyed clowns whose jokes lie too deep for tears. Miss Houston lacks material, and I am too great an admirer of this brilliant little artist to think that her part, as it is at present written, gives her a chance. In my view that ferociously witty mastiff, Mr. Douglas Furber, ought to be at once unchained and let loose upon the book. The music, by Messrs. Jack Waller and Joseph Tunbridge, is frequently and wittily indebted to Tschaikowsky. At least, nobody is going to deny that the ghost of an alleged dead man appeared to the opening phrase of the Sixth Symphony, after which chunks of that masterpiece were liberally vouchsafed. There is an old cliché to the effect that while one man may steal a horse another may not look over a hedge. This being so, Messrs. Waller and Tunbridge are entitled to plead that they should not be blamed for picking Tschaikowsky's pocket for this entertainment, in view of the fact that in a more serious theatre Messrs. Massine and de Basil between them pillage whole wardrobes. I agree.

Girl Unknown is all about a brothel, a sanatorium and a railway-station. Dull matter, one suspects, for the playgoer who does not frequent the first, hopes never to enter the second, and is bored with the third. Instead, one fell into a brown study. Why does the English theatre persist with Molnar, whose vein of sentimental butter-milk is as dislikeable to us as, let me presume, Sir James Barrie's whey might be to the Kurds ? Why do foreign actresses of distinction invariably appear in plays without any ? At what near date will broken English be the *sine qua non* for a leading lady on our stage ? So musing, and finding no answers, the present scribe, like the lover in *Marpessa*, " into the evening green wandered away."

PLOT AND PASSION

FOLLOW YOUR SAINT. A play by Lesley Storm. Queen's Theatre, Thursday, September 24, 1936.

MURDER ON ACCOUNT. A play by Hayden Talbot and Kathlyn Hayden. Winter Garden Theatre, Friday, September 25, 1936.

FRONT OF HOUSE. A play by Charles Landstone. Arts Theatre, Monday afternoon, September 21, 1936.

[September 27, 1936]

IN PURSUIT OF A THEORY of a super-Galahad we are asked to imagine a greenhorn pacing Irene Iddesleigh's " beach of limited freedom." Only in this case an Irish beach. While David French is spouting Yeats to " the chill waves of troubled waters " and flinging chunks of " Æ " on " the oases of futurity," something totally different is going on in the Regent's Park flat of Alec and Joanna Rothney. Alec, with one foot in the grave, is quaffing beakers of bicarbonate of soda in the study, while Joanna is receiving the embraces of the raffish Charles Hastings in the brilliantly lit drawing-room with the blinds up and in full view of sundry, if not all. Obviously if David is to be introduced into this household it can only be on the assumption that his mother was an early sweetheart of Alec's. All the same, why Joanna should consent to give this young man bed and board is not easily understandable until you come to remember that the title contains the word " saint," which must refer to

Joanna. Now to Alec, Joanna is only a comfortable piece of furniture, while to Charles she is an uncomfortable mistress always nosing into other affairs of his. This leads up to the boy who, again in the words of Irene, is to find his sympathy " dashed against the rock of gossip." In other words, he arrives in this country to find a prettier kettle of fish than any with which he has been familiar on the Irish coast. Does he allow that kettle to remain " within the false bosom of buried scorn " ? No ! He determines to have a finger in it. The kettle is really a very complicated one. Joanna has employed a private detective to watch Charles ; Charles, knowing that he is being watched, thinks the fellow has been put on by Alec. If it is going to come to a show-down Charles prefers to be the first to put his cards on the table. He proposes to make confession to Alec and after the divorce marry Joanna. This is one of the play's major weaknesses. There is no conceivable reason why Charles, who is a man of many mistresses, should insist upon burdening himself with a convention-ridden baggage intent upon retaining not only the whole of her lover but also the whole of her self-respect. And, of course, no experienced philanderer would dream of burdening himself with *that* ! But now Joanna rounds on Charles. She wouldn't dream of marrying him, because of the other women. She isn't even sure about continuing to be his mistress. Charles says this is nonsense and proposes two o'clock in the morning as a convenient hour in which to prove it to her. David, who has been lurking in the full glare of a standard-lamp, overhears this, and next day he shoots Charles in the course of a morning with the pheasants.

Now comes the great scene. David rushes in, tells Joanna what he has just done, and the theatre being what it is, the piece promptly goes to pot. There are several credible courses of action. One is that Joanna, who is a high-tempered little madam, would round on the boy and say : " You

Tn

blasted little fool, what do you mean by killing a man who was a man and not a puling moon-calf? Get out of this house before I ring up the police!" What is incredible is that the boy should lay his head on Joanna's lap and quote at great length from the Profundities, while Joanna strokes his hair with the yonderly expression of a nursery Duse. As a picture of life the play now gets " wusser and wusser," though as a vehicle for emotional acting not based on reason it becomes very fine indeed. Alec now appears to believe that David genuinely mistook Charles for a pheasant and that the whole thing was an accident. But David will not have it. He has killed Charles because Charles deserved killing. Subsequently the plot so thickens as to defy summary. Alec, on learning that his wife has behaved in the only manner he could reasonably expect, falls into Othello-like rages. Oddly enough the play has been good enough in places to justify Joanna saying to Alec: " Don't talk such nonsense. That I should have a lover in no way trespasses on our sympathetic companionship, which is all our marriage is. After all I am a woman and not a tea-cosy. As an educated man living in 1936 you ought to realise this and apologise for your temper!" Needless to say the opportunity is not taken. Instead Alec has to explore the deeper hell of believing that the boy is also his wife's lover, and presently he and David agree that what is to happen next can only be decided by a jury at the Old Bailey, notwithstanding that the Coroner has already accepted the accident theory. In fact the two ring up the police station in the friendliest way. The Inspector arrives, and at the last moment is put off by Joanna herself with a feeble yarn about some missing jewellery.

It is incredible that Mr. Basil Dean, the producer, should have allowed Joanna's speech, which runs something like this: " That diamond brooch which you, Alec, bought on our honeymoon because you thought my eyes were like stars reflected in the Mediterranean—that was one of the items, Inspector. That rope of pearls—you remember, Alec, saying that they were like the tears with which I confessed my love for you—that, too, is missing, Inspector. Those ear-rings . . ." etc., etc. The Inspector pretends to believe all this, and the curtain comes down on Alec telling David to pack his bag for the mathematical tripos at Cambridge and prepare to forget love among the triangles. Comes down, too, on one spectator debating not the mysteries of life, love, adultery, pheasant-shooting, and sudden death, but whether the detective who has turned out to be a bit of a blackmailer is going to receive the money which Alec has half-promised him. For it is undoubtedly a nasty thing when a woman, who has employed a detective to dog a faithless lover, then has that gallant shot by a younger lover—at least the detective thinks that this is a view which the police might hold. And, of course, to conceal a nifty bit of evidence costs money ! Doesn't Alec agree ? One is driven to the conclusion that the detective is the only rational person in the piece !

Miss Edna Best's strength has lain hitherto in the portrayal of young women glumly reconciled to being fair, chaste, and inexpressive She's. What riot, this actress has so often asked us to assume, may lie beneath a mask as placid as mirror, meadow, or milk-pudding ? Now comes a star part having nothing to do with the Milky Way, and we are entitled, I think, to ask what Miss Best can do with it. I am afraid the answer is—not very much. One does not believe in this deliberate adventure in dangerous living. Here, one feels, is a Joanna who would be perfectly content with a dyspeptic husband plus an occasional visit to the drama of Miss Dodie Smith. In the last act, in which Joanna tells Alec not to be a fool, Miss Best is better, though I think her line must always be that quietism which dramatic critics who have never seen any emotional acting are so fond of calling " restraint."

But then I am not of the Quietist School, which always reminds me of Mr. E. F. Benson's amateur pianist who gave virtuoso performances of the first movement of the Moonlight Sonata and on the score of a headache excused herself from the high-speed remainder. But all the other members of the cast worked like Trojans. Mr. Nicholas Hannen, when Alec was ultimately let loose, acted all over the stage. As Charles, Mr. Francis Lister redeemed the play from insipidity with some highly sensible maxims from the Philanderer's Handbook. Mr. Raymond Huntley's blackmailing detective, Chapman, deserved a play to himself; one longed to see his domestic foyer complete with Mrs. Chapman and all the little Chapmans, lisping at the parental knee early lessons in detecto-blackmailing. It is perhaps not unfair to the above-mentioned to say that the evening really belonged to Mr. Geoffrey Keen, who brought David movingly to life in all his scenes.

In a novel about ancient Rome written by a maiden lady residing at Putney I came across this sentence: " The lion sprang with éclat upon the Christian martyr who expired with aplomb." *Murder on Account* has the same effect on one's critical faculty. Appended, however, are one or two observations.

1. A female convict's principal reason for accepting the King's Pardon is not that her child will take the knowledge of her mother's infamy more easily at the age of ten than twenty. Nor will it be the desire to rejoin her husband who left her ten years ago having planted on her a crime for which he hoped she would be hanged. Any convict's first reason for accepting a pardon is that he or she is sick of the filthy hole.

2. This play seeks to prove that if you serve ten or twenty years for killing Jones and it subsequently appears that the body was that of Smith who was killed by somebody

else, you may then with impunity kill Jones on sight because you can't be punished twice for the same crime. I don't believe this. In such a case the law would hand you £8,000 compensation with one hand, and with the other hang you by the neck.

3. It is too late in the theatrical day for a mother to play Lady Isabel to a Jane Eyre whose Mr. Rochester is her own father.

Miss Rosalinde Fuller acted throughout with heartrending vivacity; the poor mother could not take up her daughter's photograph without clutching it to her bosom like a tigress with her day's ration of meat. Miss Dorothy Dix brought the piece within measurable distance of sanity. But the border-line was not reached until we came to Mr. Cameron Hall, whose old lag was not only a joy but a credible one.

Front of House is a play about actors and actresses, box-office officials, barmaids, programme-girls, and commissionaires, which will vastly amuse actors and actresses, box-office officials, barmaids, programme-girls, and commissionaires. It will be Greek to the general public, always presuming it is not double Dutch. The scene is the dress-circle bar of a theatre during a performance, and when the curtain is up the theatre-staff uses the place for the conduct of its private affairs. This may or may not be true. My impression has always been that during the performance the bar of a theatre is empty except for its maids, the assistant manager, and the publicity agent's second string. Now that I know that it is a hot-bed of intrigue more passionately exciting than anything likely to be exhibited on the stage, I begin to conceive an alternative field of criticism. One would, of course, return to the auditorium for the intervals. Mr. Esmé Percy as an actor-manager was wildly amusing, the rest of the cast less so.

SOPHOCLES AT COVENT GARDEN

ŒDIPUS REX. Revival of the Tragedy by Sophocles. Translated by Gilbert Murray. Covent Garden Opera House, Monday, September 28, 1936.

A MONTH IN THE COUNTRY. Revival of Turgenev's Play. Westminster Theatre, Wednesday, September 30, 1936.

TRANSATLANTIC RHYTHM. A revue by Irving Cæsar. Music by Ray Henderson. Adelphi Theatre, Thursday, October 1, 1936.   [*October* 4, 1936]

LORD, what fools these ancients be ! For if only the Greeks had cottoned to human responsibility as the key and mainspring of human drama, what a world of trouble they would have saved themselves ! Any play by any Greek dramatist is like one of those Heath Robinson drawings in which machinery to work a coalmine is necessary before the smallest walnut can be cracked. Does the dramatist take for theme the propriety of killing one's father and marrying one's mother ? To a post-Greek this is simplicity itself. He sends his Hamlet to his mother's closet at the beginning of the play, and next morning when the King is fastening his shoe-laces gets behind him with a sword and does it pat. This post-Greek play has now advanced as far as Act One, Scene Two, and in Scene Three those recriminations which are the essence of the responsible drama begin. Now consider the machinery which Sophocles has to erect before Œdipus can, so to speak, get going. Thebes must have a Sphinx dealing out death to anybody and everybody who cannot answer her riddles. Because young Prince Œdipus can answer her riddle she destroys herself, whereby the Thebans offer Œdipus the throne of Laius, whom the young prince has just accidentally slain en route, and throw in Laius's widow, Jocasta.

Then there has to be an Oracle, a thoroughly busy fellow. Some twenty years before the play starts the Oracle tells Jocasta that her babe shall murder his father and marry his father's widow. "That he shan't !" says Jocasta, and abandons the child on a mountain-top, not realising that even in the matter of babe-murder if you want a thing doing well you must do it yourself. Some ten years before the play starts the Oracle repeats the warning, this time to Œdipus. Immediately after the second warning Œdipus sets out for Thebes, kills Laius, and marries Jocasta. Presumably he has not forgotten the warning, just as the murder of her husband must have revived the earlier warning in Jocasta's mind. But they do not compare notes, and live for ten years in complete amity until a plague smites the city and the play begins. I ask you, readers of the *Sunday Times*, whether old man Ibsen himself would not have boggled at so much revelation by innuendo. What staggers me is the alertness of the Greek audience, which in the days before programmes had no difficulty in taking in all this. Or perhaps slaves went all round the arena carrying a *précis* after the manner of the boards at Lord's announcing when play will be resumed ?

The introduction of human responsibility has altered the entire course of dramatic feeling. A man who gambles away his money so that his wife and babes starve may be the subject of a tragedy, whereas the thrifty fellow whose bank goes smash is the subject of no more than a newspaper paragraph. To pretend that the concatenation of miracle-mongering which is *Œdipus Rex* moves the modern mind to anything other than a purely poetical emotion is the rankest hypocrisy. It may interest or even excite. Surely now the fellow must begin to see. . . . Surely after this he can't go on not knowing. . . . And so the play gets hotter and hotter, as the children say. There are many things in it to admire, things like the urbanity of feeling which is constant throughout. The inhabitants of this particular world take for granted that the standard of human thought and action is a noble one.

This, then, is interesting, exciting, civilised playgoing, though not emotional. Œdipus putting out his eyes that they may no longer be offended is like a man with a cold cutting off his nose so that it may no longer be blown. The final exit through the audience is one of those colossal mistakes of which only your highbrow producer is capable. Keep Œdipus within his frame and he remains Œdipus. Send him among us, and those bleeding sockets are merely red paint on the countenance of a delightful actor with whom you remember chatting at the last Test Match. The Reinhardt gang has never realised that to venture one inch beyond the proscenium arch destroys the whole illusion so laboriously created. This is the age of the picture stage, and even if you are twelve German producers rolled into one you cannot put the clock back. You may put something in illusion's place, but that isn't what I want. When I go to the theatre I want illusion, and whether the Greeks wanted it or not I just don't care. Perhaps they were too High Minded. So be it.

Sir John Martin-Harvey may not have the physical size for Œdipus, but mentally and spiritually he sizes it up beautifully. This is a noble and satisfying performance, always full of the incredulous bewonderment of a fine mind confronted with baseness. As Jocasta Miss Miriam Lewes declines to essay the task of looking like this Œdipus's mother, and devotes her amazing energy to giving Sophocles a bit of Strindberg's mind. The first business of a Messenger is to deliver his message. Mr. Franklin Dyall does the job resonantly; he needs only a pill-box hat with a tin disc to be the First District Messenger. Mr. Baliol Holloway's Creon, Mr. Fisher White's Teiresias, and Mr. Philip Hewland's Old Servant are sound and sensible performances, but I do not think that Mr. Philip Desborough's Stranger from Corinth should speak with the bright young accent of Shepherd Market. As the leader of the chorus, Mr. Harvey Braban makes an admirable fugleman, initiating his followers into a series of bar-bell exercises with the grace of a Knox and the fertility in invention of a Nervo.

It is perhaps not generally realised that the revolving stage was invented by whatever Russian first wrote plays. The Russian theatre, so far as it has been possible to know it over here, is full of an astounding actuality, which persuades us that the actors when they have completed one scene retire not to their dressing-rooms but to some other part of the house to resume a life from which they have been momentarily snatched. Any scene presented to the audience is only a section of the stage, those sections out of view seething with life though we do not see it. Or you might put it that the English playwright, bethinking him with difficulty of a central character, has all the trouble in the world to think of other personages of whom throughout three hours he may be the central one. But it is only by a kind of fluke that Mme Ranevsky, for example, is the central figure in *The Cherry Orchard*. It might have been, and very nearly was, Lopakhin, and we feel that for a quite insignificant bet Tchehov would have focused the interest on the German governess and made Mme Ranevsky, Lopakhin, Gaev, and all the others revolve round her.

So it is with Turgenev's *A Month in the Country*. Indeed, it almost seems as though the characters in this lovely play live richer lives off the stage than they do on, and that what we observe are only their reflex actions. This piece was fully noticed in these columns on a previous occasion, and it only remains to say now that it is an even more exquisite play than one thought ten years ago. As a piece of emotional counterpoint the middle act is perfection. Here, as indeed throughout the piece, Miss Gillian Scaife's performance of Natalia Petrovna gives a subtle and perfect pleasure. Here is Quietism at its best, since it is exploited by an actress in whose range are not only pianissimos but considerable fortes. Miss Cherry Cottrell as Viera must plough a difficult and lonely furrow; she does it with great sensitiveness. As Bieliaev, Mr. Stephen Murray admirably suggests the transition from a young man's total unawareness to the first beginnings of interest. One feels that if he did not run away, his affair with Natalia would be something to regret for the rest of his life. Where these Russian writers are so transcendently fine is in their provision of comic relief. Whenever there is danger of subtlety declining to tameness, in comes Mr. Cecil Trouncer as the *raisonneur*, Schpigelski, whipping up interest in everything and everybody, and leaving enough exhilaration behind him to last until his next entrance. If Mr. Dennis Arundell's Rakitin is a little dull he is entitled, I think, to plead that the character is not so much a walking gentleman as a walking stick.

Transatlantic Rhythm is a glittering, empty show. Glittering, because a great deal of money has been spent on the scenery and dresses. Empty because insufficient talent has been engaged to fill it. The last is something so staggeringly obvious that nobody seems to have said it since the invention of printing. Scores of reasons are adduced for the failure of this or that production; I have never seen it set down that the principals engaged are just not good enough. Or, in this instance, are they? It may depend upon the point of view. One of the greatly billed stars is a torch singer. Now a torch singer is a female crooner, and your view of this performance must obviously depend upon your view of crooning. At its best this misuse of the human voice is to me no better than street-singing; indeed, our lavender-sellers cry more musically. At its worst, crooning, again in my view, is like the cater-wauling of seasick tabbies. To this critic, then, the whole business is humiliating and obscene in the sense that it is an abasement of the human voice and a degradation of the art of singing. Holding this view I cannot think that any crooner is better or worse than any other.

There is a lady comedian in this show who has no voice with which to sing and hardly any with which to talk. Her dancing consists of rapid projections and withdrawals of the hip, and her impersonations of film-stars are burlesques. Her energy, however, has a certain acrid charm, and to be honest I must say that whereas the crooning of Miss Ruth Etting gives me no pleasure whatever, the antics of Miss Lupe Velez give me a little. On the other hand, Mr. Lou Holtz would be an admirable comedian if he were not hampered by any and all of his present material. When he spins the stuff out of himself he is very funny indeed. Buck and Bubbles are two engaging negroes whose engagement may possibly save the present show. They dance wittily and well. The music is dull, the wit to seek, and the sketches are too often vulgar. The chorus is capable and lively. Altogether I am of the opinion that the best thing Mr. James Donahue can now do with Mr. Felix Ferry's *Transatlantic Rhythm* is to ferry it back across the Atlantic.

TWO RESTORATION COMEDIES

THE COUNTRY WIFE. Revival of William Wycherley's Comedy. Old Vic Theatre, Tuesday, October 6, 1936.

THE PROVOKED WIFE. Revival of Sir John Vanbrugh's Comedy. Embassy Theatre, Thursday, October 8, 1936.

CHARLES THE KING. A play by Maurice Colbourne. Lyric Theatre, Friday, October 9, 1936.   [*October* 11, 1936]

THIS WEEK has seen two blazingly good new pieces of acting, counting Miss Edith Evans's Lady Fidget as nothing ! This for the reason that one has learned what to expect from this past-mistress of Restoration coquetry. Everybody in to-day's audience has seen and admired that exquisite frigate in full sail which is her Millamant. Lady Fidget, we feel, will be a companion vessel to Congreve's, say a sloop of war, a trifle more robustious because of the manlier Wycherley. And so it is. Why waste words to describe the images which this great artist conjures up—images varying from a battleship coming into port to a Rowlandsonesque cartoon of Britannia turned bawdy ? For here, if this character and this author and the whole of Restoration comedy are to mean anything at all, is a tale of bawdry pure and simple. The truth, said a later wit, is rarely pure and never simple, whereas bawdry such as Lady Fidget's is never pure and always simple.

Even the sternest moralist watching this performance must balance the merry quality of the riot against the lack of squeamishness. Personally, I do not believe that a committee consisting of Martin Luther, John Calvin, John Knox, William Penn, George Eliot, Mrs. Humphry Ward, and Mrs. Ormiston Chant would have been able to resist the tremendous fun with which Miss Evans invests Lady Fidget's indiscretions. The word pulls one up, since it has an accidental implication, and there is nothing of accident about Lady F. Her sallies are all sorties directed against circumspection, wilfully planned. Miss Evans may have faults, though I have never been able to discover any. Upon a review of the whole range of her talents I will venture to affirm, as an early dramatic critic wrote: " That *impartial* JUSTICE *must* pronounce MISS EVANS as the *First* of her PROFESSION; and that the *amazing* BLAZE of her EX-CELLENCIES greatly *obscures*, if not totally *eclipses* her DEFECTS." This was written, with due alteration of pronouns, about Garrick, which brings us back to this week's performance by a new actor, Mr. Mervyn Johns, in Garrick's favourite part of Sir John Brute.

In a little-known anthology entitled *The English Dramatic Critics*, I find this passage, culled from *The London Chronicle* of October 7, 1758:

" It is amazing to me that Mr. Garrick will *attempt* the part of Sir John Brute; a part which he not only apparently *mistakes*, but in which he is absolutely prejudicial to the morals of his countrymen. Quin made him a Brute indeed, an ill-natured, surly swine of a fellow; and I dare swear everybody most heartily despised and detested him: But with Garrick it is quite a different case; the knight is the greatest favourite in the play; such a joyous agreeable wicked dog, that we never think we can have enough of his company; and when he drinks confusion to all order, there is scarce a man in the house, I believe, who is not for that moment a reprobate in his heart. In truth he is so very much the entertainment of the audience, that, to speak in a phrase which Sir John Brute might be supposed to make use of himself, whenever he goes off the stage, we are like so many people sitting round a table after the wine and glasses are removed, till he comes on again."

Carefully avoiding the temptation to declare that Mr. Johns, whom one is seeing for the first time, is another Garrick, I say without hesitation that what the dramatic critic of the *London Chronicle* wrote of the great actor's performance in this part applies also to Mr. Johns, though we should have to see the two performances together in order to judge to which it applies the more. This is not so foolish as it sounds, for I guess that the stage is emptier when Mr. Johns leaves it than when Garrick did. This for the reason that Garrick left behind him Mrs. Cibber and Mrs. Clive as Lady Brute and Lady Fanciful. Whereas Mr. Johns leaves on the stage two actresses, one of whom, in my opinion, has not sufficient of the particular talent required, while the other, though a very talented actress, is entirely miscast. Even Mrs. Cibber, acknowledged to be a grand actress in the right part, was alleged to want a trifle of spirit in the character of Lady Brute. But I can find no justification for Miss Julia Crawley's whole-hearted melancholy. Nobody admires more than I do Miss Marda Vanne's genius for representing the sturdy, commonsensical woman of to-day. But to suggest that this is right for Lady Fanciful is like casting Mrs. Siddons for Mrs. Dombey. One of the Embassy actresses has no manner at all; the other lays it on so thick that we see through it. As a flibbertigibbet Miss Vanne puts the old play in the cart, from which Mr. Johns marvellously extricates it at each and every appearance. This is a magnificent performance which would have warmed the heart-cockles of the old playgoers. " Can any man wonder like him ? " asked Lamb about Munden. It is certain that no actor of to-day can stare like Mr. Johns.

Many things help this player. He is Garrick's size and looks like a Zoffany come to life. But I think he is chiefly helped by his talent, which is up to every demand made upon it by this magnificent part. In this actor's hands Sir John is a brute indeed, not a puling mooncalf but a roaring bull. But there is more to it than that. Mr. Johns lets us see the pleasure he is taking in the fellow's brutish gusto. There are actors who could make the man as unbearable to an audience as he was to his own circle. If Quin did this he was wrong, and Mr. Johns, by lifting a corner of the brute's mind to show us his own, is right with Garrick. The Embassy production of this delightful play contains one other good performance, Mr. Christopher Steele's most amusing thumbnail sketch of the Justice.

The week's second remarkable new performance is that of Miss Ruth Gordon as the country wife. Here again one is in the old difficulty. It is impossible to know how good an actress Miss Gordon is until one sees her in something else. The greatest recorded Margery Pinchwife is that of Mrs. Jordan, and I cannot help thinking that what Hazlitt deems sauce for the Jordan may possibly be sauce for the Gordon :

" It was not as an actress but as herself, that she charmed every one. . . . Mrs. Jordan was the same in all her characters, and inimitable in all of them, because there was no one else like her."

One performance cannot tell us whether Miss Gordon is the same in all her characters, and therefore we cannot know how much the other night she was acting. It is quite true that there is no one else like Miss Gordon, which does not prevent Miss Gordon being like quite a lot of other people.

Margery Pinchwife might have been at one moment the creation of Adèle Astaire, at another that of Zasu Pitts, and at yet a third that of Pitoëff. Several of the Barrie heroines were, so to speak, in the offing, with Dickens's Marchioness and Miss Anita Loos's Lorelei more than nodding acquaintances.

All sorts of qualities were present, glinting and giving place. The faster and the furiouser the fun, the more certain became the conviction that if ever the actress turned to pathos it would be heartrending. But pathos was not her business now, except in so far as it is inseparable from simplicity. Miss Gordon miraculously avoided the suggestion made by so many exponents of the part that Margery was a minx even before she was made into one. Instead she indicated with admirable subtlety a mind so virginal that the monstrous could grow in it as easily as the blameless. But one is labouring. Better to say that the great scene of the letter was a superb piece of comic accomplishment. Here was childish lying with its back to the wall, with all the reinforcements of prevarication called up and exhausted. Although one knew the outcome one's pulse beat faster. It may be said that Miss Gordon speaks American. Vat of dat ? It is not the first time that an alien accent has been heard in our theatre. I am afraid I thought Mr. James Dale's Pinchwife noisy rather than humorous; this character ought to be more tetchy than tyrannous. Mr. Richard Goolden was much nearer Sir Jasper Fidget's quality, and Mr. Ernest Thesiger's Sparkish was, as before, beyond praise or cavil. As against this Mr. Michael Redgrave was, in my opinion, quite inadequate as Horner. He was neither old enough, nor experienced enough, nor sardonic enough, and was altogether much too nice a youth to hit upon this play's ugly and middle-aged invention. The stage has been decorated by Mr. Oliver Messel. From a near view one might think it over-decorated, though from the middle of the auditorium the designs must appear very handsome indeed. The song from *The Beggar's Opera* which, the programme tells us, is " interpolated by permission of Frederick Austin," should at once be dis-interpolated with or without anybody's leave. At the first night it was poorly sung and atrociously accompanied, and in any case it has nothing to do with the period.

It is clear from *Charles the King* that the Cavaliers and the Roundheads were equally in the wrong. That monarch is obviously a fool who tries to shove an uncongenial prayer-book down a Scotsman's throat at the same time that he is putting an unwanted surplice on his back. As against this, the dissenter who drags an altar into the middle of the church and uses it for his Saturday afternoon game of nap is an ill-mannered boor and an anachronist to boot. It is quite obvious, again from this play, that a monarch who condones a Star Chamber is not fit to wear his own Garter. But it is equally obvious that a democrat like Cromwell will develop into a tyrant more trying than any despot.

The piece, then, is one of conflicting ideas, and as such is to be highly respected. But a play which concerned itself solely with theories of government would, unless Mr. Shaw wrote it, be as dull as a page of John Richard Green, who isn't dull either. What I am getting at is that in the theatre what we are really concerned with is Charles's Van Dyck beard and Cromwell's Rembrandtesque bib. Mr. Colbourne's view in this play is rightly that of Lady Callcott: " Charles showed that, if he had been mistaken as a king, he was a good man and a right high-minded gentleman." Yes, there can be no doubt that history for the stage is most effective when it is written in the manner of Little Arthur. Perhaps Mr. Colbourne has contrived most movingly in the long deliberation about Strafford. After all Charles cut off
Un

his friend's head possibly not to save his own but to save his wife's, which suggests that absolute monarchs should keep absolute wives in some other country. Henrietta Maria was a nuisance in real life, and she is a bit of a nuisance in this play. Even Miss Ffrangçon-Davies can do nothing with her except make her look Lelyesque in a lovely red gown. Now it is no use engaging a brilliant actress unless you give her a scene in which to deploy her brilliance. With this object in view Mr. Colbourne has given Henrietta Maria ten minutes' leave-taking on Wapping Old Stairs. But whether it is Wapping or whether Miss Ffrangçon-Davies is brilliant nobody knows, as it all takes place in the dark at midnight.

I am conscious, however, of wasting the reader's time. All anybody wants to know about a play concerning Charles I is the amount of pathos possessed by the chief player. There was once an actor in this part who so blinded the spectators with tears that they could no longer see the stage and when they groped for the exits could not find them. Mr. Barry Jones is not in Irving's class, but he gives a moving performance of considerable sweetness and dignity. His faults are monotony and a total absence of those ill-tempers which even Charles's admirers admit to. And at what date, pray, did the king's hair, like that of the lady in Wilde's comedy, turn golden from grief? Mr. Morland Graham makes a really exciting Archbishop Laud. Owing to the way the part is written Mr. George Merritt's performance of the Protector-to-be was not so much Cromwell without the wart as the wart without Cromwell.

ANTON AND CLEOPATROVA

Antony and Cleopatra. Revival of Shakespeare's Tragedy. New Theatre, Wednesday, October 14, 1936.

Jane Eyre. A play, adapted by Helen Jerome from Charlotte Brontë's Novel. Queen's Theatre, Tuesday, October 13, 1936.

[*October* 18, 1936]

The tail-end of your theatre programme is invariably composed of what Cleopatra would call " lady trifles " and " immoment toys." Thus you will read " Shoes by Thingummy " and " Stockings by Thingumbob." One turned to the New Theatre programme the other evening to see whether among the informative rag, tag, and bobtail, one would find : " Words by Shakespeare." One did not. The time-honoured phrase was in its usual place under the title of the play. But alas ! the information turned out to be, in part and in the most important part, false. Cleopatra's words may have been Shakespeare's ; they were spoken in the accent of Count Smorltork. But of this more later. Beneath the words " by William Shakespeare " one read in thicker and blacker type : " The Production is devised and directed and the Scenery and Costumes designed by Komisarjevsky." But not a word about the disgraceful messing-up of one of the grandest of Shakespeare's openings. It may be useful to recall how it goes. The curtain rises, and to the unimportant Philo is given one of the most tremendous sentences in the whole of Shakespeare :

Nay, but this dotage of our general's
O'erflows the measure: those his goodly eyes,
That o'er the files and musters of the war
Have glow'd like plated Mars, now bend, now turn
The office and devotion of their view
Upon a tawny front: his captain's heart,
Which in the scuffles of great fights hath burst
The buckles on his breast, reneges all temper,
And is become the bellows and the fan
To cool a gipsy's lust.

There in ten lines is the whole of Antony. Next Philo bids us mark the entrance of the lovers, but still harping on Antony, and with Cleopatra dismissed in the single word "strumpet." "Behold and see," he tells Demetrius. Then follow the lovers' exchanges, beginning with Cleopatra's: "If it be love indeed . . ." An attendant enters whom Antony will not hear. Let Rome in Tiber melt and the wide arch of the ranged empire fall sooner than he shall be bothered with Cæsar's foolish politics. "Speak not to us," he says to the messenger, and leads his queen away.

All this is Shakespeare's "wide arch," the opening through which he desired that we should enter his play. Mr. Komisarjevsky will have none of this. He does not cut the scene, which would be bad enough. He postpones it, which is worse, and in favour of a tweeting soothsayer and a pair of gossipy girls. I do not think that foreign producers, however distinguished, should permit themselves to take such liberties. For this is a liberty which matters. Shakespeare meant to open his play grandly; this opening niggles.

Like all other producers of this play, Mr. Komisarjevsky has been faced with the old difficulty about the multiplicity of scenes. He gets over this by pretending that no difficulty occurs. He has two formalised settings, one before the interval and one after. It is all exceedingly simple. If a Roman appears, then the place is Rome; if an Egyptian, then Egypt. This is fairly easy for the producer. But just as it is always said that easy writing makes hard reading, so easy producing means hard playgoing. Simplification has other dangers, one of which is that the spectator, having been induced into the mood of simplicity, may decline to get out of it. Consider the famous scene whose stage-directions are " Enter, below, Antony, borne by the Guard " and " They heave Antony aloft to Cleopatra." Even if these directions are not Shakespeare's, the text clearly indicates that Antony is to be drawn up into the monument, and, I suggest, even on the Elizabethan stage in view of the Elizabethan audience. Mr. Komisarjevsky has Antony carried round to the rear so that nothing is seen save the backs of the hauling women, while Antony's broken: " I am dying, Egypt, dying ! " has to be shouted at the top of his lungs by an actor in obviously excellent vocal condition. Here the playgoer's induced simplicity comes in. Why, he aks, go to all that trouble when from the spot where Antony has fallen to the top of the monument there is a perfectly good staircase of six steps only ? I am afraid this production is one of those cases in which what is wanted is a little less imagination and a few more scene-shifters.

I cannot hope to emulate the phonetic daring of one of my colleagues. But I confess to rubbing my ears on hearing Cleopatra say to Antony:

Wen you suet staying,
Den was de time for Wurst.

What had English tallow and German sausage to do with this Egyptian passion ? It needed genuine effort to recall that what Shakespeare had written was:

> *When you sued staying,*
> *Then was the time for words.*

And so Mme Leontovich continued throughout the entire play. Let me not be misunderstood. If except for the matter of accent this were a great Cleopatra, then one would make every effort to forgive the Russian accent just as one forgave Modjeska's Juliet her Polish intonations. But Mme Leontovich is never Shakespeare's Cleopatra, though she might make a very good shot at Mr. Shaw's. We know our Russian visitor to be an extremely accomplished comédienne; the difficulty about Shakespeare's baggage is that she is a part for a great tragic actress who has a comédienne up her sleeve. And, alas, I do not think that Mme Leontovich, born comédienne though she is, has any of the physical dispositions necessary for a great tragic actress. She has an eager, inquisitive little face resembling that of Spinelly. She has hardly any voice, and what she has is pitched too high, with the result that poignancy becomes a squeak. The artist put gait and gesture to notable use in the earlier scenes, but when tragedy grew we noted the lack of inches and the too constant use of a statue-like pose with one knee advanced. This was probably intended to compensate for the lack of height, but merely suggested a not very expert sculptor. Since we could hardly bear to listen to this Cleopatra we were forced to fill up occupation with our eyes, and therefore could not help noticing how little of majesty or queenliness there was in the little figure skipping about the stage. Incredible though it sounds, Cleopatra attended the sea-fight in a costume consisting of a Roman helmet, a golden breastplate, and a slashed skirt of forget-me-not blue satin, the whole irresistibly reminiscent of Miss Renee Houston in some naval-cum-military skit. But then absurdity was never far away from this Cleopatra's frocks, whose trains covered the floor like a peacock's, but afforded no protection elsewhere.

Of the essential Antony, Mr. Donald Wolfit, alas, gave little ! At the beginning of the play he glowed like plated Mars, and he went on glowing to the end. But the whole point of the man is that he has ceased to glow and is now only the ruins of what has once been great. Antony is a lean wolf, bloated, out of training, with a middle-aged spread; a lean Wolfit, who is chubbier than he was, is not the same thing. The actor did his best, though his tragic expression was rather like that of the desperate leader in a tug-of-war whose team had given ground at the word " go." I suspect him, unfortunately, of not having much natural pathos of the kind possessed by Mr. James Craven in the small rôle of Eros. On the other hand, Mr. Wolfit may very well take up the challenge and ask what pathos I expected from an Antony whose pathetic passages had been cut. If Mr. Komisarjevsky does not know, he must be told that " Call to me all my sad captains " and " To-night I'll force the wine peep through their scars " are to the English ear and mind sacrosanct. While one is on this point of arrangement and rearrangement, what a mess was made of the " music of hautboys as under the stage." I recall how well this was done in the last revival at the Old Vic. It was night, and the Guard was set one at each corner of the stage. Then came the unearthly music, the First Soldier's : " What should this mean ? " and the Second Soldier answering him across the empty stage : " 'Tis the god Hercules, whom Antony loved, now leaves him." Mr. Komisarjevsky had this said at high noon by a soothsayer !

Mr. Ellis Irving preferred a forthright rendering of that polished snake, Octavius ; this honest manly Emperor would never have conceived the impertinent : " Which is the Queen of Egypt ? " As Menas, Mr. Lawrence Anderson elected for a gum-chewing gangster of our own day, and as Lepidus, Mr.

Vernon Kelso was less anachronistically amusing. In the matter of Enobarbus I can only say that Mr. Leon Quartermaine, by turning the bluff soldier into the silky diplomat, was utterly and entirely wrong from the first syllable of the part to the last. Yet inasmuch as all the other syllables were pure and dulcet English exquisitely manipulated I forgive him. But then, I would at any time pay half-a-guinea to hear Mr. Quartermaine recite a page of Bradshaw's Railway Guide. The cleverest thing about Miss Margaret Rawlings's Charmian was that she refrained from wiping Cleopatra off the stage till after she was dead. The Queen once dispatched, the tiring-maid let us know in six lines who should have been playing what. Here were the voice and the manner and the English language. But the world of the theatre is a rum place, and it would not in the least surprise me if Mme Leontovich's next part should be that of Katie O'Shea.

Shakespeare, who could be right even about the theatre, pronounced correctly when he said: " One *wow* doth tread upon another's heel, so fast they follow." After *Pride and Prejudice* Miss Jerome's next play just had to be *Jane Eyre*. But then, isn't it the same story—Jane's pride versus Rochester's prejudice ? I now look forward to an agreeable procession of these hybrids. Since there can be thousands of them, and if Miss Jerome should desire a hint as to critical preference, I shall suggest E. P. Roe's *Barriers Burned Away*, Rhoda Broughton's *Cometh Up as a Flower*, Elizabeth Wetherell's *The Wide, Wide World*, Charlotte M. Yonge's *The Daisy Chain*, Miss Braddon's *Aurora Floyd*, Edna Lyall's *Won by Waiting*, Mrs. Henry Wood's *The Shadow of Ashlydyat*, and Emma Jane Worboise's *Thornycroft Hall*. Being in the tentative vein I shall opine that whereas anybody can dramatise Jane Austen, nobody can dramatise Charlotte Brontë. This for the reason that in dramatising Jane you merely pick out the funny bits and string them together, whereas there are no funny bits in Charlotte. What I am trying to say is that the essence of the latter's book is the emotional thunder and lightning of its background against which the story seems to be a mere interruption. Whereas the story and the chatter *are* Jane. Charlotte used her personages to explain her own tempestuous mind; Jane smiled, embroidered figures on a tambour, and went on smiling. Now, though you can make a novel out of a background you cannot make a play so, and therefore the best dramatisation of *Jane Eyre* will always be less effective than the worst dramatisation of *Pride and Prejudice.* This being granted, the present version is effective enough. Miss Curigwen Lewis plays Jane like a German stove—plenty of heat inside and nothing visible. The part is not one for display of acting; all that is wanted is an actress who can look like Queen Victoria in early widowhood. Mr. Reginald Tate has great fun with Rochester, which would have greatly surprised that grim Murdstone-cum-Dombey. But then I suggest that there may have been more innocent fun in M-cum-D than the casual spectator might imagine. It remains to say that Miss F. Marriott-Watson is a quite remarkable Grace Poole. This is " stone cut from the Brontë quarry." I forget who first said this. It may even have been me.

WYCHERLEY'S LITTLE JACK HORNER

[*October* 25, 1936]

ALL THE WORLD has been reading with great interest and amusement the discussion between Mr. Sydney Carroll and Lord Lytton in the *Daily Telegraph*. Readers will remember the famous fight in *Alice*, and how Tweedledee, when he got really excited, would hit anything he could see, while Tweedledum hit everything within reach, whether he could see it or not. At this point Alice expressed the opinion that the brothers, who chose a wood to fight in, must hit the trees oftener than they hit each other. Readers will remember Tweedledum's reply: " I don't suppose there'll be a tree left standing, for ever so far round, by the time we've finished ! " If I seem to butt in, it is with the intention not of stopping the fight, but of making clear to each what the fight should really be about. Mr. Carroll, having himself produced Wycherley's *The Country Wife* at a commercial theatre and therefore for profit, cannot go all out and say that this is an obscene play and nothing more. " Not even its sincerest advocates," he tells us, " can deny that it is a play containing the grossest improprieties in situations, thought, and language." This play " cannot justly be said to have the slightest cultural or educational value." Its choice by the Old Vic " represents a complete abandonment of the Old Vic's standards, and is a step that no brilliance of production, beauty of décor, or vigour of acting can, in my opinion, excuse." Why then did Mr. Carroll produce this play at the Ambassadors two years ago ? Because " it has the merits of wit and blunt speaking," because of " its reflection of the decadent and corrupt age in which it was written."

Mr. Carroll's contention, as I see it, is that while it is lawful to produce a blunt and witty play of corruption, the fact that the plain-speaking and the wit are centred in corruption prevent that play from having any cultural or educational value. There I join issue with him. Mr. Carroll called upon the governors of the Old Vic to explain to him the cultural and educational value of *The Country Wife*. I call upon Mr. Carroll to produce in the entire range of British playwriting from the death of Shakespeare to the birth of Mr. Coward a more brilliant example of pure comedy than the famous letter-writing scene in *The Country Wife*. I will even throw in Mr. Coward ! Surely it is obvious that a person who knows this scene is more highly cultured and educated than a person who doesn't ? I will go further and say that a person who knows his Chaucer, his Boccaccio, his Rabelais, and his droller Balzac is more highly cultured and better educated than a person who doesn't. And it seems to me that Wycherley is in the same category.

Before coming to Lord Lytton, I should like to say a few words on the Englishman's habit, when confronted with something nasty, of pretending either that it isn't there or that it is something nice in disguise. An Englishman confronted with an unpleasant object will look through the object, or round it, or above it or below it, or in any direction except into it. As I once observed in connection with a totally different kind of play, when an Englishman says a subject has been exquisitely handled, he always means exquisitely avoided. Lord Lytton says : " I can well imagine a production of *The Country Wife* which would be only unpleasant, in which the coarseness of the plot rather than the satire on the immorality of the age would be emphasised, and by which the audience might be encouraged to think that the conduct satirised in the play was worthy of applause and imitation." But this is an age-long difficulty. In his new book, *From Richardson to Pinero*, Professor Boas has this passage:

> " Richardson, though he had undertaken ' not to raise a single idea throughout the whole [of Pamela] that shall shock the exactest piety,' found himself confronted with the dilemma which meets every writer who turns fiction or drama to moral uses. If he turns away his gaze from the evils against which he wishes to warn his readers, he can appeal only to the ' fugitive and cloistered virtue ' which overcomes the world by shunning it. If he paints scenes of depravity and temptation, his art may make them so lifelike that they may kindle a flame in the senses and imagination which his didacticism cannot afterwards extinguish. Rousseau, fervent admirer as he was of Richardson, said that in his novels he lit a fire that he might bring up the pumps and put it out."

According to Lord Lytton, the production at the Old Vic has re-kindled the flame which was Wycherley, but by choosing an innocuous exponent for the part of Mr. Horner has dowsed that unholy glim which is the play's central character. I can make nothing of this contention. Let us suppose that a play is written round a character whom we will simply label A. Let us further suppose that an actor is chosen who fulfils A and makes the audience believe that A does and says those things which are set down for him. Let us suppose that the result is, in Lord Lytton's words, " a dirty entertainment." Now let us suppose that another actor is engaged who does not suggest A, and who persuades the audience that A is incapable of doing and saying the things

which the author has set down for him. The result, says Lord
Lytton, is a clean entertainment ! I would prefer to say that
it is an incredible entertainment, because you no longer
believe any of it.

Imagine for a moment that there existed in this country
the same antipathy to melancholy that there is to obscenity.
What, then, would Lord Lytton propose to do with a production of *Hamlet* ? By his own showing he must engage an actor
with the roundest possible cast of feature and so hilarious of
temperament that we should not believe a single word
Hamlet said. Such an actor would at the line, " sicklied o'er
with the pale cast of thought," do his best to look like a full-
blown peony. His " nighted colour " would be some cheerful
combination of magenta and vermilion, and the " thousand
natural shocks " would be attended by a thousand un-
natural chuckles. The result might be a clean entertainment,
but it would not, I submit, be a performance of Shakespeare's
Hamlet. In so far as Mr. Horner at the Old Vic is played by
an actor " whose inherent niceness is so transparent " that
it " makes the whole play a clean and not a dirty entertainment," the part of Mr. Horner, the scenes in which he
appears, the play's total gesture, and the author are all
betrayed.

*I hold that " The Country Wife " is a play which may be per-
formed with propriety in any theatre so long as that theatre in its
placards and newspaper-advertisements bears the announcement that
it is a play for adults only. I hold that it is cultural, educational, and
entertaining. In simple language, it is a work of art.*

Now about this wretched business of entertainment tax.
In my view all plays performed at the Old Vic, Sadler's
Wells, and the Open Air Theatre should be free of entertainment tax. And remain free until such time as a committee,
not of tax-gatherers whose education is general but of persons
highly educated in the particular way of æsthetics and the

drama, should decide that the privilege extended to these theatres was being abused—such a committee to consist of Mr. Shaw, Miss Rebecca West, and any Bishop. One of the obligations attendant upon that privilege would be the nice discrimination and notification of plays suitable for adults only. *The Country Wife* being a play of educational and cultural value, its production would not constitute even an infinitesimal breach of privilege; I should even deem it an upholding and justification thereof.

We come now to the complication caused by the intervention of Mr. Gilbert Miller. Mr. Miller intends to use the present Old Vic production as the basis of a production in New York in which, presumably, his object will be commercial rather than cultural or educational. (This is perhaps the place to say that any theatre-manager is fully entitled to produce plays for wholly commercial reasons, and that no stigma whatever attaches to him because such plays are not necessarily cultural or educational.) I do not know what share Mr. Miller has taken in the cost of the present production or what will be his share, if any, of the profit, if any. All I have been told is that the production is to go to America, and all I presume is that a success over here may have some bearing on success over there. Let us keep red herrings out of the argument. The play of *St. Helena*, which was afterwards produced commercially in the West End, was not put on at the Old Vic as a stepping-stone to West End production. It was put on because Miss Baylis thought that it was a good play. That she was right in so thinking is nothing to the point. Nor is comparison between the two cases to the point. They have nothing in common. Let us realise that this entertainment tax is not only nonsense but delicate nonsense. I think possibly this is a case in which the tax authorities might have done a little bargaining. I think they might have suggested to Mr. Miller that out of his New York profits he should refund some portion of the tax remitted at the Old Vic. Or even out of his New York losses ! If Mr. Miller should utterly reject this, with what regret must they impose the full tax on the Old Vic ! In which case I feel sure that Mr. Miller's sense of arithmetic would have come to the rescue.

To sum up:

(1) Mr. Carroll is wrong in saying that *The Country Wife* is neither cultural nor educational.

(2) Lord Lytton is wrong in saying that you can make a dirty play into a clean one by pretending the dirt isn't there.

(3) Both are wrong if they think that a play with an obscene subject cannot be a work of art.

(4) Both should ponder Ally Sloper's maxim: " A dirty mind is a perpetual feast "—a quotation which had the sanction of the most august of our literary weeklies in its palmiest days.

(5) Both should consider the application of this maxim to Wycherley.

(6) Both should ask themselves if Lamb's airy defence of Restoration immorality was not the only one which could have been printed in *The London Magazine* in the 1820's.

There is, I think, no more to be said on the matter.

A ROUSING MELODRAMA

Young Madame Conti. A melodrama by Bruno Frank.
English adaptation by Hubert Griffith and Benn W. Levy.
Savoy Theatre, Thursday, November 19, 1936.

[*November* 22, 1936]

A wise critic is one who refrains from looking before
and after or pining for what is not. A wise critic, instead of
asking for the little more, gives thanks that he was not fobbed
off with the little less. A circus critic, if there are such things,
would not complain of a tight-rope dancer that she did not
attitudinise like, say, Miss Tilly Losch. He would commend
her for having danced without falling off. I think it was
Arthur Johnstone who praised Bizet for not pretending that
Mérimée's *Carmen* was anything more than a pothouse story
which might have happened in the Waterloo Road. Somehow
or other this rule of criticising the thing for what it is and not
for what it might have been, would not seem to obtain in the
theatre. Somebody modestly proposes a melodrama, and at
once the critics mount all their highest horses and ask why,
instead of telling a tale of violence, didn't the author withdraw to one side and treat them to an essay on pity for human
suffering. It is as though some musical critic of the period
should have solemnly reproved Beethoven for writing a
Sonata Appassionata when he, the critic, would have liked a
Sonata Compassionata.

Messrs. Benn Levy and Hubert Griffith did doubtless all
they thought needful in the way of forestalling this when they
wrote the words " a melodrama " at the top of Herr Bruno

Frank's play. But they didn't do enough. They should have
written "a melodrama with terror but without pity." That
perhaps might have done it. At least one is tempted to suggest that a melodrama, complete with terror and pity, ceases
to be a melodrama and becomes a tragedy. What our higher-
flighted critics are really after, of course, is the pity without
the terror and also without the melodrama. Which in my
view is like reading Francis Thompson poetising about
cricket, but hating to see a man of brawn hurl himself at the
stumps only to be hit out of the field for his pains. The great
advantage possessed by these plays, in which Pity, like a
naked new-born babe, galumphs about the stage dropping
tears from escritoire to mantelpiece, moaning mouthfuls of
misericordia—the great advantage of such plays is that they
can be acted with the actress's back to the audience, or a
full-faced mummified rigor with no more than a finger
twitching the corner of a mourning veil. One knows twenty
actresses capable of recollecting paranoia in tranquillity for
one who can portray paranoia itself.

   The part of this play's heroine needs something which I
shall call horse-acting, in the same way in which one talks of
horse-sense, meaning a greater degree of sense than usual and
not a sublimation into sensibility. Consider what she has to
do. In the first scene we see her as a flourishing courtesan
rejecting the love of a sentimental boy. This is a luxury
which women of Madame Conti's class know that they must
automatically deny themselves, provided the young man is of
any class at all. For if they do not they will have to go
through the tedium of explaining to the earnest young man
that they don't want all that Marguerite Gautier meant when
she murmured to Armand:

   "En une minute, comme une folie, j'ai bâti tout un
   avenir sur ton amour, j'ai rêvé campagne, pureté; je me suis
   Wɴ

souvenue de mon enfance,—on a toujours eu une enfance, quoi que l'on soit devenue ;—c'était souhaiter l'impossible."

They have seen the play too often not to know that *on revient toujours à ses dernières habitudes*. No, the young man they are looking for is an *amant complaisant*, one whom they can support during the intervals when he is not in prison for being so supported. The redeeming point about such a scoundrel is that he must return the affection which he inspires, and it is mere childishness to pretend that this aspect of the relation between courtesan and souteneur does not exist. Madame Conti has such a protector, with this unforgivable difference that he despises and loathes her. At least, she is not going to forgive him; indeed, she is going to shoot him, and the curtain comes down on the first scene just as the revolver is levelled.

There are many admirable things about this *pièce de théâtre*. The first point is that the next scene opens, not on a bewigged and romantically assembled trial-scene, but upon the court-room in the horrid light of early morning with the charwoman cleaning up and the whole business of the law shown for the grim reality it is. Another point is that the author, not being afraid to drop his curtain occasionally, gets rid of the tedious business of swearing witnesses, and so can proceed from salient point to salient point without the intolerable detail of a murder trial. The greater part of the evening is taken up with the trial. Now there are two ways of doing this, according as an actress (*a*) can act, or (*b*) can't. If she belongs to (*b*) she sits glum, like a Mona Lisa, without a smile. If she belongs to (*a*) her face will not be a beautifully-bound, closed volume but an open book in which the audience can read all that she is going through. In a piece of this sort the prisoner is almost certain to have an Outburst, in which case the (*b*) school will choose another play. The part gives immense opportunity for both the mute and the vocal kind of distress.

Later there is a scene of terror in the condemned cell. This is
Painful To Witness; indeed, it is painful in exact proportion
as the actress can do it or can't. And as though this were not
enough, the last scene shows Madame Conti recovering from
the dream—you may, if you like, call it " imaginative projec-
tion "—of what the business of being hanged really amounts
to, and nevertheless resolving to proceed with the job.

Here, then, is a part for an actress to get her teeth into,
which is something the Quietist, tight-lipped school never
attempts. Miss Constance Cummings acts every ounce of the
part, and immediately takes rank, even on the strength of one
performance, as an incontestably fine emotional actress up to
anything from pitch-and-toss to manslaughter. The piece is
explicit melodrama, and Miss Cummings acts it explicitly,
without a word left unsaid and none of the ineffabilities belonging to the tragic or great order of acting. But the task
being what it is, she performs it in a way in which very few
English actresses would be able to attempt. That possibly
may be because such parts are not often written nowadays,
and if so one cannot escape the reflection that young English
actresses would be all the better for a course of blood and
thunder. Mr. Bernard Lee makes the most of a very difficult
moment of ultimate terror; Mr. Raymond Huntley is responsible for a superb exposition of the realities of capital punishment; Mr. William Dewhurst, as the judge, keeps exaggera-
tion at arm's length; Mr. William Fox plays well within
himself as the boy lover; Mr. Phillip Leaver, as the souteneur's friend, gives a glimpse at once frightening, amusing,
and valuable of the underworld in which this play has its
roots; and lastly, Miss Olga Edwardes contributes a very
clever little sketch as Madame Conti's maid. But it all comes
back to Miss Cummings, who makes a roaring success out of
what in other hands might so easily have been an inarticulate,
elegant flop.

A GREAT PLAY

WASTE. A tragedy by Harley Granville-Barker. Westminster
   Theatre, Tuesday, December 1, 1936.

O MISTRESS MINE. A comedy by Ben Travers. St. James's
   Theatre, Thursday, December 3, 1936.

[December 6, 1936]

THIS PLAY is much too good a stick to flog the Censor
with. Let us instead talk about how good a play it is. If
Galsworthy beat Mr. Granville-Barker at the game of
success it was because Galsworthy stuck closer to the rules of
the game. All Galsworthy is playwriting; there are parts of
the present author which are not playwriting but dissertation.
This accounts for those *longueurs* which are *longueurs* in the
theatre only, and would be of vital interest anywhere else.
I refer particularly to the second half of the second act, all of
which could go by the board. Montague, writing about
Ibsen, has something vital to say on this point. " Many
dramatists never, to the end of their careers, grasp all that
the special conditions of theatrical representation mean and
demand. Their plays remain essentially novels, or lyric or
didactic poems, or pamphlets, or Socratic dialogues. Ibsen
learnt his trade to begin with, and learnt it well. When one
of his characters speaks you feel that you really must hear
the reply. When one of them comes upon the stage you feel
that for some minutes you have been coming to need his
presence. He plays on you like a flute, and knows every vent
and stop of your attention."

The trouble with the second half of our second act is that

suddenly you find you are not attending. You feel that instead of waiting for Cantilupe to arrive on the stage, you have been coming to need his absence. Here one must safeguard oneself by making a provisional correction. Is it possible that our lack of attention is due to decreasing interest in Church Disestablishment ? This may have been a burning question thirty years ago; there is no conflagration now. To one school of thought it is obvious that one form of error has no more right to establishment than any other; to another that every village is entitled to its pump, though individuals may prefer to wash elsewhere. There is a minority of thinkers, among whom I class myself, who hold both opinions, and with equal fervour.

Every one of Mr. Granville-Barker's plays shows this tendency to discursiveness. Wherefore, the other evening, was that half-hour during which one reflected how exasperating it is when a major dramatist falls into a trap which a minor one would have avoided. One felt that Pinero would have written a much better play on the same subject. Except, of course, that Pinero would not have thought of the subject, or had the mentality to deal with it if he had thought of it, or risen to any of the heights or said any of the magnificent things in which this play abounds. But he would never have inflicted Cantilupe's pribbles and prabbles upon us. Cantilupe is nicknamed " His Eminence "; Pinero would have made great fun of the nicknaming and let the arguments for eminence be taken for granted.

Professor Allardyce Nicoll holds that in *Waste* the drama is " that of the woman with no motherly instincts faced by the philoprogenitive man." It seems to me that this is to misread the play. It may be that in Mr. Granville-Barker's rewriting ten years ago the insistence on Trebell's philoprogenitiveness disappeared. Very little of it came through the other evening, the only hint of it left being Trebell's remark to his sister:

" I keep thinking of the child," and this only because the child is a symbol of the Parliamentary Bill which now lies in ruins. What did come through with enormous force was O'Connell's condemnation of his wife as " a worthless woman," and his pronouncement amounting almost to a bond with Trebell: " I think we are brothers in misfortune." Every word of this fell like a stone into the consciousness of the audience. Add the only thing which Trebell, who is a man of conscience and honour, can find to say about Amy O'Connell after she is dead: " I wasn't in love with her. It didn't last long. The little trull ! " Trebell's sister immediately says: " How can you be so vile as to say that ? "

This passage is vitally important and worth exact consideration because Mr. Granville-Barker is too fine an artist to use words carelessly in a play written with so much intensity and passion. He writes " trull " and therefore means " trull," and a play which is all about a man throwing the world away for love and then finding that he was not in love at all must be a comedy and not a tragedy. Now a tragedy on the subject of duty and inclination must be conceived on the lines of Antony's: " Let Rome in Tiber melt . . . The nobleness of life is to do thus." In other words, the world well lost, and all the rest of it. But why should we suppose that Professor Nicoll is right in saying that this play is " fundamentally a domestic tragedy with an individual hero " ? As I see it, there is no tragic hero in this piece, but only a tragic subject, and that subject is waste. The play is called *Waste*, and it ends with Trebell's secretary saying:

" I'd like to go through the streets and shout that he's dead—that they've lost him and wasted him, damn them. With his work all undone. Who's to do it ? Much they care. . . . Oh, the waste of him—oh, the waste—the waste ! "

If any dramatist ever meant anything Mr. Granville-Barker meant that reiterated " waste "; he meant it as Sibelius means whatever he says in those last strident chords which end his Fifth Symphony. And when a composer or a drama-tist says something as urgently as that I see no reason to look round for something else that he might be supposed to mean.

Some day I suggest that Mr. Granville-Barker should write the comedy inherent in this subject. For it is one of the world's most ironic. Trebell is thrown over because nobody in Horsham's Cabinet really cares whether his Bill is passed or not. But suppose the country to be at war and Tre-bell to be an inventor whose ray can keep away the airplanes which will be over Downing Street to-morrow morning. Would Horsham write to tell Trebell that because of his private life he and the country have no more use for him and his ray ? There is an admirable model for such a comedy. It is a short story written in French. It is called *Boule de Suif*. But Mr. Granville-Barker chose the tragic key, and we must not be led away from it. The play contains scores of things whose fineness stands up from the rut of common thought like the dome of St. Paul's above the City slums. I have only space for one of these fine things, which is the reply to the remark that the best of what Trebell is trying to do in his Bill seems too good to be true. Trebell says : " If I were God, that's the one blasphemy I'd not forgive ! " The total gesture of this play is that waste is the one unforgivable blasphemy, and that if the principles of Mrs. Grundy mean the waste of something more valuable, those principles must go by the board. The critic is not called upon to give or refuse his sanction to such a proposition. It is his business to say that this and no other thing is what Mr. Granville-Barker's play declares, the right or wrong of such a declaration being left to the playgoer's individual conscience.

The piece is very well acted on the whole, and in one or two of the smaller parts superbly. Nothing better has been seen for a long time than Mr. Felix Aylmer's ex-Prime Minister looking like a mixture of Delius and the late Lord Curzon and attaining to an Olympian and even Balfourian degree of cynicism. Or than Mr. Mark Dignam's wronged husband, aflame with the dark passion of Irish injury. Miss Catherine Lacey has to call up all the resources of her cleverness to make one and the same character out of the smiling fascinatress and the woman aggrieved and abandoned. One keeps saying to oneself: " Who'd have thought the serpent to have had so much venom in it ? " But Miss Lacey does brilliantly, and makes us feel how good a play it is in which so much brilliance can still be beside the real point. There are other good performances, but one must draw to a close. Mr. Nicholas Hannen bears the brunt of the evening with very great distinction indeed, and if he is to be faulted anywhere it is that he has too much natural charm. The essence of Trebell is that he is hard, dogged, and unlikeable. His Bill is the fire of a fine spirit, but it is fire struck from a rock. Mr. Hannen cannot quite suggest that here is a man whom nobody likes but who is necessary to his time. One comes back to the essence of the whole thing, that the waste of Trebell is not his tragedy but the community's.

O Mistress Mine is all contained in the second act, the previous one being merely occupied in explaining why a Ruritanian queen should be occupying an Anglo-Austrian's bath in a Mayfair flat, to the astonishment of English ladies taking her for a French *cocotte*. The third act removes these apprehensions. Her Majesty, having washed and dried herself, occupies the dead vast and middle of the play dining bestrewn with the jewels of everything except wit. And that, in a word, is what is wrong with this little play. This sort of nonsense is only tolerable when on the slenderest basis of plot is erected immensity of wit, like a triangle standing on its apex. In other words, geometry *à la Private Lives*. Unfortunately Mr. Travers has not the courage of Mr. Coward, and has constructed an enormous apex without any triangle. This cannot fall flat because it is flat to start with. Does one think that, as somebody else remarked, the characters will be witty by-and-by? One soon realises that if they are going to be witty it will be in the sweet by-and-by. Yet the piece ought to be a success since it is full of people pretending (*a*) that they can't speak English, and (*b*) that they can. My suggestion is that Messrs. Cole Porter and Vivian Ellis should be mobilised further and kept without food and drink till they have written thirty-six more songs. That a chorus should be imported, and the whole thing turned into a musical comedy when, of course, it would at once seem to be, in comparison with other musical comedies, outrageously witty. For the St. James's Theatre it is just not witty enough.

Mlle Yvonne Printemps acts rather better than her lines permit. But I confess to watching her " opposite number " with something of a sense of waste. For here is a magnificent French actor doing something of which young Englishmen just down from Oxford are capable. In fact they do it better, since they imply a sense of fulfilment, while there is no major dramatist at whom this beautiful player could not fly, from Corneille to Obey. In fact, one wants M. Fresnay to be more *effréné*.

WHAT IS A GREAT ACTRESS?

THE WITCH OF EDMONTON. Revival of the play by Dekker, Ford and Rowley. Old Vic Theatre, Tuesday, December 8, 1936.   [*December* 13, 1936]

At THE FALL OF THIS CURTAIN, as nearly as I can remember, M. Michel St.-Denis said, among other words, the following: " It is a pleasure to work with Miss Edith Evans, who is a great actress. She is a great actress in a great way. Not only does she transform herself every time, but all her transformations are convincing." Rejecting the theory that M. St.-Denis had carefully primed himself from this column in the *Sunday Times* of three years ago all but four days, I cannot refrain from thanking him for those few kind words. And not only kind words, but intelligent also. And not only intelligent, but comprehensive. And not only comprehensive, but going back to first principles and everything that has ever been written on the subject of great acting. " Miss Evans is a great actress in a great way." What else is this but a re-statement of the first sentence in G. H. Lewes's essay on Edmund Kean: " The greatest artist is he who is greatest in the highest reaches of his art." And again: " Miss Evans transforms herself every time." This brings us back to the charge against Bernhardt that she was always Bernhardt, against Irving that he was always Irving, but not for some odd reason, to any charge against Duse that she was always Duse. Exactly the opposite is true. There were half a dozen Bernhardts, and at least a dozen Irvings. Anybody who ever thought that Sarah in Racine's Phèdre, in Hugo's Doña Sol, in Dumas's Marguerite, and in Maeterlinck's Pelléas was the same woman is a multitudinous ass. As for Irving, don't take my word, take Max's. Irving may not have been able to transform himself, and about this Mr. Beerbohm has said: " Irving's voice, face, figure, port, were not transformable." But mark what follows: " Intransformable, he was—multiradiant, though." Which means that though all the parts were Irving, they were not the same Irving. Which, again, means that there were always enough Irvings to go round.

As for Duse, I really do not know. Mr. Beerbohm's " prevailing impression " is that of " a woman over-riding, with an air of sombre unconcern, plays, mimes, critics and public." There is a legend of gaiety and the right kind of unconcern when she played Mirandolina in Goldoni's comedy, and I myself remember being simultaneously dazzled and saddened by her Adrienne Lecouvreur. Here it occurs to me that an actress who can do these two things at the same time must be in the way of greatness. But then came the time when Duse started to play everything with grey hair and a grey face, and so gave us an excuse for thinking that an actress capable of playing Marguerite Gautier in this guise was, like Habakkuk, *capable de tout*. Why not say that Sarah sometimes not herself, Irving always grandly himself, and Duse at least in her later years sombrely and unconcernedly herself, were all three great players? More important, perhaps, is to discover the justification for saying so. Because— and this is the great point—because each of them possessed, and would in any evening of any week and given the right play, offer triumphant proof that they possessed, that quality which Frederick Myers said was characteristic of Homer, " the sense of an effortless and absolute sublimity." Even Mr. Shaw, who throughout his critical career attacked Irving unceasingly, admitted when he was dead that the old man had been not only eminent, but pre-eminent. And no player can be pre-eminent who does not suggest effortless and absolute sublimity. Equally, the player who can do this at once passes into the strict and narrow rank of great actors. With this proviso, that sublimity must be exhibited in the sublime. The thing is not achieved when an actress peers over the edge of a teacup and suggests an oblation to the gods. Let her never mind the suggestion. Let her oblate. Duse, Bernhardt, Irving, all oblated.

Miss Evans oblated when as a Welsh housemaid in *The Late Christopher Bean*, in which she was appearing at the time of our article three years ago, she washed up the tea-things and yet contrived to look like a canvas of Perugino. But if sublimity were all, acting would be a dull business. Again multitudinous asininity would be that man's who thought that Gwenny and Agatha Payne in *The Old Ladies* (April 1935) were the same woman. " A slow nightmare of macabre genius . . . some insane doll that increases continuously in physical stature and spiritual decay," wrote Mr. Morgan. Next came Juliet's Nurse (October 1935). " As earthy as a potato, as slow as a cart-horse, and as cunning as a badger," wrote Mr. Darlington of this. Then Mme Arkadina in *The Seagull* (May 1936). " Taking the eye like a drawing by Toulouse-Lautrec—a lovely performance of shimmer and sparkle and quite rightly without one atom of heart to it," wrote somebody. Her Lady Fidget in *The Country Wife* (October 1936) was " a Rowlandsonesque cartoon of Britannia turned bawdy." Next Rosalind (November 1936), and I find that ten years ago I was moved to write about " bubbling seas of Renaissance wit." As for her Witch in the present play, this is just good straightforward melodramatic Mother Shipton plus a note of heart-searching pity which brings you up sharp in the middle of cruelty's guffaw.

Very well then. Here we have an actress who can be

macabre, doll-like, and insane, suggest the cart-horse, the potato, and the badger, make oblations to the gods, imply a bawdy cartoon, and at the same time ride bubbling seas of wit. If that is not transformability, then we must find a new Lewis Carroll to tell us what is. Mark finally that Miss Evans has been on the stage for twenty-four years, or exactly eight times the length of the period we have been analysing, and that never once in all that time has she repeated herself. One has only to mention Shakespeare's Cressida with which she began, Rebecca West (*Rosmersholm*), the woman in *Heartbreak House*, the singer in *Evensong*, that extraordinary daughter of M. Dupont in Brieux's play, the Serpent and the She-Ancient (*Back to Methuselah*). And while she has been doing these things Miss Evans has given us her Millamant, which is not only the finest reproduction of eighteenth-century manners the twentieth century has seen, but is, I venture to guess, as good as anything seen by the eighteenth century, and you can throw in the nineteenth as well! There is no doubt that Evans must take rank as one of the great comic actresses. Is she a great actress in the sense of effortless and absolute sublimity? If not, it is only because the sublime has not come her way. But in any case, as Sir James Barrie's Cinderella said about the love-letter, " it's a very near thing."

Dekker's play, the peg for the foregoing, is a poorish peg. The interest as to the first two-thirds is purely antiquarian. They are the sort of thing which in the early seventeenth century any competent dramatist could put together to bemuse contemporary oafs withal, and of the many reasons for reviving a play the antiquarian one, unsupported, seems to me to be the poorest. Why, with Miss Evans in the company, not give us her Evadne in *The Maid's Tragedy* of Beaumont and Fletcher? This is not only old, but old and magnificent. The third part of the present play is another

pair of shoes altogether, since here Ford and Rowley have
hit upon something to say and Dekkered it out with all the
paraphernalia of horror which Webster made, and which
still is, so effective. There is even poetry here, which in the
earlier parts is to seek. Let me just note the sympathetic and
interesting playing of Mesdames Anna Konstam and
Beatrix Lehmann, the brilliant embroidery of Mr. George
Hayes, and the first-class tragic passion of Mr. Marius
Goring. M. St.-Denis suggests that we should accept the Dog
who represents the Devil as symbolical of mental conflict. As
to which *vide* any German notion of the ghosts in Shakespeare ! I prefer to hark back to Hamlet's " 'Tis an honest
ghost," and suggest that this is an honest dog. Mr. Hedley
Briggs plays the cur as honestly as the late Charles Lauri
would have done, but with an uneasy difference admirably
calculated. Which enforces the conclusion that the play is a
mixture of *Dr. Faustus* and *Puss in Boots*.

SIR JAMES BARRIE'S NEW PLAY

THE BOY DAVID. A play by Sir James Barrie. His Majesty's
Theatre, Monday, December 14, 1936.

[*December* 20, 1936]

SIR JAMES BARRIE's last full-length play was *Mary Rose*,
and I take this opportunity of refuting any allegation that I
am not a fanatical admirer of this great playwright by saying
that only last week I journeyed to a little theatre in Rich-
mond to see a performance—and a good performance—of
that heart-searching fantasy. When first the present play was
mooted it was put about, or let me say that it got about
without any putting, that Miss Bergner was so great an
actress that nobody except Sir James could cope with her
dramatic needs, or, alternatively, that Sir James, having
looked upon Miss Bergner's greatness, had been once more
moved to draw his trusty but by no means rusty blade.

Now there is no reason why any playwright should not
write a play for an actress if he feels so disposed. But when a
claim for greatness is made in the one case and admitted in
the other, we naturally look for something by-ordinar', as
the Scotch say. Suppose Prospero in his oldest age to have
surprised his granddaughter playing at conjuring. Suppose
Miranda had invited the old gentleman to perform just one
more trick for the child's enlightenment. Do we not feel that
the Master would have either refused point-blank or pulled-
off some magic worthy of his once so potent art ? The trouble
with *The Boy David* is that its author has fobbed off little

Mirandolina—meaning to-day's public—with something less than his full genius. He has taken a tremendous theme and out of it made a little play whose hero is not to be identified with " the mighty valiant man, and a man of war." In this historietta it is Little Boy Blue who blows David's horn.

Barrie—for he is big enough not to have " Sir James " tacked on to him every time—once more shows in his plays a likeness to Lewis Carroll, who doted on little girls till they were twelve and then turned his back on them. It is this kink—I wish I could find a more respectful word—which makes him more interested in David the child of dew than in David the patriot-sensualist-poet. Our Puritan inheritance has inculcated in us the belief that a man can only fulfil his best self by self-denial. What a theme, then, in David, king of Israel, fulfilling himself not by garnering his spirit but by spending it ! Mark that what Mirandolina has been fobbed off with is not even the Boy David but the Little Boy David. The lion dies " with a look of wonder on his face." And well he may ! Any lion may reasonably entertain surprise at being strangled by this mite. A lion who knew his Ibsen would die gurgling: " Kiddies don't do such things ! "

Miss Bergner's presentation of childhood is inescapably lovely. It is childhood with the vision splendid still about it. It is almost dream-childhood, not so much the state of those who refuse to grow up as of those who, in Lamb's words, must wait upon the shores of Lethe millions of ages before they have existence and a name. He would be a block, a stone, a worse than senseless playgoer who was not moved by this actress looking down with head a little averted so that you see her in three-quarter face. But there are playgoers for whom wan rapture unaccessoried makes too spare a banquet, and for these poor fish this play provides little else. It is true that there is Saul, who asks why his evil spirit should punish him so, only to be answered that his personal torment is irrelevant, the important punishment being that of the people of Israel upon whom, for their evil deeds, his evil kingship is inflicted. Think what Shaw would have made of such a theme, and note how Barrie, having stated it, puts it gently on one side, content to show a Saul suffering from attacks of something half-way between what Dr. Rutty, the Irish Quaker, called "hypochondriac obnubilation from wind and indigestion" and the aphasia which overtook Kipling's Blastoderm.

Mr. Godfrey Tearle plays Saul with relish grand and grim enough to make us wish that he were the hero of a play which did not come to a full stop at the end of its second act. There is a third act in which Barrie glances unconvincingly at, and David dreams improbably of, the events that are to lead up to Saul's death. And this is all, except for an epiloguish winding-up concerning David's pact with Jonathan. The Goliath scene fails with me largely because Mr. Augustus John's Spanish setting leads me at any moment to expect an arrow to ping past some prehistoric Escamillo's hat, and a 3,000-year-old Micaela—which is the age of most Micaelas —to enter opining that naught shall frighten her here. But this, I freely confess, is just bad playgoing on my part. Even so, I must further confess to finding this little play strangely old-fashioned, and to thinking that M. Obey has a better knack of doing this kind of thing. And in a voice too small to reach Glasgow let me whisper that Mr. Bridie also knows a newer thing or two ! For the other actors it shall be said that Sir John Martin-Harvey's Samuel is noble, Mr. Ion Swinley's Nathan well-spoken, Mr. Leon Quartermaine's Ophir a shade disappointing (the part is a poor one), and Master Bobby Rietti's Jonathan roundly unhappy, with an accent much envied in Highgate.

As for Miss Bergner, this play lessens the darkness as to those capacities in which we have lived for three years.

XN

Enough has been said in praise of that quality of which she gave us proof then and repeats that proof now; the point has always been what else Miss Bergner could do. She was given an opportunity in this piece, and this occurred when David came to the Lament over Saul and Jonathan. Mr. Maurice Baring has said of a great actress that when she recited the La Fontaine fable in *Adrienne Lecouvreur* one felt " that for the perfect utterance of beautiful words this was the Pillars of Hercules of mortal achievement." This gives the measure of what was wanted for David's Lament, and we have to note that Miss Bergner did nothing with it that a normally gifted lay-reader might not have done. She was not acting here, by which I mean re-creating old emotion and old beauty and causing the spectator to receive the words as though they were being felt and uttered for the first time. Miss Bergner was just reading at a desk. Whereby one is justified in asking with what, in grown-up parts, this actress replaces the childish wistfulness upon which in this country she has hitherto relied. At the moment no other means are in sight. Yet if the claim for greatness is to be upheld, these other means must exist, and if they exist they should be produced. Take a parallel from another art. Should we, in the case of a pianist who never performed anything except Schumann's " Album für die Jugend " be justified in acclaiming that pianist as a world-executant ? Will not Miss Bergner hear and accede to the general petition that she should do something to prevent those who must do their playgoing and play-judging in this country from harking back as a final pronouncement to what Liszt said about Chopin: " Son genre n'était pas grand, mais il était grand dans son genre " ?

MR. OLIVIER'S HAMLET

HAMLET. Uncut Version of Shakespeare's Tragedy. Old Vic
Theatre, Tuesday, January 5, 1937. [*January* 10, 1937]

BEFORE PRONOUNCING whether an actor can act Hamlet,
one has first to decide whether he can act at all. If this is
too sweeping let me for " at all " substitute " poetic tragedy."
Has the young man a feeling for poetry, and a sense of the
tragic ? And since everything that an actor does must be
conveyed through his physical means, this is equivalent to
asking whether he has a distinguished and mobile countenance, a resonant voice, a noble bearing, a princely gait, and
sufficient stature. An actor may be twin-souled with Shakespeare, but if he be plain, rasping, cringing, creeping, and
dwarfish, he must confine himself to Thersites and Caliban.
What is at the back of an actor's mind is not nearly so
important as the back of his head, always provided the man
can act. For if a man can act, his performance, though mis-
conception stands the part on its head, will still give pleasure
of a kind. Whereas conception alone, however right, if the
means to convey that conception be wanting, gives nothing.

Now consider Mr. Laurence Olivier in the frank, brutal,
and altogether sensible way in which the old dramatic critics
considered the old actors. What is the first thing G. H. Lewes
tells us about Frédéric Lemaître ?

" Lemaître was very handsome. He had a wonderful
eye, with large orbit, a delicate and sensitive mouth, a fine

nose, a bold jaw, a figure singularly graceful, and a voice penetrating and sympathetic. He had great animal spirits, great daring, great fancy, and great energy of animal passion."

And what is the last thing that he perceives in him ? It is this : " A note of vulgarity, partly owing to his daring animal spirits, but mainly owing, I suspect, to an innate vulgarity of nature." Apply these things to Mr. Olivier. Mr. Olivier has a well-turned head, a pleasing, youthful face, a magnificent voice of a bow-string tautness and vibrancy marred by a few commonplace intonations which could easily be eliminated, good carriage, a springy, pantherine gait, and the requisite inches. Mr. Olivier, then, can act, since in addition to the foregoing he possesses the mimetic talent. Now we must ask : Can he act Hamlet ? I have just used the word " commonplace " because I wanted to avoid the word " common." I detect in Mr. Olivier none of the vulgarity which Lewes found in Lemaître. But I do observe a modern, jaunty offhandedness which is presumably a legacy from parts of the Beau Geste order. I do not refer here to the one quality in which Mr. Olivier's Hamlet excels any Hamlet of recent years—its pulsating vitality and excitement. After Claudius has left at the end of the Play Scene this Hamlet acts literally all over the stage, his " Why, let the stricken deer go weep " being accompanied by a tremendous leap from the perched-up throne on to the mimic stage below, and thence down to the footlights in an access of high hysteria. That is matter for the most compelling admiration. The jauntiness complained of occurs in the philosophic passages, which too often take on a note approaching pertness. This is due to, I will not say a fault, but a characteristic of Mr. Olivier's playing which prevents him from being Hamlet.

The same great critic whom we have been quoting has

a significant passage about Charles Kean, which I would apply almost word for word to Mr. Olivier:

> " The fluency of Shakespeare's movements, the subtle interpenetration of thought and emotion, the tangled web of motives, the mingling of the heroic with the familiar, the presence of constant verisimilitude under exceptional and exaggerated conditions, all demand great flexibility of conception and expression in the actor, great sympathy of imagination, nicety of observation, and variety of mimetic power. In these Charles Kean is wholly deficient. He has the power of coarse painting, of impressive representation when the image to be presented is a simple one; but he has no subtlety of sympathy, no nicety of observation, no variety of expression. . . . It is because there is no presence of poetry in his acting that we all feel Charles Kean to be essentially a melodramatic actor. The unreality and unideality of a melodrama are alike suited to his means. If he attempt to portray real emotion he leaves us cold; if he attempt to indicate a subtle truth, it is done so clumsily and so completely from the outside conventional view that we are distressed."

Or you might put it that Mr. Olivier's Hamlet is the best performance of Hotspur that the present generation has seen. One more quotation from Lewes, and I have done with him. " For myself," he writes, " I confess to have the smallest possible pleasure in a French actor when he is *profond et rêveur*." And for myself, I confess to the smallest possible pleasure in a Hamlet who is neither *rêveur* nor *profond*. Mr. Olivier's Hamlet is entirely without melancholy, and its lack of profundity may be gauged from his delivery of the line to Rosencrantz and Guildenstern:

> " I will not sort you with the rest of my servants; for,

to speak to you like an honest man, I am most dreadfully attended."

Here Shakespeare has the grimmest of double meanings; Hamlet is referring either to the Ghost or to his antecedent: " I have bad dreams." Mr. Olivier speaks the words as though Hamlet were complaining of the attendance in a service flat.

But let us take the performance in a little more detail. This Hamlet at the beginning of the play is puzzled. But it is rather the honest, frank perplexity of a modern young man at Oxford or Cambridge whose annoyance that his mother should have re-married with such indecent haste is not going to prevent him from helping himself that afternoon to a hundred of the best off the sister University's bowling. There should be more " to " Hamlet than this, even at the outset. We ought to feel that even if there were no Ghost and no murder, Hamlet is still an invincible neurasthenic. We feel that the present Hamlet has not in him anything " which passeth show," that in him everything, as it should be in the case of healthy young men of his age, even though they are mourning a father, is on the surface, which does not mean that it is superficial. A little disappointed here, we seize at the skill with which this Hamlet receives Horatio's " My lord, I think I saw him yesternight." Hamlet hears this without taking it in, and this is the first of many bits of straightforward acting which Mr. Olivier does excellently. The scenes with the Ghost and immediately after are crammed with all that excitement which is to be the note of the performance, and provide the first occasion for the welcome letting-out of that too rarely heard thing, a voice up to the demands of high tragedy. And now follows the admonition to Horatio and Marcellus. It may be that here the actor has to choose between Forbes-Robertson's

heartbreak in " For every man hath business and desire "
and the wild and whirling delivery here indicated; Forbes-
Robertson was not wild and never whirled. Mr. Olivier is
entitled to take " Look you, I'll go pray " at immense speed.
But he must not, I think, make so little of the " antic disposition " passage. This is the point at which the actor must
declare himself in the matter of Hamlet's madness.

For myself I have no doubt that Hamlet was completely
sane, and I have never been able to detect one single word
in the entire part suggesting the contrary. Johnson (" It
never does to neglect Johnson ") says:

> " Of the feigned madness of Hamlet there appears no
> adequate cause, for he does nothing which he might not
> have done with the reputation of sanity."

Some little time ago somebody said to me about the most
méchante langue in London: " Lady X—— is not intentionally
witty; she speaks exactly what is in her mind, and this in
an insincere age is wit ! " Now, wit at a court is wit out of
place, and hence madness. Hamlet in his teasing of Polonius
is merely speaking his thoughts aloud, and this, together
with his melancholy and neurasthenia, would at the court of
Denmark easily pass for madness. The point is that Hamlet,
while remaining as sane to me as he does to Horatio and
Marcellus, must convey madness to the rest of the court.
Mr. Olivier skates over the " antic disposition " passage as
quickly as possible, and the question of madness real or
assumed is then dropped as far as Hamlet is concerned. But
I must not be too long. The passages of which Mr. Olivier
makes notably little are, first, the scenes with the players. It
is incredible that he should be unconscious of the sheer word-
beauty of " this brave o'erhanging firmament, this majestical
roof fretted with golden fire." When Forbes-Robertson said
this, Rosencrantz and Guildenstern were struck into a

Michael-Angelesque dumbness. He disappoints, too, in the
" Get-thee-to-a-nunnery " scene and in the Closet Scene.
To conclude the tale of blame, Mr. Olivier does not speak
poetry badly. He does not speak it at all.

Now for the good points. The soliloquies are delivered with
remarkable cogency, and immense power and fire in the
right places. I do not think I have ever heard the Fortinbras
soliloquy better treated. The lines:

> *I do not know*
> *Why yet I live to say " this thing's to do,"*
> *Sith I have cause, and will, and strength, and means,*
> *To do't. . . .*

are trumpet-moaned as though it has at last broken in on
the young man that indecision is his bane. Up to that time
Hamlet has been the one person in all Denmark likeliest to
get his own way about anything from pitch-and-toss to
slaughter. Of the Play Scene and all that follows I have
already spoken. The rest is a jumble of the good and the
insufficient. The Grave Scene lacks reflective emotion, and
there is not enough banter in the little scene with Osric. On
the other hand, the fencing with Laertes—a moving performance by Mr. Michael Redgrave—is done with real
virtuosity, which fades before the Death Scene. Mr. Olivier
just cannot say: " Absent thee from felicity a while," and
he will have to live some time yet before he knows how to
die. To sum up, this is obviously a performance carefully
thought out, consonant with itself, and taken at admirable
speed. On the other hand, it is not Hamlet, but a brilliant
performance of the part such as Stanhope in *Journey's End*
might have put up in some rest-interval behind the lines.

The King will be better when Mr. Francis Sullivan plays
him outside his robes instead of in them, and the Queen of
Miss Dorothy Dix conveys the impression of not being in

the play at all, but of looking in now and again to do a bit
of acting. As Ophelia Miss Cherry Cottrell strikes me as being
unripe. Mr. Torin Thatcher makes an inaudible Ghost, and
Mr. Frederick Bennett's First Gravedigger is the one gloomy
spot in the entire production. Horatio *ne fera pas*, since
" won't do " sounds so rude, and Fortinbras, instead of
being dumpish and insignificant, should always be played
by Mr. Shayle Gardner clad in gold armour. On the other
hand, Mr. Alec Guinness contrives to make a character out
of Reynaldo, and Mr. George Howe continues to be the best
Polonius anybody has ever seen. Lots could be said about
Mr. Tyrone Guthrie's highly imaginative production, but
not, I think, at the fag-end of an article.

MR. COCHRAN'S REVUE

HOME AND BEAUTY. Mr. C. B. Cochran's Coronation Revue. By A. P. Herbert. Music by Nikolaus Brodszky and Henry Sullivan. Adelphi Theatre, Tuesday, February 2, 1937.

THE ORCHARD WALLS. A play by Merton Hodge; adapted from the Hungarian of Ladislaus Fodor. St. James's Theatre, Wednesday, February 3, 1937.

ON YOUR TOES. A musical comedy by Richard Rodgers and Lorenz Hart. Music by Richard Rodgers. Palace Theatre, Friday, February 5, 1937.

[*February* 7, 1937]

THIS TITLE is only two-thirds of what the tenors used to sing. In all seemliness shouldn't there be a little more England about a *Coronation* revue called *Home and Beauty* ? The chief composer's name has a Czecho-Slovakian ring, the scenery by M. Raoul Pene du Bois is French, the star of the revue is frankly Hungarian, while the nationality of the two pianists, Rawicz and Landauer, invites, shall one say, conjecture ? Is it possible that one comes from Buda and the other from Pest ? It is all very well to tell me that art knows no frontiers. But having no frontiers, what can art have to do with coronations ? I suggest that Mr. Cochran would have done better to leave the great occasion out of it rather than to skimp it. There is only one scene which lives up to the event, and this is dragged in between two others occurring in a dressing-room and a bathroom, and just because a little boy has found a harp in a box-room ! Even here the costumes

have been executed by the not notably British-sounding
Mme Karinska.

At the end of the first scene the front door of the country
house known as Mulberry Moat is thrown open, and Miss
Gitta Alpar, before she has been shown her room or taken off
her bonnet, bursts into song. You have seen, reader, an angry
sea dash itself against an imperturbable breakwater. Miss
Alpar's arias, with their crests and troughs, sprays of trills
and foam of fiorituri, scudding grace-notes and sea-bird
swoopings, left me, I am sorry to say, patriotically unmoved.
This country, in the year which this revue celebrates, is still
Queen of the Seas; let an English singer tell her so. To consider the matter with more general reference, I thought the
quality of Miss Alpar's voice hard and unpleasing and that
her intonation was frequently faulty. There were, however,
some English breaks in the orgy of foreign cantilena. There
was Miss Binnie Hale with her blackbird flutings, so delight-
fully unforced and so perfectly in tune. Miss Hale is a revue
artist to the ends of her finger-tips, and her parodies of Miss
Dorothy Dickson and Miss Jessie Matthews were lawfully
devastating, though I think she would have been better
advised not to attempt Mr. Billy Bennett. Then there was
Mr. Nelson Keys in terrific form as the M.F.H. whom it
would take the pen of a modern Surtees to describe; and I
doubt whether anything funnier has ever been seen than his
world-financier with a cold. Apart from these brilliant performers there wasn't, always excepting Miss Norah Howard's
poise, very much else. Mr. Brodszky's music is grandiose. But
why not Mr. Walton? We English claim to possess composers; let them be used at such a time. There are some
charming *little* tunes by Mr. Sullivan. Mr. Herbert's wit?
One could not tell, with all that *bel canto* to drown it.

One or two other questions remain to be asked. Why in
this year of Coronation grace does Mr. Cochran entirely

cold-shoulder Terpsichore, the muse to whom he has ever been most beholden? Where are the colour, the variety, the fantastication which are the heart of Cochranesque genius? When the general talk is of empires and crownings, why pitch on a circumscribed tale of a country house? Surely a Coronation revue should echo the spirit of Kipling's opening to *The Seven Seas*:

> *Hear now a song—a song of broken interludes—*
> *A song of little cunning; of a singer nothing worth.*
> *Through the naked words and mean*
> *May ye see the truth between*
> *As the singer knew and touched it in the ends of all the Earth.*

I am not suggesting a ballet of nations as provincial panto-mime understands it. But I do suggest (*a*) that country-house japes would do as well at another time and (*b*) that they do not need Mr. Cochran to produce them. Our greatest impre-sario has accustomed us to think of him as an Antony from whose pockets realms and islands drop like plates. This time he has dropped them like hot plates, and his spectacle is the poorer. Instead we have scenes like that one in the nursery in which babes divorce; this is the very apotheosis of bee-in-bonnetry. Or that burlesque of Handel which needs a Henson for it to become funny, and even then would hardly be.

I regret to have to write in this strain, which will probably cause Mr. Cochran and his lieutenants to rage furiously to-gether. But they have imagined a very nearly vain thing, and it is my duty to say so. Am I misliking what they have done because of what they did not set out to do? Perhaps. But I am afraid that even within its scope I like this revue less than I am accustomed to liking shows which, in non-Coronation years, have never failed to be the most exquisite of their kind.

The Orchard Walls is so wilfully and defiantly bad that it is worth while explaining why. Worth while because it will probably run a year or two, and if plays as bad as this run a year or two, why, then, farewell to playwriting as an art for the theatre, and hail the advent of the straggling strip of cinema-fodder ! The third scene of the first act was the Continental departure platform at Victoria Station. In this scene the luggage van of the departing train stuck after following the coach in front of it some ten yards or so. I have never been so pleased with anything in my life. This was not only poetic justice with a vengeance, but vengeance with poetic justice. The only thing which would have delighted me more would have been if the coach itself had stuck, leaving half the *dramatis personæ* waving lily but static hands.

The reason for this ghoulish delight in discomfiture ? Simply that the scene had no business to be there at all. It did not get the play as many inches further as the train had moved yards. It was, in fact, wholly unnecessary in the theatre and wholly in place in a film. The scene prior to that (the second of Act I) had exhibited Miss Irene Vanbrugh being amusingly manicured. This scene also was wholly unnecessary and had been preceded by one even more needless (the first of Act I), in which we were shown the foyer of a London theatre. The whole business of these three scenes had been to establish that Hilda McKenna, in love with John Engleton, chose to marry Lord Felstock, a millionaire manufacturer of hot-water bottles. This for the reason that her father, Sir Michael, was overdrawn at his bank, though we did not understand how this could be, since the famous surgeon was so full up with engagements that he could not get away for his daughter's wedding, and even failed to catch her ought-to-have-departed train.

The younger generation regards Ibsen as a dud. But let me tell it that that demoded jobber would have raised his curtain with the fourth scene of this play, being the hotel in

Venice during Hilda's honeymoon, in the course of which he would have told us all we wanted to know about her father, mother, and impecunious lover who was hoping to set up solicitor. Let us wash the mind with a page of the old man to show our young folk what good playwriting is. It is perhaps necessary to say that the talk is of Hedda Gabler's honeymoon :

MISS TESMAN (*produces a flat parcel wrapped in newspaper and hands it to Tesman*) : Look here, my dear boy.

TESMAN (*opening the parcel*) : Well, I declare—have you saved them for me, Aunt Julia ? Hedda ! Isn't this touching—eh ?

HEDDA (*beside the whatnot on the right*) : Well, what is it ?

TESMAN : My old morning-shoes. My slippers.

HEDDA : Indeed. I remember you often spoke of them while we were abroad.

TESMAN : Yes, I missed them terribly. (*Goes up to her.*) Now you shall see them, Hedda.

HEDDA (*going towards the stove*) : Thanks, I really don't care about it.

TESMAN (*following her*) : Only think—ill as she was, Aunt Rina embroidered these for me. Oh, you can't think how many associations cling to them.

HEDDA (*at the table*) : Scarcely for me.

Hedda's boredom throughout the whole of that ghastly honeymoon comes through in that exacerbated " Well, what is it ? " just as Tesman's following her about is a picture of the married life she is to look forward to. Does not the younger generation of playwrights see that good playwriting is like a game of lawn-tennis with the footlights acting as the net, and implication and inference exchanged like the ball in some prolonged rally ? In good playwriting the spectator

takes a hand in the game ; in bad he must sit out and list-
lessly look on.

The first of the play's two reels ended with Hilda's discovery that her solicitor-lover, John, had married the nitwit
Frankie. The second reel began in John's office, it being the
rule of the cinema that when husband and wife want to
divorce they must both consult the young solicitor who,
though married, cherishes a deep passion for his female
client. John, at this point, wanted to elope with the young
woman in her Rolls, caring nothing that he would be struck
off his own for professional misconduct! Only Nitwit was going
to have another little nitwit, which meant an entirely superfluous scene in a maternity hospital, surprisingly sistered by
Juliet's Nurse. The final scene took place at Coblentz years
later, where Hilda had fallen for a riding-master, whither
John had come with an airwoman, and whence Lord Felstock
had fled to find chalybeate comfort at Carlsbad. Come to
think of it, " a werry strong flavour of warm flat-irons "
exactly describes this play. The title ? That, I think, was
merely put in to make it seem more difficult, since there
isn't a ha'porth of Romeo in John or a pennyweight of Juliet
in Hilda. Risking this opinion to a young highbrow, I was
met with the cold suggestion that I had overlooked the
parallelism of the Nurse. But I still fail to see any resemblance
between a lover who climbs walls and one who doesn't. The
play ended, so far as one could gather, with John and Hilda
climbing the wall and proposing to sit on love's fence *sine die*.
Or am I sedulously missing the point ? Is Mr. Hodge's or
M. Fodor's point that these lovers are not star-crossed, but
star-, or rather jelly-, fish drifting about love's sea in gono-
phorous indecision ? In any case, *The Orchard Walls* is a grand
example of how not to do it. Or how to do it for the film, where
audiences like railway platforms and hospital wards for themselves and without reference to what happens on or in them.

Miss Valerie Taylor and Mr. Evelyn Roberts, as Hilda and her husband, lent their parts a beauty and an interest which simply were not there. At times they even gave them a kind of sense ! Mr. Hugh Sinclair as the inadequate John was more than adequate. If the younger generation of actresses think that they are ever going to approach within forty thousand miles of Miss Irene Vanbrugh they are mistaken. They have not mastered the rudiments of any one of the eight or ten arts of acting of which Miss Vanbrugh is the complete mistress—wit, charm, poise, manner, gait, repose, enunciation, and *vis comica*. To watch this brilliant artist make bricks out of straw was a complete lesson in acting. Mr. Arthur Sinclair had the even more difficult task of making straw out of nothing at all. A bomb would not have blown up this play more effectively than one single intonation of this great comedian, who needs an O'Casey to stand up to him. The play was rapturously received by an immensely smart house. But I know ruder audiences whereby the more than talented players must have shaken the yolk of inauspicious eggs from their play-wearied flesh.

No space—write like Jingle—theatre rum shop—*On Your Toes*—no world announcements—no ransacking Balearics for ballerinas—just original and witty burlesque of Russian ballet by people who can dance—audience flabbergasted—decide to laugh and risk it—Jack Whiting—better actor than Astaire—pig's whisper—no gammon—Olive Blakeney fine actress—shouldn't sing though—delicious fooling and dancing Vera Zorina—Gina Malo and Eddie Pola fill in—impressionist scenery and impudent costumes—who said Toulouse-Lautrec ?—music catches exact Rimsky-Korsakov note for ballet—when banality wanted, catches that too—best light entertainment for years—everybody's eye wiped—ungentlemanly—very !

INDEX OF PLAYS AND PERSONS